Praise

"What an extraordinary book. *Hope for the Worst* is a tale of high ideas and high longing, with an untrustworthy guru and New York in its most desperate years. I loved the wild turns the story takes in the Himalayan edges of Asia, and the dangers the writing leads us through. It's a riveting book that will make its mark on all readers."
JOAN SILBER, AUTHOR OF *THE SECRETS OF HAPPINESS*

"*Hope for the Worst* is a novel that speaks to our moment. It is concerned with the largest questions: how do we live? how not to suffer? how to be where we are? In all seasons the narrator names the world as it passes before her, vibrant, reverberating in time. But by the end of this remarkable story the narrator not only takes us to where she is. By her patient chronicling she allows us to see our own lives with new eyes."
KATHLEEN HILL, AUTHOR OF *SHE READ TO US IN THE LATE AFTERNOONS*

"In her startling, sensual novel, Kate Brandt embarks on a thrilling journey into the heart of Buddhist thought on pain, truth, and desire. Her hero is searching for wisdom while on a perilous journey of self-discovery, but as a deceptive teacher attempts to shape her and control her, she risks losing herself in the quest. With a thoughtful, sensitive eye for detail, Brandt makes the pressing questions of female spirituality, and the place of women in contemporary Buddhism, feel vital. This story will pull you deep into the thorny beauty of American Buddhism — and leave you wondering and moved."
BLAIR HURLEY, AUTHOR OF *THE DEVOTED*

"In exquisite prose, Brandt's novel pulses with vivid observations of what we do in the search for love. I was gripped by deeply wounded and philosophical Ellie Adkins, an insomniac, as she navigates an uneven power balance with her lovers in 1980s New York City and Tibet. Capturing the twists and turns in Ellie's quest for healing, the novel is structured in lyrical journal entries and letters. This is a novel with many lessons for living, rendered in beautiful form."
JIMIN HAN, AUTHOR OF *THE APOLOGY*

"Kate Brandt's extraordinary novel is just the kind of book I love—
intimate and finely observed, yet chock-full of big ideas and profound
questions. We fall in love with her unforgettable young narrator, Ellie,
who, new to New York City, struggles with loneliness, depression and
a hunger for meaning. With a wry eye, Brandt draws a vivid portrait of
the snake-oil guru who preys on that vulnerability with the promise of
deeper truth. We follow Ellie across the globe in her effort to escape her
obsession and find her own truth. I could not put this book down. I look
forward to reading it again and again."
DEBORAH ZOE LAUFER, PLAYWRIGHT OF *END DAYS*

About the Author

Kate Brandt's work has appeared in *Tricycle: The Buddhist Review*, *Literary Mama*, *The Westchester Review*, *Ginosko* and *Redivider*, among other journals. She teaches adult literacy students in New York City and lives in Westchester County, New York.

katebrandt.net

Kate Brandt

Hope
for the
Worst

Dear Notebook,
you may be the last person I talk to.

For the Healers

To study the Buddha Way is to study the self. To study the self is to forget the self. To forget the self is to be enlightened by the ten thousand things.

Dogen

Tuesday, June 3, 1986, 2 a.m.
107th Street & Amsterdam
The Red Notebook

Dear Calvin,

I've stopped sleeping.

I keep thinking about the day in Union Square Park. A weekday afternoon. No leaves on the trees yet but the squirrels were hopping about, and people had disregarded the signs and sat on the grass. You in your blue shirt—with the white beard, your wild man look. People stared at us—they always did when we were together—the age difference. I looked back, not caring.

"Everything is on fire," you said. "The grass is on fire. The trees are on fire. See those lovers? Burning. And if you think there's water, the water is on fire too." I was listening, but there was a question in my mind: why weren't we in our usual place. Maybe I was already starting to know.

When you told me you weren't going to see me this summer, everything in me stopped for a moment and held its breath. A woman over at the benches leaned over laughing toward a man with a headband. Cars swished by. A pigeon took off. It couldn't be the same world, but it was.

"Why?" I asked.

"Out of the country," you shrugged.

"Where?" I asked, but you wouldn't tell me. "Can I write? Will it be forwarded?"

"You can write." Something in me slid away, out of my body.

"I'm in love with you," I said. "I think of you all the time." Do you understand what I was trying to say to you? *It's too late. How can you stop it now?*

9

Here is what you did because I know you will not remember. You took up my hand that had been lying in my lap and raised it in the air. You shook it slightly and put it back down.

"I'm sorry." You looked up at the sky. "I don't feel that way. It's almost like an old car—the shocks don't work anymore." Then you smiled at me, benign as Santa Claus.

When I lie down in bed, I can't stop talking to you inside my head. Hours go by. An old apartment and the heat is stifling. I get up and stalk naked through the rooms filled with the orange light from the streetlamps outside on Amsterdam Avenue. I see myself in the mirror: a face that doesn't mean anything; an orange-tinted ghost.

Tuesday, 5:30 a.m.
107th Street
The Blue Notebook

My mother never wanted me to keep a diary. She wanted me to go out and *do something*, the last two words delivered emphatically. She was—is—that kind of person: a doer. Maybe that's why I hid my notebooks in the closet and wrote at night—the forbidden-ness of it. My father, of course, approved. *Know thyself, Ellie. That's what Socrates said.* Mysterious words that I liked the sound of. The truth is, when I was young, the diaries were mainly lists of events in my day: *brushed teeth, went to bed.*

Now there's a whole shelf of them, black-and-white composition books with photos or magazine pictures glued to the front; spiral notebooks with loops of wire that get tangled and I have to patiently pull apart. Sometimes I title them—*L'Enfer C'est Les Autres; The Truth is Invisible to the Eye.* Seth made fun of me for it: *your notebooks have names?* Cass used to ask me about them, too. I told her the truth: my notebooks are the only place I'm safe. Cass always understood the concept of safety.

The last four notebooks have been Calvin Notebooks, but now a new one: blue. An Ellie notebook. I need to write myself into being.

5:30 a.m., the view down Amsterdam Avenue: a few short trees, spots of green over the gray road lined with cars on either side: a blue sedan, a dilapidated station-wagon, a white van. The church with its triangular roof, a rectangular tower beside it. Barely visible in this light; maybe I'm just seeing what I know is there. In *The Iliad* and *The Odys*sey, the day always starts with the rosy-fingered dawn. But in The City, dawn is not rosy-fingered. It is gray and then the white summer light is everywhere. Everything is painfully present; a picture that has been taken with a too-bright flash.

I'm dressed for work: short sleeve blouse, linen pants, saddle shoes. The office doesn't open for four hours, but I woke at five after falling asleep at two. That's how it is now: three hours at a time, after I take a Benadryl and down a few shots of tequila. My legs ache. My eyes are crusted. My head is an anvil.

When I wake now, there is maybe a nanosecond of me being who I used to be, then I think of Calvin, and become who I am now: a harpy, swooping down to take bites out of myself.

Last night in the neighborhood, some sort of fight happened around about midnight. There were shouts, a loud bang, then lots of voices jumping into the middle of it all. It must have been the block up the street because I couldn't see much, even when I went to the bedroom window at the north end of the apartment. It died down fast enough: a fire that caught, flared briefly, moved on.

When I first moved here, the noise drove me crazy. The salsa swayed and jiggled all night; car alarms went off, rhythmic honks that wouldn't stop. If we were the kind of family we used to be—normal—and my parents had come to help me move in, it would have been a place they worried about—their young, white, middle-class daughter in a neighborhood known for its drug problems. It wouldn't have looked good to them: all those people sitting out on the street, the mustard-yellow stucco on my building's hallway walls, each scoop of dried yellow plaster filled with dust. The chocolate brown of the bannisters; the stray dead mouse in a corner of the stairs.

Fights like the one last night happen a lot here. When I first moved in, there was a drug shooting right on our street in the middle of the night; a guy named Junior with a loud, raspy voice who was always out on the street. About midnight, we could hear him shouting and pleading in Spanish. There were a couple of pops and he screamed.

"His foot!" someone yelled in English. "They shot him in the foot!" My quasi-boyfriend, Seth, had stayed over that night. He rushed to the window, laughing in a scared-but-excited way.

"Oh my God, they shot Junior," he said. Seth grew up in New York; he's used to violence. In the seventies, he said, he saw a riot in Washington Square Park in which one man sawed off another man's leg.

That night, people came to their windows, opened them, talked to each other from window to window. There was some laughing— the neighborhood took up a running commentary in Spanish about what had happened to him. I could hear the varied reaction in the tones of people's voices, even if I didn't understand the words— there was wonder, humor, analysis. The human drama, all here on our block. I thought of that Kitty Genovese story from the sixties— she died alone in the street, and nobody came to help. This is 1984, but maybe not that much has changed.

According to Calvin, most of us live in a state of delusion. That was the theme of his first lectures: we're all brainwashed. We all think it's about getting ahead, or conversely about not getting ahead, not playing the game. "It's neither, folks" he said. "It's just about being completely present in the moment that we are."

People think Buddhism is about getting away from it all," he said. "Buddhism is about being awake. "WAKE UP PEOPLE," he yelled at us. "WAKE UP TO YOUR LIFE."

That was a year ago. I remember how exhilarated I was; how uplifted. Calvin had shown me the possibility of being more than I was.

Now I am less than I was. I stand in my apartment for hours and my mind is a high-speed movie that can't stop cranking out the same scenes: I have undressed in front of Calvin, and he aches for me, reaches out an arm. I have asked a question that has revealed a contradiction in what he says, in Buddhism itself; made him realize that I am not only young and beautiful, but also wise. I have written something so poetic and tragic that he is moved to tears.

This is how hours go by. It feels like minutes, but when I look at the clock, most of the night has slipped by. It's almost the next day.

Last night when I realized I'd been sitting on the couch for three hours without moving, I made myself get up, go into the bathroom, look at my own face in the wood-framed mirror that balances between a small ledge and a pipe. I took myself in: the frame of long, brown hair, high forehead, slightly ski-jump nose, lazy s-curve of the cheekbones. "He's not going to call you," I said out loud. "You don't mean that much to him."

Which is impossible. When I first met Calvin and heard him lecture in that loft on 14th Street, I knew. I sat in the back, didn't speak, didn't even make eye contact with anyone, but I knew he'd plumbed mystery. Someone who could turn the world upside down and shake it so the truth came tumbling out at your feet. I've known that ever since; it's the one thing I've been sure of.

So when I looked in the mirror last night, it didn't seem possible. That he just lied to me. Not after all this.

Tuesday, 9 a.m.
City Hall Park
The Blue Notebook

I am having a crisis.

I write these words when I interrupt my five-minute walk from the subway to the office. Sitting on a green bench, I look at the hexagonal concrete tiles that make up the sidewalk and watch people walk by: a thin, jittery white woman in an immaculate linen suit and running shoes; a man in a suit with a crew cut and a face like a shovel; a bicycle messenger pumping the air below his feet.

Everyone is so purposeful. I do not have purpose.

It might help to say it to myself: Recognize the problem. In twelve-step programs, that is the first step: *I am an addict.* A statement of fact.

I look at a stick of a tree, its base imprisoned in a tiny, metal cage that surrounds a square of littered dirt. I remember what Calvin said about misfortune: *Let me tell you something about pain, folks. Pain lets you know you're awake!* He roared it at us, in that room where we all met. I actually shuddered. But then I saw the truth of it right away, and I was grateful. Not many people will yell a truth like that at you. Mostly what I've seen around me in New York is the opposite of truth. The walls of the subways implore me to buy Coke; tell me how happy I will be if I open an account at Chase/use Dove/drink Heinekens.

Tuesday, 9:30 a.m.
The Center for Urban Research
The Blue Notebook

When I first got this job, I told anyone who asked that I liked it because it was boring. "You can sit at your desk, hide your notebook on your lap under the desk, and write in it," I said.

The Urban Poverty Research Center has pink walls. This is a decision we arrived at collectively. When we moved from Chambers Street, this place was renovated. We all had a meeting and decided on pink. That is the kind of agency it is. When I was first hired, our director, Amber, told me that the Center was a horizonal organization. I did not know what that meant; it turned out that it means there are a lot of staff meetings where everyone sits in a circle. It was at one of those meetings that we agreed upon pink. Now it looks as if our entire office is covered with calamine lotion.

When I came in today, there was the reception desk with Vicky, brown-haired, sweet-faced, and with a belly swollen from liver disease. A former drug addict, she is the face of our agency; that is the kind of agency we are. There is the long corridor with walls that do not reach all the way to the ceiling. On the other side of them are the cubbies where the "academics" sit; Beth Hoffman in her tent-y dresses; Ed Fanborough, always in a white shirt and tie (*he's not one of us*, Beth jokes); Amber, our big-faced boss, who wears flowered skirts and ballet slippers, and has one long black braid that hangs down her back.

What we do here, according to Amber, is "cutting-edge sociological research reviews to inform urban policy, particularly around poverty." But mostly what I do is type labels.

At the end of the corridor, Amber's office and mine, a tiny cubby, right next to it. I was pleased to see I was alone.

16

A To-Do list on my desk: three reports to photocopy; a mailing.

A wave of despair: I am already so tired my body is a cinder block. *It's nothing*, I tell myself. *Just type some labels.*

I am lucky to have this job; I know that. For the year before I got it, I temped. I got used to people being perpetually annoyed at me: I did not type fast enough/understand memo format/know how to transfer phone calls. But here they are academics; people do actually wear Birkenstocks and fuzzy sweaters to the office. They have mugs that say things like *Speak Truth to Power* and *The Solution to Oppression is Education.*

The first thing on my to-do list is a mailing. One hundred labels to type, A to Z. Make copies of the latest report, stuff them into manila envelopes, seal them, slap the labels on, then carry them to the post office. Each time a new report is finished, we send it out to half of the City's officials. According to Amber, that's how we have "impact." We have to get our work into "as many hands as possible." For me, it means a lot of labels.

10:30 a.m.

Beth just came to the opening of my cubby. I shoved the notebook under the desk. She was wearing the usual: a tent dress. Her blue eyes gazed at me over the hooked nose.

"I thought of you over the weekend. I ran across a store that was half saddle shoes."

I smiled up at her, starting to thread labels into my typewriter to look busy.

They make a big to-do about my saddle shoes here. They want to be friendly, and they don't know what else to say.

When I first came here, it was like working for a bunch of grandmothers. It's not that they're so much older than me, just that I was not an adult in the way they were. They liked me just for my youth—the new things I brought.

Ed Fanborough stuck his head in after Beth. Casual today, in a polo shirt for once, he asked me how the novel was coming. That's his big joke with me: I am really a writer, writing my best-selling novel in my notebook on work time; taking on the guise of a lowly secretary typing labels when anyone appears. I always pretend to enjoy the joke.

It's true that they all like me. It's also true that they don't like me as much as they used to when I first got here and was always willing to volunteer for things—typing someone's report, staying after to collate pages. At our "horizontal" staff meetings, Amber would say "we need someone to …" and I would always volunteer.

I'm not as pliable now. When people ask me for things, they come and do a little deferential dance in my doorway. "Ellie you're *so good* with Word Perfect. Could you help me with something?" Now I don't jump up to help the way I used to; I make people wait. I wanted to be liked back then. Sometime in the last year or so, I stopped caring.

11:30 a.m.

Amber arrived. I was on "H" in the alphabet. She hovered in the opening to my cubby, her long country-girl braid down her back, her flowered skirt hanging over her sandaled feet.

Amber is from Michigan. She has an aw-shucks way of talking to people, but she did not get to be the head of this agency by being a pushover. I've seen her bring people here to tears, sending reports back six or seven times until they say exactly what she wants them to say. This morning she stood in the doorway and asked how I'm "doin'," before getting to her real questions. Will I be able to get that mailing out today? (Yes). Did Amanda Finn call? (No.) How is the filing in her office coming? (Almost there). Satisfied, she went away.

It's from Amber that I've learned about euphemisms at work. When she isn't happy with you, she'll say she has "concerns." When I call in sick, she'll call me at home to see "how I'm doing." The first time she did that, I was touched until I realized she was checking to make sure I was really sick.

Generally, I'm okay with her; the main thing I want in a boss is civility and a manageable workload; Amber provides both. I do make fun of her quirks to myself: the way she keeps triplicates of

her phone messages and files them. The way she saves every draft
of every report she's ever written.

3 p.m.

Celeste and I went to lunch. I think I need to stop this—having
lunch with her, I mean.

She always fills the doorway of my cubby when she comes: fleshy,
big-lipped face; giant brown curls bustling around her head; enormous breasts that look as if she will fall forward any minute.
Today, she wears straight-legged pants and a cranberry-colored
peasant blouse. Her small, plump hands twitch at the ends of her
sleeves.

The usual arch beginning. "Care for a promenahhhde?" she said
in a faux-English accent. That is one of the things Celeste likes to
do at work; speak in a faux English accent. The other things:

- Talk earnestly about urban poverty;
- Gossip about the other people who work here, especially
  Amber;
- Analyze me.

Celeste was hired as a new research associate about three months
ago. Before she came, I was basically on my own; people liked me,
but they were a few levels above, and Vicky the receptionist and I
had nothing to talk about. Her third week here, Celeste walked into
my cubby, pulled out the extra chair, and plopped down on it. "So
Ellie," she said. "I want to be your friend." I blushed, I remember;
turned my face toward the wall so she wouldn't see.

"Don't think I don't see you scribbling in that notebook. You're the
most interesting person here, you know that?" she said. I widened
my eyes to show that I was skeptical of that. But when she invited
me to lunch, I accepted right away.

Today we went to our usual place: a bench near the South Street
Seaport that looks toward the East River. That's about as far as
Celeste can walk with the bad leg; getting there, with that step-
drag that she has, takes twice the time it would have taken me on
my own. Still, I'm patient.

You're the most interesting person here.

I was happy at first. The sparkle of light on water, the sound of the ropes on the sails of the boats slapping the masts; constant motion as Wall Street-types walked around in their office clothes to buy ice cream; pigeons pranced in circles; tourist families looked around up at the skyscrapers in wonder, consult maps.

And I wasn't alone. I had a friend. Since Cass left, it hadn't been like that.

At first it was a lot of complaining about Amber. Among the bosses I've had so far, Amber seems fairly benevolent, but Celeste has lots of criticisms. Amber chooses the wrong topics for research; Amber doesn't manage well.

Today, it was the fact that Amber chose Ed Fanborough to write the report on homelessness when she, Celeste, worked on the homeless commission *for three years*.

Everything was okay until she started in on me.

"So Ellie," she said. "How's life?"

I looked away. A group of laughing businessmen passed.

"Pretty tired," I said.

"Still not sleeping, eh?"

"Still awake at 4 a.m."

"I've been thinking about you," she said. "I think you're in danger."

I laughed out loud.

"I'm not in *danger*, Celeste." But I could already feel it inside: the falling.

"Ellie," she said, firmly. "Insomnia is a *very* bad sign. You need to see someone. A professional. And I think you need anti-depressants."

I laughed lightly. "But I have you."

Among the many jobs she's had, Celeste worked for a while as a therapist. When we started our "sessions"—that's what Celeste calls them—she said I was doing her a favor, letting her keep her hand in. We talked about me—my parents' divorce; what kind of child I had been. After a while a theme emerged: *so much untapped potential.*

"I've thought about it," she said today. "I don't think it's just temporary. I think you're clinically depressed." I looked down at her thigh which balanced a paper tray of crinkly French fries. Celeste is overweight, but she doesn't care; she eats what she wants. A pigeon pranced the ground near our feet.

"You have all the signs." She ticked them off with her fingers: "you're not interested in anything; you have low concentration; you're indecisive." She glanced over at me: "definitely low self-esteem. You spend all your time by yourself." I looked at her hand in the air, counting off my faults. "And the insomnia. Classic."

I nudged the pigeon away. "Lots of people are like this."

Celeste looked over at me, her lips firm. "No, Ellie they are not." My chest hurt.

"There's a new anti-depressant out. Prozac. I think you should try it."

"There's nothing wrong with me," I said.

"There's nothing wrong with you except you don't help yourself. You have to *want* to feel better, Ellie."

"I'm coming to work, aren't I?" I heard the squeak in my voice.

"Is that what you want to reach for? This is *life*, Ellie. You're in your twenties. These should be your best years, and you're miserable." I watched a woman in high heels and a briefcase struggle across Fulton Street, a bike messenger passing her the other way. I felt my throat start to close. Since we'd come out here, everything had changed. The vista of cobblestone street and waterfront looked like an old-fashioned TV set with the picture slowly fading to a single dot.

"Can we stop talking about this now?" I pleaded.

"You know you don't have a bad life, Ellie," she said, thoughtfully. "You're *very* well educated. You've had a *very* privileged childhood. "It sounds to me like you never really had to work for anything. Maybe that's part of the problem?"

A weight was pinning me to the bench.

Something entered my upper chest, right in the middle, and twisted. I got up.

Now I'm sitting on top of a toilet in the hall bathroom, locked in a stall, hoping no one comes in. My notebook is out on my lap. If I writewritewritewritewrite, maybe it will get out of me.

I shouldn't have let Celeste start those sessions.

Compared to me, Celeste is an adult. She's already been through several careers: certified social worker, director of an education program for high school dropouts, counselor at a halfway house. She's always telling stories about intervening between fighting addicts or firing teachers who are doing a bad job. I cannot imagine doing anything like that. I cannot imagine doing anything except what I do now—making copies, typing the labels for the reports, stuffing them into manila envelopes until they make large, lopsided piles on the mailroom countertop, then throwing them into plastic mailboxes and taking them downstairs.

I wonder how long I've been in here.

I'm shaking.

Write fifty times: *I am fine, I am fine, I am just fine.*

Tuesday, 6:30 p.m.
107ᵗʰ Street
The Blue Notebook

Walking up Broadway, I couldn't stop talking to Celeste in my head. *Fuck you; you can't talk to me like that. Why don't you mind your own business.*

I should not be so angry. I know that. I said yes to the sessions, didn't I?

At Duane Street, a woman in short shorts and espadrilles walking a poodle. At Canal, a snarl of cars and the sun beating down on a half-full dumpster; two or three kids on skateboards.

You should leave me alone. Why do you talk to me if you just want to make me feel worse.

At Houston, a homeless guy on the sidewalk, reading a novel, a can in front of him.

You fucking think you know everything. You don't.

Tuesday, 8 p.m.
107th Street
The Red Notebook

Dear Calvin,

I remember what you said about pain: Pain wakes you up. "Why do you think the Buddha pursued enlightenment?" you said. "Dukkha—dissatisfaction—pain."

Sometimes I think how it would be if I never met you. I would have lived my life. I might have been happy.

I do not understand how I could have once been acceptable to you, and now I am not.

I tell myself that you are bad; I should not have listened to you. But the things you taught us are all I have.

And they still seem true.

Like tapes.

I'm sure you won't remember; you always said you didn't. It was your second lecture.

Ever notice how you go off for a walk, you're going to figure out your whole life. You walk for about half an hour, and what do you notice? You're talking to people in your head, and you're going around in circles. It's a broken record in there, you laughed. *I call those "tapes."*

Of course yes, I remember thinking when you said the word. *Of course; of course.* That day, after your lecture, I walked up Sixth Avenue all the way from the New School to Columbus Circle, elated.

Truth.

Today I was upset. I walked up Broadway, and it was exactly like you said, my mind going in circles.

The most important teaching is when the teacher is not even in the room, you said.

You were right. You are out of the country, but you are still teaching me.

24

Tuesday, 9 p.m.
107th Street
The Blue Notebook

I look down Amsterdam Avenue; the light is still strong and the sky above the buildings is a blue diluted nearly to white. In the street, an old woman walks along pulling a shopping cart behind her; a mother with two kids walks by—one of the little girl's braids sticks straight up. The men sitting under the bodega's awning watch everything, joke, and talk. The salsa is the air of this block. We are all caught in it; we jerk back and forth with its rhythm.

Today while I walked home from work, I thought about what Calvin told us to do when we were upset: just think *I'm no one.* Remember what the Buddha said about the Self—it's an illusion. *You're nobody, so what does it matter if nobody gets hurt*, he said.

Someone asked him how to do that. *So you're walking down the street and you just note things. Forget about "I." Just see what's there.* I did that—walked along and named things: blue car blaring music at the stoplight; stick-thin girl in high-heeled boots; mother with children on scooters; roaring bus with advertisement for Crazy Eddy's on the side; flyer stuck on wall for the Fresh Air Fund; swirl of graffiti on brushed metal streetlamp.

It did help for a very short while. But then my mind started, and I thought about Celeste again and it occurred to me that she was probably right—there is something wrong with me. My throat got hot and I was crying and walking at the same time, and finally I couldn't keep walking anymore so I got to a bench at a community garden in the village and I sat.

I know what Calvin would have said about that. *Self-pity—what good does that do?* I thought about his advice. *Stop thinking about it*, he said. *Change channels. Think about something else.*

25

So I tried it; I bought a *Times*. There was an article about black holes in space—there is a theory that they are at the center of galaxies, that gravity inside them is so intense that everything is crushed to a single dot. Incidentally, the temperature in outer space is -455° Fahrenheit.

When I got to the steps up to my building, Junior was there—it turns out, when he was shot in the foot, it wasn't that bad. He was in shorts past his knees and a tank top that said *Puerto Rico*. His hair was kind of greasy, but he didn't smell; I wonder where he takes a bath. Usually I don't see him around the neighborhood— I just hear him with that raspy voice speaking in Spanish, but today he was there on the stoop. He has been hanging around our building lately.

When he saw me, he said, "How you doing, Mamí?" and when I shrugged he said, "Why so sad?"

I said, "Life is sad," and then he told me that he had grown up on a farm in Puerto Rico, and he wished he was back there.

"I wish I never came here, Mamí," he said, shaking his head.

Before he left, Seth told me that I should not let Junior into the building because he was an addict, but Junior didn't ask me to let him in—I guess he can take care of himself. Climbing the stairs to my apartment, I thought *this is what I've come to—my main company is a crack addict*.

But maybe that isn't so strange. He is addicted to crack. I am addicted to Calvin.

It's a relief to be home. Things are familiar at least. The lumpy plaster walls in the kitchen and the rhythmic cooing of the pigeons in the alleyway outside the kitchen window and the living room with its loose windows banging in their frames, but at least there is light.

I hope I sleep tonight.

I hope I sleep tonight.

I hope I sleep tonight.

Wednesday, June 4, 1 a.m.
107th Street
The Blue Notebook

One a.m. A ghost writes.

I sit here on the ragged white loveseat that Seth and I took from the street. There is the plywood shelving that the former tenants left here, the dark-green, threadbare rug, the paneling that is coming loose from the white walls. I'm naked. Shadows of the trucks trundling up Amsterdam Avenue cross my white ceiling, pass over me, industrial angels that appear briefly on the tops of my thighs before moving on. Outside, the salsa that usually bounces through the block has died down to a hum. Three old men in undershirts sit on upside-down white plastic buckets under the bodega's metal awning across the street, murmuring in Spanish.

I went to bed at 11. *Going to go to sleep now.* Like a normal person: lie down in bed. Close eyes. Sleep.

But that's not possible anymore. Now it's non-stop conversations in my head with Calvin. In one I undressed, told him anecdotes about people at the office. He smirked, enjoying my cleverness. He longed for me: the swing of my narrow shoulder, the outthrust of my hip.

In another, I was full of self-righteous indignation: *how could you? I was your student.* The imaginary Calvin answered me back: *You chose it, didn't you.* I had to admit to myself it was true.

Then begging. *I don't understand what it is you don't love about me.*

Then despair.

When I looked at the clock again, it was 1:30. I got up, walked to the bathroom, looked in the mirror at my own face:

27

You stupid idiot.

Stupid fucking bitch.

"Read the Gita," That is what one of Calvin's students said to me. I did. Here is what Krishna says to Arjuna:

If you can understand what comes between being and nothingness, Arjuna, I'll give you a second head to hold your enlightenment.

Now I am here between being and nothingness.

There is no oxygen and it is extremely cold.

2:30 a.m.

It was Seth who persuaded me to take the writing class at the Y.

"You do it all the time anyway," he said. "Why not meet some other people who do it too."

An Introduction to Memoir. Our writing teacher, Sarah Hamsted: petite, with large hair that swept down in one curve in back of her neck. She wore short skirts and pastel scoop-neck shirts; flats that were like the cloth shoes they sell in Chinatown. She was kind to all of us: the scared young ones, the old ones who talked on and on.

Everyone has a story, she said. *Tell the story that only you can tell.*

The red notebook is the Calvin notebook. The blue notebook is the story of me. It is time to sit and write down what happened: put it in order. If it is in order, maybe it will make sense.

I guess if it has a beginning, that beginning is Seth. It starts with the day there was a knock on the door of my campus apartment; I opened it, and there he was. Beak nose, plump cheeks and small eyes, and a shag haircut left over from the 1970s.

It was the eighties. He dressed cool, in Hawaiian shirts and tight jeans, but that didn't hide how thin he was—scrawny.

Of course I knew him—everyone on campus knew Seth Federman. He had run for class president with the slogan *Seth is Best*. He knew everyone on campus—the jocks and the artsy types and the nerds and the punks; he was the kind of guy who could relate to everyone without anyone thinking he was being fake.

I blushed when I saw who it was. Seth asked for a spatula, and I said we didn't have one.

"Are you sure?" he asked. "Could you look?" Seth then offered, "Making scrambled eggs," because I hadn't said anything. And then he said, "Not much of a conversationalist, are you?" and I laughed stupidly. I thought he was going to go, but he just stood there.

There was a stilted conversation about my major: I said I was in "lit-crit." He wanted to know what books I liked.

When I mentioned Proust he said, "You're kidding me. You really *are* a nerd."

I shrugged and said, "Well, I walk to the beat of my own drummer." I had stupid comebacks like that back then; things I had rehearsed for when I had to hold my own in conversations, which wasn't very often because even in college, I managed to hardly ever go out.

Before Seth, I was alone most of the time. There was Cass, but Cass was the daughter my mother would have liked to have—a doer—so most of the time I was on my own. I walked around rehearsing sentences that I was going to write in my papers to impress my professors, but after Seth the sentences in my head were different—I was talking to *him*.

Seth and I had a lot of fiery conversations. He liked to provoke me and say that literature was a bourgeois pursuit and why didn't I do something to make a difference. I would get passionate and say *that's who I am*, and he would sit back with a lazy grin and say *look at that fire in your eyes, girly,* and then I would say *Girly!* in an outraged voice and he would laugh.

Let's face it: I loved him.

Let's face it: I still do. But I hate him too.

I never went to parties. Before Seth, it was Cass and I hiking in the woods behind campus, talking about Cass's favorite subject: survival. First rule of survival, she said, when I met Seth: don't put all your eggs in one basket. She said she saw what I was doing—I was becoming dependent. I said she was right. But I didn't change.

With Seth, I could be part of things. There were so many party invitations. I would get butterflies in my stomach—I was going to have to make conversation—but the truth was Seth was such a talker, and so comfortable in a crowd, that I usually didn't have to say anything. That suited me. I liked being Seth's silent partner, having people say things to me like "how do you put *up* with this guy!" It felt good to be in the stream of things but attached to someone else doing the swimming. When I stood next to Seth at some party and he told a funny story about his growing up in New York, it was like I was part of it.

Cass didn't like it. She said I depended on him too much.

When it was just me and him, we would talk about authors—Seth majored in poli-sci but minored in literature so we could throw around names like Bellow and DeLillo and feel sophisticated. Seth thought my taste in literature was old-fashioned and he teased me about it. "Jesus!" he'd say—you're like a 19th century schoolmarm!" I would pretend to get mad, but I guess I secretly liked it. I was someone. I had an identity. Who would have thought.

And then there was the sex.

Seth was the first I would ever call a boyfriend. Before him, it had been one-night stands; furtive encounters with boys who I would have sex with in cars, in the back rooms of parties, on golf courses that were closed at night. The next day, they would always pretend they didn't know me.

But with Seth it was different. It was ... reverent. Beneath his cool clothes, Seth was emaciated; he had an intestinal disease, diverticulitis, and I think that was partly why he wanted me so badly—because whatever people said about me on campus, they all agreed that I was *beautiful*—that was always the word.

For Seth, once we started, it was like he was in a trance. "Why don't you turn this way. Take that off," he'd say in a dreamy voice. I remember the second time we ever had sex; he asked me to undress while he watched, and when I was standing there naked, he looked at me and said "you're so hot" in a choked voice. He took my breast in his mouth like a sacrament. When we finished, he was jubilant. He went back to being his irreverent self: eating Corn Flakes in bed with his bed jacket on and watching the football game.

That was something we sparred about. "How can you watch football when we're at college, an institution of higher learning?" I wondered, and Seth sat there with the pink bed jacket on, which was really the inner lining of an old coat and said, "I refuse to be a pseudo-intellectual."

A memory:

I was wrapped in a blanket eating a bagel that had been hanging out in Seth's refrigerator. Seth was being very funny, and I remember thinking I could feel the happiness from him. There was just the bed and the TV. The sky outside was that deep blue it gets before it gets black, and the orange streetlamps were all coming on outside all around campus so the light in the room was artificial and dreamy. I caught a glimpse of myself in the window and I thought *I have someone* and there was a kind of wonder that went with it.

But when we graduated and moved to The City, all that changed.

Seth found me the apartment—somebody's friend's brother was leaving it. It was always like that with him; he always knew someone who knew someone else. I remember the day he took me to see it—I couldn't believe the luck—four big rooms with high ceilings and windows all around with the light streaming in and the view down Amsterdam Avenue all the way to the church. Old-fashioned transoms over the doorways, paneling, in the kitchen a deep sink like the kind you'd find in a janitor's closet. I had not had any idea how I was going to survive after school, and now here we were, a whole apartment, and rent-stabilized, too.

"So are we going to live here together happily ever after?" I said archly, looking down at Amsterdam Avenue. I had assumed that was why he had found the place.

"Ellie," he said, "are you crazy? That's a *terrible* idea. This place is for *you*. Living together would ruin *everything*."

I was looking down at the men hanging out under the awning of the bodega and I remember how my head went silent inside. It was like a movie when the sound goes off. I watched two young guys in cutoffs walk along the sideway. A bus roared by. I noticed the steeple of the church like a black needle in the sky.

Later, of course, my mind started up again. *What kind of person are you? Why would you do this? What is it, am I not good enough? Cass was right—I shouldn't have let myself depend on you.*

We left and I said I would get back by myself and walked rapidly away, with him kind of skipping along beside me saying, "Ellie, Jesus, what is the problem?" I was able to lose him in Grand Central and I took the train back myself. When I got to the campus, I went into my apartment. Later, when he knocked on the door, I would not let him in.

For a week, it was just me and Cass. I told her she was right—I should never have started with him. I asked her if she wanted to move in with me. We started to make plans. I was done with him.

But he kept coming. He kept knocking on the door and he persuaded one of my apartment mates to let him in, and then he came to the door of my bedroom and talked through it, groaning, "Ellie why are you doing this to me why do you think I got you the apartment because I wanted us to be able to see each other why are being like this Jesus talk to me." And finally I did.

I can't stand people going away from me.

Maybe I should have kept the door closed. But I opened it and listened while he told me that it was for me, that he wanted us to be able to keep what we had. "I've seen so many people fuck it up by making it into an institution," he said. He looked so earnest. I listened.

When I told Cass, she said she wasn't going to move in with me. "It's getting too complicated," she said.

We graduated. I moved into the apartment.

Seth got me to give him a key and he would come over whenever he wanted.

When he was over, he would gloat about how good it was.

Do you know how *lucky* we are, Ellie," he said. "Other people would kill to have what we've got. We're both *free* ... Everything's clear."

When we graduated, I had to go out to temp agencies to get work. Sit in a big room filled with other women in job interview clothes: ugly A-line skirt, blazer, blouse. Wait for my name to be called and take a typing test. Say stupid things like "I want to apply my organizational skills in an entry level position with possibilities for advancement."

Cass got a job at a gym.

Seth used his connections and got himself an internship at *The Nation*, where he got to meet all sorts of cool people: someone who had been McGovern's mentor; some girl named Margo who dressed in black and had a ring in her nose. He had met Alexander Cockburn himself, *The Nation's* founder. He had danced with Susan Sarandon at the annual benefit.

There was a lot of talk about Reaganomics and the New Left. I just listened. It was like it had been in college; Seth was the one who brought the world to me.

And there was the lovemaking. Usually at the time of day when the sky was the color of a tropical ocean, just a rectangle of it visible from where we were on the bed. Seth would speak to me in that urgent whisper. *Can you take that off? Turn this way.* Sometimes, after, he would put on music. A couple of times we slow danced in the living room with the light just right, the salsa in the street outside. Threadbare rug, furniture we'd carried up from the street. The room was orange-dark, and I knew I was lucky, young, alive.

There were a lot of fights. There was a fight the day he asked, "Why don't you wear black? I'd like to see you in black." When I asked him why, he said, "Just try it."

Is it because Margo the punk wears black?" He admitted that it was. "This is who I am Seth if you don't like it maybe you should leave."

Seth made fun of me—"Wearing dowdy clothes is who you are? You need to look like you stepped out of a 1940s movie?"

I told him to go. He called and left messages on my answering machine and I listened to them but did not pick up the phone.

For five days.

I called Cass. She wasn't terribly sympathetic. "Boy am I glad I didn't move in with you," she said.

Then it didn't seem to matter anymore. I was talking to him in my head without stopping anyway.

And I wanted him. I wanted that way he looked at me when he needed my body and the way I could tell him things and the things he brought—talking about politics, things I knew nothing about, being in the world. Seth was always in the world.

The worst fight was when he decided he was going to California to work on the campaign for Jerry Brown. We were in the kitchen and I was chopping onions to make us a chicken dish.

"So I'm thinking of going to California," he said. "I've been talking to Margo—she thinks Jerry Brown could be the next president, and I think she's right." I was chopping but I could feel the emotion filling me up like heavy water, rising in my legs and torso and arms.

"Do I mean anything to you, Seth?" I asked. I didn't wait for him to answer. "Because I listen to you talk and I don't think I do." That was the first time I yelled. "You know you're a fucking asshole. You know you don't know how to love. You think you can do whatever you want and I will still be here." I made him give me the key. I told him not to come over anymore. That time I meant it. Of course, in the end I got too lonely.

Wednesday, 3:30 a.m.
107th Street
The Red Notebook

Dear Calvin,

In my neighborhood there is a homeless lady who walks with her pet rabbit in a shopping cart behind her. She wears a big hat, and layers of dirty rouge that crease when she grimaces cake her face. Beneath the hat her lips move. She pulls the cart behind her and the rabbit rides in it: a fat, white bunny with its eyes closed to the light.

I need to stop writing to you. I know that.

I try to look at myself from all angles. When I listened to your lectures, it was like a door opened to the night sky and I felt I would walk out that door and understand everything.

But a year has passed, and nothing is any clearer. Each time I turn a corner of myself, it is just another angle.

In the room where I met you, everything was light; I cried out and you lay beneath me, and held me with your eyes, and saw me. Saw who I was. There was the wall with the crack, the small window holding the world below. Everyone has always said I am beautiful, but when you said it, it meant something different. It meant you were seeing inside me and what you saw was good.

Wednesday, 4 p.m.
The Center for Urban Research
The Blue Notebook

I guess it was Celeste who left the book on my desk: *The Antidepressant Solution*. There was a sticky note on it: *Take a look, Ellie. I think this could help you!* She'd underlined certain parts for me.

Most were about some woman named Anna who "checked all the boxes" of depression. Once she started taking Prozac, she was transformed. She had lots of friends, started dating, got a big raise at work.

Could be you, Celeste had written in the margin.

I stopped reading. I hate it.

Wednesday, 11 p.m.
107th Street
The Blue Notebook

My legs hurt after all that walking. After work, I went to the Reading Room at 42nd Street Research Library. I like it there: the discreet, apologetic throat clearings and weight shifts; the long communal tables; the people who quietly rustle pages there: the young Black man in the luxurious cashmere turtleneck; the nervous white woman in boots and swinging plaid skirt; the hassled young white guy in the suit. Up front the board with the crazy quilt of lighted numbers, the little window where you receive your stack of books.

I got three:

The Theory and Practice of Mandalas.

The Namtar of Dorje Gyaltso

The Sorcerer of the Iron Castle.

Pleased with myself for tracking them down through several card catalog searches. Here is what I think I look like in the 42nd Street Library: I am dowdy, in the linen pants and saddle shoes, but people still see my beauty, wonder about me, the wan girl with the serious face.

My expeditions to the 42nd Street Reading Room started when I moved to New York. I was after magicians.

First, Wan Po, the painter in the imperial court of ancient China who painted a vast landscape, and when the Barbarians were crashing the city gates, magically escaped into it. Then the Athara Veda, Kali.

Wan Po was from a story my father told me. He loved stories like that: the magic of art.

Once I met Calvin, it was all sorts of things. Tibetan folktales, books by Giuseppe Tucci with pictures of secret tantric paintings; biographies of the siddhis, tantric practitioners. I wrote the titles on slips of paper, filled out the book requests, paged through them, puzzled, but was unwilling to give up the hunt.

Today it's *The Sorcerer of the Iron Castle*. He can remove his heart from his body, hide it in a metal box in hidden rooms of his vast castle. This makes him invincible. The landscape around his castle is petrified, stopped in time. Travelers who venture into it end up as his slaves.

I want to do the same: remove my heart from my body, hide it in an iron box.

In my living room, an hour has passed. It is 11:30 but the block is still in full party mode. Someone must have a boom box just below my window because the salsa jingles up, insistent, crazy with its own frenzied dance moves. Someone shouts in Spanish; another person cackles. A breeze shifts the screen I've braced between the bottom windowpane and the sill, moves through the room.

Almost bedtime. I can't face it.

Thursday, June 5, 8:30 p.m.
107th Street
The Blue Notebook

I don't know what Celeste was doing today—she was out. I know she came in at some point, though, because there was an article on my desk when I came back from lunch: "Depression and Insomnia: the Biological Link." Inside a checklist:

For how many days have you ...

... Had little interest or pleasure in doing things?

... Had trouble sleeping or sleeping too much?

... Felt down, depressed or helpless?

... Felt bad about yourself—or that you are a failure or have let yourself or your family down?

I want her to leave me alone.

Wednesday, June 10, 9 p.m.
107th Street
The Red Notebook

Dear Calvin,

It is my second letter to you in two days. "You can write," you said that day in the park, but you haven't written back. This one I am writing in my notebook. If I want to send it, I will have to copy it over onto another piece of paper. At least that makes it harder.

My co-worker used to be a therapist. I am depressed, she says. I need to take a pill. I know what you would say about that: *stop being wrapped up in yourself.*

Low self-esteem—that is one of my problems. I remember when a student asked you about that. She was thin, reedy, dressed in droopy clothes. Her voice was wavering. "But what if you have low self-esteem?" she said. We all sat without moving. We had been wondering the same thing—what if you feel like you are nothing?— but none of us were brave enough to ask you. You smiled pityingly. You shook your head gently, drew in a breath. "Stop thinking about yourself so much," you told her, smiling warmly. "Think about other people instead." She sunk back into her chair in shame, and we all had our answer.

Thursday, June 11, 10 p.m.
107th Street
The Blue Notebook

As I watch, a toy person goes into a miniature store. It's close to 108th Street, sandwiched between the fake pizzeria and the fake deli. A man in jeans and a flannel shirt comes to the door, looks out.

I've been in that store. I went in to buy deodorant when I first moved here; the man behind the register said something in Spanish and they both laughed. "I cannot sell," he said. I looked confused and he said it again. "No for sale," he said.

Later, when I told Seth about it, he laughed at me too. "Those aren't real stores," he said. "They're fronts for drugs. You didn't know that?" That was why he liked this neighborhood, he said—it wasn't gentrified yet. "But it will be," he said, "it's the eighties."

So far that hasn't happened.

Beside the fake drug store, a dry cleaner that really does have plastic-jacketed coats, pants, and dresses hanging from the ceiling; a 99 cents store with wares out on the sidewalk; a bodega.

The inside and the outside: that is what I am thinking about. When I first moved here, I looked at myself in the mirror and admired my own face: the straight, brown hair, dark eyes and gently declining chin line; the mauve circles under the eyes, a beauty that didn't let people in. I could answer for myself: I had the job, a place to live, a quasi-boyfriend. Inside me was a person trying to keep her balance in an earthquake, but no one needed to know.

I wore my life. I had my "signature style"—linen pants, saddle shoes—and I could answer the usual questions: where I worked,

41

what I did, where I lived. I wore Seth, too: his flippy hair, Hawaiian shirts that hid his skinniness; his quirky hipness, brash political statements, internship at *The Nation*. We both liked saying where we lived. We'd toss it out in conversation—Spanish Harlem—to show how tough we were, that we could move through multiple worlds.

Friday, June 12, 1 a.m.
107ᵗʰ Street
The Blue Notebook

If I go through it all chronologically, maybe things will fall into place.

At 11 p.m. I watched myself in the bathroom mirror as I swallowed two aspirin with a swig of vodka. Then I lay down. My mind would not let me go.

Now it is 1 a.m. the next day.

In the street below, the old men sitting outside the bodega look like performers under stage lights. In the darkened street, a few voices fly up from people sitting in doorways, hidden from sight.

I am thinking about the first time I saw Calvin.

It started with a mysterious flyer in the East West Bookstore: *Free Lecture, The Secret of Happiness*, first Saturday of the month, and an address on East 14ᵗʰ Street.

Cass and I had been meeting at the East West Bookstore after her yoga class; it was right across the street. Cass loved yoga and tried to get me to go. I wouldn't, but she was able to seduce me into the bookstore. "You will love it, El," she said. "It's you."

She was right. I loved the mysterious titles: *Man and His Symbols; I and Thou; The Secret of the Blue Diamond*. And then that sign: *The Secret of Happiness*.

"You *have* to go, Ellie," said Cass. She couldn't come with me; she had to work.

When I got there, I pushed a bell next to a door on the street; then a click and the door opened to a long staircase. At the top of the staircase, another door.

Inside, a forty-foot-long loft, windows at the far end that looked out on 14th Street, metal folding chairs with all kinds of people sitting on them: a girl in a rainbow-striped leotard with a huge ponytail on top of her head; a hefty, graying woman in a cotton dress; a man in his twenties in orange; a nerdy type with the face of a gargoyle; three young girls with long hair to their waists that giggled and beamed at each other.

And Calvin. Face of a Greek god but without the helmet; the aquiline nose, proud, glittering eyes. A hippie-god: crazy white beard sticking out all over the place. Bright yellow tee shirt with blue Sanskrit lettering on it, work boots, and janitor pants with his belly slung over the belt. Already he stood out to me as slightly dangerous. I went to the back to avoid him.

At first I didn't know he was the one who would be speaking: he was talking to someone up front. Later, I noticed the same two people at every lecture—the heavy woman with gray curls framing her face, plump hips that swayed under long skirts and the bald guy with bulging eyes. I realized Calvin had an entourage. But not that first day.

Finally he moved to the front of the room, plopped his blue JanSport on a table, and rummaged through it. He turned and cleared his throat.

"Just at the East West Bookstore," he said loudly. "Guy at the front wants me to check my backpack." He holds the backpack up. "Store policy," he says.

Calvin shook his head from side to side, chuckling to himself. "I said to him, 'Well, you're going to have to have a different policy … because I'm not going to be checking this bag.'"

We were all in shock, I think—at least, the new people. We'd come here expecting magic, and what were we getting? An irritable, working-class hippie.

But none of us were about to leave. Not in a place like that, where everything you did was out in the open, subject to comment. You could tell Calvin was the kind of man who would call you out in front of a crowd.

That day, Calvin told us that by coming there, we were starting a journey, just as the Buddha had. If we were here, it was because of dukkha. Dukkha, he said, could be translated as suffering, but a better way to think of it was dissatisfaction. And what were we dissatisfied with?

Samsara.

"So what is samsara?" said Calvin. He shouted the answer: "The rat race, people. The endless cycle of existence. Stop the world I want to get off."

I could feel the shock in my body when he yelled. I kept my eyes busy with the details: blond-wood floorboards with black cracks between them, black holes where the nails were. A bookshelf with a snow globe on it.

The next minute his voice was reasonable again, even benevolent. "Once you discover samsara, you start thinking the way the Buddha did. So what did the Buddha think?" Calvin nodded his head, agreeing with himself. "Better find a way out."

Then Calvin started talking about Siddhartha. "Prince Siddhartha," he said. "Talk about having it all. The palace, the beautiful wife, the baby son ... If Siddhartha lived today, he would have been ... hmm, let me see." His face lit up. "JFK Jr.," he said. A cautious titter from the rest of us. "Gucci shoes, Brooks Brothers suits ..." More titters. "He would have had an in-ground pool. He would been one of those people who got into Studio 54."

People were tittering loudly then. Calvin laughed too from the pleasure of it. He looked up, his face to the ceiling. With his mouth open, his bad teeth sticking out, I remember feeling embarrassed for him.

He told the rest of the story: "But then what happens?" He raised his eyebrows high, looked at us intently. "Siddhartha goes to town. What does he see in town?" Calvin shouted again: "The human condition, folks: birth, old age, sickness, death. SAMSARA, folks," he roared. "Even the best day of your life is not good enough."

The rest of the story went quickly: Siddhartha leaving the palace, his wife, his young son. Going into the woods to meditate; vowing not to come out until he had achieved enlightenment. The many austerities; the temptations from the demon Mara.

And then, enlightenment.

"So now," said Calvin, "you are all here because you are like Siddhartha. You experience dukkha, and you want a way out. So now it starts—your journey away from samsara."

I felt embarrassed, but also good. It was as if we were at church; consecrated because we wanted to be better.

Of course, it's the end of the lecture that I remember most clearly. That was when Calvin showed us the bottom of the painting, rows and rows of small, cross-legged buddhas. He told us that people new to Buddhism had a misconception that there was only one Buddha, but in Tibetan Buddhism, there was no "The Buddha." We all had Buddha Nature. We were all going to be buddhas someday. In fact, he said, we were already buddhas because we had Buddha Nature.

Then he got the idea—we were going to go around the room. When he pointed at us, we had to stand and introduce ourselves as buddhas. He started in the front row—the heavy-set woman in the long skirt. She stood, giggling self-consciously.

"Judith Buddha," she said.

"Judith the Buddha of the Lower East Side," said Calvin. Everyone laughed.

Then the bald guy with bulging eyes. When Calvin pointed at him, he made a grotesque face, stood up.

"Edwin Buddha," he said, in a thread voice.

The girl in the rainbow-striped leotard made everyone laugh by making hers sexy. "Devorah Buddha," she said softly.

It went on and on. A stocky woman with the face of a frog and a bandana over her gray hair. A tall, ironic man in his thirties, dressed in a long button-down shirt and khakis. An older blonde woman in a halter top and with one glass eye.

Finally me.

I was trying with everything in me to keep cool and not to blush, but when I had to stand, I could feel the heat radiating from my cheeks.

"Ellie Buddha," I eked out.

"I-can't-hear-you," Calvin stage-whispered. Someone laughed. I could feel my face get hotter.

I said it again, my voice croaking. "Ellie Buddha."

"Wispy," said Calvin, interested. I was a bug in a jar he held up to the light, shook to see what would happen.

More laughter. Calvin's eyes swept the room.

"You LAUGH," he roared. A shocked silence.

Into the silence: "It's always the wallflower, folks. It's always the wallflower who gets there in the end."

When Calvin stopped talking, it broke up. People got up out of their seats; wandered forward. I fled.

2 a.m.

When Seth left for California, I moved my bed into this small room. It's the room next to the fire escape, with French doors into the living room. That's why I like it; not as much light as the living room, but not as dark as the bedroom where Seth and I used to sleep. I painted the floor a light sea green.

When writing your story, said Sarah Hamsted, *think deeply about cause and effect.*

I am trying to think of the reason for Calvin. I guess it was partly the way things were going with Seth.

A day I remember:

We were in bed together. Sunset. Seth had put on Joan Armatrading, and I swayed to it while standing naked over him. In bed with Seth, I was always happy. That was the only time Seth really needed me. When he got that look in his eyes, a mixture of worship and hunger.

"I went to a lecture," I said. "Last week. Buddhism."

"You did?" I enjoyed the look of surprise on his face. Seth never thought me capable of taking initiative.

"Yeah." I did a little half step on the foam mattress, felt it condense under my feet.

"How did that happen?"

"I saw a flyer."

"So now you're enlightened?"

"Ha ha."

"I'm just saying. It's not always all about politics. There are other ways to look at the world."

"What's this guy's name, anyway?"

"Calvin Ross. He looks like Jerry Garcia," I giggled. "Huge beard, white hair, psychedelic tee shirts. He wears janitor pants," I said.

"Okay, so enlighten me. Help me see the light, Ellie." He looked up at me, skeptical.

"Well, I don't understand everything ..." I said. "But the Buddha had everything, he was a prince, and then he realized that even if you have everything, it's still just basically pain, you know? Sickness, death, old age ... so he decided—'I'm going to find a way out,' and then he meditated till he became enlightened!"

"Not sure I get it."

I gathered myself. "People are so selfish," I said. "People are so ... I mean most people are not good, you'd have to agree with me."

"I'm not sure I would."

"Would you agree that most people are like 'me, me, me?'"

"Not sure I would agree with that either."

"Well *I* think most people are selfish and *I* think that's why wars happen. And I *don't* think wars are going to stop because of politics."

I stopped, looked at him triumphantly. Seth was lying in bed eyeing *The Baseball Encyclopedia*, his favorite book. He had his Hawaiian shirt unbuttoned and his skinny chest showed through the opening.

"Ellie, things aren't going to change because Baba Ram Dass in janitor pants starts talking about Eastern religion," said Seth. "Things are going to change through political grassroots action. They have always changed that way. What you are talking about is religion. How, exactly, has religion made the world better?"

"It isn't religion, Seth. It's looking *inside* yourself."

"Everybody wants something, Ellie. Even Mr. Ram Dass. You just have to know what it is."

"I don't think things are like that."

"I bet he just wants to get down your pants."

"Jesus! You always make everything *dirty*. He didn't even notice me. And besides he's old."

"How old?"

"He has a white beard."

"So what?"

"You always make everything dirty," I said again.

48

"Everything *is* dirty," said Seth.

"No it isn't."

"Yes it is."

Things turned out badly, that day. We were supposed to go out to dinner together, but Seth told me he was meeting someone from *The Nation*.

"You can come," he said.

"We had a date," I said.

He shrugged. "Harry Flock is a senior editor. This is the only time he could give me. Don't make it mean something it doesn't, Ellie," he said warningly. But I was already up and walking away. He followed me toward the bedroom, but I shut the door, locked it.

"Open this up, Ellie," he said.

"Leave me alone, Seth," I said.

"But that's exactly what you DON'T want."

"Well I want it now," I said.

"*So* Buddhist of you, Ellie," he said, sarcastically.

I didn't answer. I lay in bed and thought about leaving. Packing a suitcase, trundling down to the street. He would come over and I wouldn't be here. I went through it in my mind: throwing everything I owned into a suitcase, going.

But when I got to the part of the fantasy where I walked away, I always had to stop. Where would I go?

Friday, 1 p.m.
South Street Seaport
The Blue Notebook

I am having lunch by myself, sitting on the bench Celeste and I always go to. It's humid, cloudy. There is a hot breeze coming from the bay; the usual traffic around the food truck. Small figures swarm the "sloop" with its high mast and white sides.

Celeste was not around again today.

Good.

Here is another thing Sarah Hamsted told us about writing: *When you write your story*, she said, *go towards what glows.*

What glows.

Laurel.

The rows of colonials on streets with names like Andrew Place and Daisy Road; the arching tree branches over Main Street; the low rhododendron bushes near the war monument at the center of town, with its polished granite surface chiseled with names: *Frederick Burton, Thomas Kull.*

A memory:

I am in my father's studio. Windows that look out on a patch of sparse trees. Beyond, the playground. Inside, a series of rusted iron rings like flat donuts that my father has hung on his wall; a large, wooden key; a fluttering photograph from a magazine; two or three index cards with parts of poems typed on them. The studio is a museum of my father's mind.

I am lying on the floor. My father is painting in oils. His brush makes soft passes against the canvas. Peace.

My father, Max Adkins: 6'4" in jeans whitened at the knees, flannel shirts. Blond hair all shades from wheat to white. Bemused expression; distant smile. Eyelashes so light he looks as if he has none at all.

My father is telling me about some artists he knows. Sven Harmond makes dioramas of shopping malls. Dwight Cala makes paintings that are just slashes of color across the canvas. Peter Fannon makes giant metal sculptures that are big enough to walk through.

"Wow," I say. That is all I can think of. My father has been talking to me about art since I was six or so. Showing me pictures, talking to me about what to notice. I know that you have to say "Paul Clay" instead of "Paul Klee," that you say "Van Go" and not "Van Gog." I know what surrealism is.

"I'll tell you a secret though," he says.

"What's that?" When my father offers to tell me secrets, I try to sound casual, not get too excited. I'm only a child. Sometimes he doesn't seem to notice.

"There's an artist who I've discovered, who makes me want to give a show."

"Oh yeah? Who?"

"A figurative artist. A woman—Avery Snow. She does tiny, photorealistic images of objects—apples, sewing needles, drinking glasses, printer blocks ... I thought I would hate them, but I *love* them."

My father's voice is full of wonder. His own work couldn't be more different—huge, wall-sized abstracts with lots of colors. I am always trying to see something recognizable in them: a building, a person.

My father "giving a show" is an ongoing topic of conversation. He has often been tempted to do it, but he also refuses to "sell out" and "suck up" to gallery owners. My father calls gallery owners "philistines." He explains why they so often don't like his work— he hasn't sold out. He isn't commercial enough. "But that isn't what art is about," he always says, shaking his head. "It was never about that. Art was never about catering to a crowd. It was never about making a buck. So strange, but I find it incredibly inspiring. I want to do a show with her where there are these tiny, meticulous images next to what I do." He looks up at the sky but then he turns to me and grins. "Space."

Two of my father's paintings are leaning against the far wall. There are vague bandshells of color on them: lime green color spread thin so it fades to white then darkens again at the edges; deep red.

I know a secret about them: they are not really abstract—they really *are* pictures of something—the astral realm.

My father has been telling me about the astral realm for over a year now. You can train yourself to go there. You can stay awake in your dreams, and then you will learn to fly through the astral air and visit people before you return to your bed and sleep at night. My father reads books about it—"All religions speak of it," he says, "if you know where to look. We can all do this. We just have to train our minds."

At ten, reading my father's books is beyond me, but I spend a lot of time thinking about the astral realm. When I am alone in my room, I write stories about it. I have created a character—Princess Crystal, who travels through the astral-sphere and saves people: old women who have gotten lost; little dogs tricked by unscrupulous pranksters. Princess Crystal can see past appearances. She can see people's astral bodies, hear astral conversations that no one else does.

When I am done, I bring the stories to my father's studio and read them aloud to him while he works. He listens, nodding thoughtfully, then shakes his head back and forth. "You've got it, Ellie," he'll say. "You're perceptive as hell, you know that?"

That's a sentence I carry around in my head when I am out of the house—walking back and forth to school with books on my arm. At school, I get good marks, but no one likes me.

Perceptive as hell.

It is late morning. Inside our house the rooms will be filled with the roar of my mother's vacuum, a monster that moves through the rooms. If I were not here with my father, I would be inside the house, helping my mother. She would have me cleaning or sorting piles of art supplies. In addition to her job, my mother volunteers as an art teacher at a halfway house. My mother believes in being useful. She says this emphatically. Sometimes her head bobs when she says it, as if she's pecking at the word.

This is my mother's mental burden: I spend too much time in my father's studio. Mooning, she calls it. I do not have friends my own age. She says this so frequently it has become a song that follows me around the house: *friends your own age.*

My mother, Bonnie Adkins, is wire-thin with dark brown hair cut close to her head, a wide lipsticked mouth, and sharp cheekbones. She runs the physical therapy department at a rehab center, supervising five or six physical therapists. She sometimes tells stories about the other therapists—Myra who has "husband problems," Wendy, whose oldest son is "nothing but trouble."

When she is not working, she is perpetually busy. She cooks, shops, pulls stiff, dry clothes off the line. Whisks me around town to the library or the supermarket, where we always run into people she knows: the secretary from my school; a co-worker; a lady who works at the pharmacy—and shouts with laughter at something that does not seem funny to me. The weather. The way the supermarket doesn't have a certain ingredient just when you need it.

There are things about me my mother does not like. The way I would rather read a book than *do something*, for instance; the way I cry easily. That's why I am so often in my father's studio.

On this day, I have been thinking. My mother believes in *caring about people and having friends*. She is always exhorting me to *think of others*. My father, I know, thinks differently. I can tell from some of the things he says: *most people don't think very much; hell is other people* (he always says this one with a look of delighted naughtiness.)

I ask my father if he thinks it's bad that I don't have more friends.

"That's your mother talking," he says. "Her credo."

"What's a credo?"

My father goes back to painting. "A belief system," he says. "Basically, it's a form of ingratiation."

"What's ingratiation?"

"When you do something for someone so they will like you," he says.

"People like Mom?" I ask.

"Yes," says my father.

I wait.

"But how do you know what's true?"

My father stops again, brush poised mid-air. When he answers, his voice is sonorous. "The truth is liquid, Ellie."

"What does *that* mean?"

"It's not *fixed*. It's not divided into right and wrong." He crinkles one eyes, smiles at the canvas. "The world has light and dark, Ellie. The darks are just as important." He looks over at me.

"Are you and mom different?"

My father wipes his hand on his thigh, leaving a streak of blue.

"Like black and white," he says.

"So what am I?" There is a faint note of distress in my voice.

He stops, looks at me, thinks for a minute. "You, my dear, are a very nice shade of gray."

Seth used to make fun of me when I talked about Laurel. "I lost it, Seth," I'd say in a hurt voice. "You don't understand."

"Jesus, Ellie," he'd say. "Just live your life."

Saturday, June 13, 2 p.m.
East Village
The Blue Notebook

At the table across from mine, a guy with a safety pin through his ear is eating a mushroom burrito. The girl next to him, black skirt hiked high over her onion-white legs, leans over, takes a bite from his fork. I am in the courtyard at Café Olana in the East Village, surrounded by brick walls. This is the place to be.

But I don't really care about that. I care about one thing:

Cass is back.

Cass with her bitten-down nails, sharp face all pointing forward; dark hair; with her thin, jumpy legs.

She just paid her bill and left, but I stayed to write in my notebook before I forget.

I came home last night and the green light on my answering machine was pulsing. When I pushed play, Cass's voice filled my living room. "Hey Ellie, I'm back let's meet."

Happiness.

She looks different from when she left. Then, she was all business: short hair, camouflage pants, hiking boots. She liked to talk about camping gear: the pros and cons of a JanSport versus a North Face; the best kinds of sleeping bags. She was going to live in a fire tower in Oregon for the summer and kept talking about what a difference the gear made. "Not going to be a lot of bathing going on," she said. "Going to have to keep it simple."

It was just when Seth started to talk about going to California that Cass announced it. My whole body hurt when she told me. *What about me*? I almost said, but even if I'd said it, it wouldn't have made a difference, she would have gone. My first thought when she told me: that I deserved it. Hadn't I stayed with Seth?

"What if something happens there?" I asked. "A young woman, alone ..." Cass rolled her eyes at me.

"If there's one thing you know about me, Ellie, it's that I'm a survivor."

Which is true. Cass's mother is agoraphobic. Since college, she's been telling me the stories: by the age of ten, she was doing the food shopping by herself. Her mother did not take her to doctor's appointments. Her mother did not come to her graduation. Her mother would get up in the morning, eat a piece of toast, turn on the television, and sit there all day. By the age of twelve, Cass was leaving. She would trek into the woods and camp there, just to get away.

The Cass who left me was an outdoorswoman. The Cass I met today was completely different: black pants, tee shirt, cargo jacket. She has dyed her red hair black, with one magenta streak through it. The effect is jarring: blue eyes, black hair, chalky skin.

"Cass?" She turned her face to me. Surge of relief. It was her. "You've *completely* changed yourself."

She laughed. Cass's eyes are a little too big for her face. They pull at you; glossy and intense.

"What happened?" I asked, sliding down next to her. "You've turned ... *goth*."

She shrugged. Her eyes flicked over the tables next to us. "Something different." That's how she's always been, isn't it? As soon as one thing ends, she wants to do something completely different. Reinvent herself.

A menu was delivered. I didn't look at it. "So how was it?"

She grimaced. "Disappointing."

"Why?"

She rolled her eyes. "Crowded! It was supposed to be in the middle of nowhere and it was crowded!"

"A *fire tower*?"

"It was evidently some famous place that people liked to hike to."

"Oh. Did you have to let them into your bedroom and stuff?"

"No. But they were *there*. It was supposed to be me and the wilderness. How many acres and they all have to come to my fucking spot."

"That sucks."

"And the supervisor was an asshole. Some rednecky guy who kept coming to check that I

wasn't doing drugs or anything. I think he was hoping I'd invite him into my bed or something."

"Oh."

"In the end, I had to move into my car. He was giving me the creeps." She looked across the courtyard, made a face.

I think about it now: how strong she is. I would have fallen apart. But of course, I wouldn't have gone in the first place.

"I could never have done what you did," I said. "Off in the wilderness like that? And then living in your car?"

She turned her face away, looking for the waitress. "No I can't see you doing that. Reading Proust and having tea in your car. Do you even drive?"

That's Cass's idea about me, isn't it? I'm the intellectual-living-in-a-bubble. She's the woman of action.

At the next table, a man is demonstrating kung fu moves with his fingers on the checkered tablecloth. His friend, with slicked-back hair, is laughing harder than he needs to.

I met Cass my first year in college, even before Seth. Getting takeout at the local diner, and there she was in a waitress uniform. I didn't even know she went to our school until she blurted out "Have you taken Filmore's lit class?" Unlike the rest of us, Cass didn't have anyone putting her through school; she was paying her own way. She was flunking and in danger of losing financial aid. When I wrote her paper for her that very night, she sat and watched me, knees jiggling. The entire time, she chanted "thank you, thank you, thank you," in a continuous whisper.

I loved her right from the beginning.

"So now what?" I asked. "Where are you living, anyway?"

Her face changed. "I have an idea," she said. "Are you ready?"

"Okay."

"Everest."

"You're going to Mt. Everest?"

"I'm going to climb it."

"Oh." I worked to keep my face muscles stiff. "Doesn't it cost a lot of money to do that?"

"It does," said Cass, "but I met someone and I think I can go for free or very low cost."

"Oh. Where did you meet him?"

She leaned forward again. "In a bar. His name is Faraday but no one is allowed to call him that." She grinned. "We have to call him Tommy Hilfiger."

My eyebrows flew up. "Because?"

"He says we are all famous. We should all take the names of famous people because we will all do great things. He says we should have a world without rank."

"Isn't climbing Everest pretty dangerous?"

"But I'd be going with the group."

"What group?"

"The New Heights Group."

"What's that?"

Cass leaned forward, her eyes grabbing me. "The New Heights Group," she said

dramatically, "is a thought experiment. What if we did inspiring things to inspire people to do the right thing?" She leaned back, one white hand crossing her chest to grasp the other arm. "They climb mountains and raise money for destitute people," she said.

"Wow," I said.

She came forward again. "I actually thought of you right away when he told me. Remember how we used to go to the East West Bookstore together?"

"Yes."

"You went to that lecture and then you were so interested in the Asian stuff? Buddhism? Taoism?"

"Yeah."

"What if we could *go there*."

"I'm not going to climb Everest, Cass," I said. "Maybe I need to do something, but it isn't going to be that."

She blinked her eyes; the jet-black hair shook around her face. "I want you to," she said petulantly. I laughed.

"I'm not an athlete, Cass. You know that. Climbing Everest would be like ..."

"You could get in shape," she said.

"I'm not like you, Cass. I'm not ... active."

"You could start working out," she said. Her face slanted into a grimace.

I guess I've been sitting here twenty minutes. At the table next to mine, the same guy is demonstrating kung fu moves with his fingers. Across from him, two girls in green army jackets.

I'm sitting here thinking about what happened when Cass said Mt. Everest. I thought: the Ralung phurbu.

Calvin never stopped talking about it. He would give out one of those tribute poems to his teacher, Geshe Thondup. In the beginning, I was embarrassed by them: "Geshe Thondup, precious guru, the sky bows at your feet ..." I didn't think Calvin was much of a poet.

Calvin would read them out loud to us, and then he would talk about the phurbu.

There was a prophecy: whoever had the phurbu would be Geshe Thondup's dharma heir. It was in Tibet, at a monastery. It had been buried in a secret place when the Chinese invaded. Only Geshe Thondup's students knew the location.

It was what Calvin had gone to Tibet for, two summers ago, but he hadn't been able to persuade the Chinese guide to go to Ralung. He'd wanted to get the phurbu before a rival student, Eckerman, but he'd failed. When Cass said "Everest," I saw myself, just for a minute. I had gone to Tibet with Cass and gotten it, and I was handing it to him. He was looking at me like I was more than he'd ever thought.

Voices rise up in the courtyard; the waitress is peering at me, wishing I would go. I think about Cass showing up with dyed black hair, completely changing herself. How I'm the opposite, dressed in my earth-colored linen pants, saddle shoes; trying to blend.

Safe.

Saturday, 7 p.m.
107th Street
The Blue Notebook

Outside my window, the tops of heads pass by; bodies leave doorways, make forays, come back to where they were. There are eight or ten people sitting on plastic chairs outside on the sidewalk, the salsa jumping through the air.

We had to read other essayists in Sarah Hamsted's memoir class. One of them was Joan Didion. "We tell ourselves stories in order to live."

Here is how I thought it would be when Seth and I moved in together: we'd have brunch on the weekends, eggs and bagels that I made for us in my thrift store clothes. We'd read *The Times* together, have lamb chops in the dim kitchen with the pigeons cooing in the alley behind the window, and we'd talk about the things we'd talked about in college: politics, how things really were.

But once we graduated, it wasn't like that. Seth came over to have sex, but the rest of the time he had people to meet: new friends he'd made while interning at *The Nation*; friends he'd had in public school.

We tell ourselves stories in order to live.

Saturday, 8:30 p.m.
107th Street
The Red Notebook

Dear Calvin,

These days it is still light enough at 8:30 for me to walk to Riverside Park and look at the lights across the river. You live in New Jersey; that much I know. I suppose you are somewhere else—"Out of the country," you said—but I need a direction to turn to. I talk to the horizon as if it is you.

Coming back, I passed a mother and her young child. I walked behind them, heard their conversation.

The child could not stop crying. "If you don't shut up, I will send you to an orphanage," said the mother. The child's wail became a column in the air.

It is not a kind world.

What does it mean to be a bodhisattva, you said. *It means that you put everyone else's salvation ahead of your own.*

You were right. People are suffering, and what am I? A selfish mess.

But I do not seem to know how to change myself.

And I didn't think falling in love with you was wrong.

A bodhisattva. I do not understand why you invited me if I wasn't good enough.

Saturday, 10:30 p.m.
107th Street
The Blue Notebook

Outside, the sound of a siren. Night, finally. From the floor of my living room, I can only look through the top panes of my windows: dark blue of the deepening sky and the top rows of windows in other buildings—yellow lighted squares. From below, the carnival of voices. When a truck passes, my own windows bang against their frames, but bring no breeze.

If a story is keeping you up in the middle of the night, get up and write it down, said Sarah Hamsted.

Samsara. Before I met Calvin, I did not only research magicians. I was also into animal rights. I collected pictures: the pig chained to an abattoir conveyor belt with fear in its eyes; chimpanzees intentionally addicted to cocaine; kittens with iron helmets fitted to their heads, needles permanently inserted into their brains. *This is what the world is.*

At the library, I looked up Saint Paul the Hermit, who left his riches and lived in a cave in the desert; St. Padre Pio who worked 19 hours per day for 51 years, healing the sick, caring for the poor.

I read, marveled—how did they do it?

Love—it sounds so ennobling. *I am in love.*

This is not ennobling. This is the addict shoving the needle into her ankle because it's the last available space on her body.

Saturday, 11:30 p.m.
107th Street
The Red Notebook

I need to remember that I wished for Calvin before he came. Even before I walked into that loft, there was an empty space, waiting for him.

The first indication that Calvin was magic: he read minds.

"The real teaching happens when the teacher is not even in the room"—that was something Calvin said in one of those early lectures.

Same loft with the folding metal chairs, long blond floorboards, thangkas on the walls. Roughly the same group of people: the girl in the leotard; the heavyset woman with the gray curls and hearty laugh; a man in a faded tennis hat; Calvin in the orange tee shirt with the ZZ Top beard.

I had, in fact, started to think about him when I was not in one of the lectures. Think *to* him, asking questions. *How could it be that ...? Why did you say that ...?*

So when he announced that, at the beginning of the lecture, "The real teaching happens when the teacher is not even in the room," I remember blushing, looking down into my lap.

Sunday, June 14, 1 a.m.
107th Street
The Red Notebook

Just because a wish comes true doesn't mean it isn't scary. When I met Calvin, my first instinct was to keep my distance. I could see—anyone could—that he was dangerous. I went to the lectures, but I always left as soon as they were over.

The lectures were once a week, Saturday afternoons.

The hawk nose; the wild man beard. Once I walked into that loft, I always asked myself if I shouldn't walk out again.

But I couldn't stay away. There was the loft itself— the thangkas, with their weird many-armed figures, surrounded by tendrils and flowers; the objects on the walls—scenes under glass (Niagara Falls; Hawaii) made of butterfly wings. On the long table at the end of the loft, a tall, empty glass globe; animal skeletons. Then there were the people; cool-looking, in their upper twenties or thirties in scruffy-looking village clothes; girls in tie-dyed tee shirts. When you come to The City from the suburbs, I suppose that is partly what you are looking for ... you are looking for the circus. Calvin was certainly that.

That second lecture was the first time he showed slides. He told us we couldn't really understand Buddhism unless we went to Asia. "But don't worry," he said. "I am going to take you there." Whoever owned that loft had also provided a slide projector and screen. Calvin turned the projector on, showed us slides of a pyramidal, blood-red building of painted brick rising up in the middle of a desert. A monastery in Tibet.

Tibet, he said, to Westerners, a fantasy-land, and maybe rightly so.

"A lot of magic in Tibet," he said. In the stories he told, there were oracles; lakes you can see the future in. Gods come down and briefly inhabit people. I think he talked about the phurbu then, too: magic objects that can rip a hole in the fabric of the universe, show you other worlds.

The version of Buddhism that existed in Tibet was Vajrayana. "So what does that mean?" he said. By then we were used to Calvin's style of questioning—ask a question, as if he were us, the audience, then answer it. "Vajrayana Buddhism," he said. "The lightning path—enlightenment in one lifetime. Traveling in Asia is a good way to be on the Path. You're trekking in Nepal during the monsoons. You look down at your feet and see the mud curling a certain way. Without even telling yourself, you start to run— mudslide!" He stopped, nodding. "Mudslides can kill you," he said. "But that knowledge—the moment you look down and you know without telling yourself—that's Vajrayana consciousness."

"No one ever laid out the Buddha's path for him, folks," he said. "If you want to follow the Buddha, you're going to have to deal with some uncertainty." He stopped, looked out at us with raised eyebrows—were we ready for this? "Think of it this way: it's when your feet are off the ground that you are on the Path." He stopped. No one spoke. "So if you're going to follow THIS path," he said, "you're going to have to put on your Vajrayana socks—your off-the-ground socks."

When the lecture was over, we sat there, a bit stunned. It was like we were waking up from a movie we had just watched; the lights had been turned on and we were all blinking our way back to real life. I was about to leave when Calvin said loudly that tea was going to be served. "Anyone who wants to be enlightened has to stay for tea," he announced.

That was the first time I actually spoke to Calvin. I went to the far side of the room: beside the animal skeletons, the long table held a large shell mounted on a dowel, an Indonesian shadow puppet, a row of silver balls on wire threads. Calvin came up behind me.

"Contemplating samsara?" he said companionably.

I blushed, turned toward the window to hide it.

"So how did you hear about us?" he asked my back. I murmured something about the flyer at the East West Bookstore. He narrowed his eyes, looked at the wall above my head. "Ah yes, the flyer." He looked at me. "How did you come to be in the East West Bookstore?"

I shrugged. "I like it there," I said lamely.

"Searching for esoteric wisdom," said Calvin. I didn't answer. "And may I ask what you do for a living?"

"I'm a secretary," I said, fighting down the blood in my face.

He laughed shortly. Close up, I could feel the heat from his body. "No wonder you come to a lecture about happiness," he said. "Do you like your job?"

"It's okay," I said. "I mainly type labels. If you see a mailing somewhere, chances are it was typed by me." I gave him a half-smile, and Calvin raised his eyebrows.

"A label-typer who goes to the East West Bookstore to shop for happiness," said Calvin. "You must have been seeking wisdom." I widened my eyes. "That's a good thing," he added.

I looked out the window: down below a woman with a kerchief around her head bent over a stroller in bright sunshine while a bus went by.

"You can't find unless you seek," he said.

Someone called to Calvin from the other side of the room, and he went to them. But when I left, he called across the room to me.

"We have lectures every week, label-typer," he called. "Don't forget to come back."

Tuesday, June 16, 2 a.m.
107th Street
The Blue Notebook

At the end of the article Celeste left for me, there were "tips" for a good night's sleep:

- Go to bed at the same time each night.
- Do not watch television before going to bed.
- Don't lie in bed if you can't sleep.

So I don't. I rise, stalk naked through the half-darkness, sit on the white loveseat and watch truck headlights approach, rattle past, wipe the white walls of my living room with blades of light. Get up and go to the window: a camaraderie of voices down there.

Today after work, I walked from Wall Street all the way to Midtown. On the corner of 14th and 4th Avenue, a man with half a pant leg, the bottom half exposing a wound that was wrinkled and gray at the edges. He cursed the air out. "You *fucking* mother-fucker; get the *fuck* out of my face."

"Tapes," said Calvin.

At Park Avenue South, I was in corporate land; the chiseled stone buildings rising directly up, towering above me. I walked fast, trying not to look at myself in store windows, but at the corner I stopped, looked over, and there I was, in my dowdy office pants and flats, reflected in the polished black marble. I hated myself: a ghost face; a pale balloon with two uncomprehending eyes.

Wednesday, June 17, 10 a.m.
The Center for Urban Research
The Blue Notebook

There are no windows in the mailroom; the calamine-lotion walls surround me. There is a high counter that runs along three walls of the room; I am sitting in the corner. Just a few paragraphs in the blue notebook before I resume.

Here is what I have been doing for the last hour: binding reports. It's a four-step process: take the stack of papers, line them up, pull down the lever to make a row of perfectly rectangular holes. Then, take the plastic spiral thing and thread the teeth through the holes. After that, slip the report into a manila envelope and affix the label, then use the porcelain roller with water in the well to seal the envelope. One report takes about seven minutes. I have been doing this since I got here; it's about noon, now. I have at least one hundred to get through. There are reasons why I like it here: a safe, windowless room that does not ask anything of me is one of them. All I must do is repeat the same sequence of motions. This I can do. This I am capable of.

I still wasn't asleep at three last night. I couldn't write in my notebook anymore; I paced through the rooms of my apartment, an urban fog that I moved through—the flashes of the outside through the living room windows, the long hallway, the dark, creepy kitchen with the one window looking out at a four-foot-wide alley where no one has been since the building came up.

Not a good idea to go out into the neighborhood at that time of night, so I just walked, the shadows in the living room like cobwebs I broke with my legs. *Whatthefuckiswrongwithyouwhatthefuckisw rongwithyouwhywon'tyousleep.*

At four, I sat on the loveseat in the living room. I remembered what Calvin had said to me: That I was *wallowing*.

Don't wallow, I wrote on a piece of paper. I etched in a border to it, drew diamonds at each corner, vines.

Then I laughed. *I am embroidering my self-pity*, I thought. Ghosts have a sense of humor, too.

Behind me, through the open door to the reception area, the voices of people arriving. Beth Hoffman arrives, greets Vicky with her warm-cocoa voice. I like hearing people while they are out of sight. Ed Fanborough arrives. His joke with Vicky is that she is a movie star who is only here to research what it is like to be a receptionist for a part. She always laughs. Hearing his voice, I smile at the wall.

If Ed Fanborough knew I was in here, he would step in and talk to me. He would call me Office Cinderella—that's his joke with me. I am amazed with myself that I can do this: that I can joke and be light as if I am a person from a TV sitcom about work, and not what I really am: a ghost who has barely lived through the night.

Behind me, through the open doorway, Celeste's voice, asking Vicky if she has seen me. I stay where I am, unseen, but Vicky remembers that I am in here.

Shit.

11 a.m.

Damn she is annoying.

Step-drag. Step-drag.

"*There* you are," she says.

I don't turn around. My whole body a message to her: *I'm busy*.

"Big mailing to do," I say.

"You have to eat lunch, don't you?"

"I don't think I can go out today, Celeste. I have to finish this. I have to get this out today."

I keep my back to her while I bring the lever down. Shaky.

Take the ream of paper and thread the holes through the plastic teeth.

She's still standing there.

"I know you're mad at me, Ellie."

I blush, looking at the wall.

"No I'm not."

"You know what a friend does? A friend tells the truth, even if it's hard to hear. I'm trying to *help you*."

I sigh audibly. *Don't look at her*. The pink shelf, the rectangular stacks of Xerox paper.

"I'm not mad about it, Celeste. You know—whatever. I'm sure it's true."

"I'm worried. You are twenty-seven and still working an entry-level job. You're not happy here—anyone can see that. You're white, middle class, and educated, and you have lots of choices."

"You're right, Celeste," I say loudly. "Can I work?"

"You can't keep kicking the can down the road, Ellie."

"I have to do this now."

"Suit yourself, Ellie."

Step-drag.

Step-drag.

She's gone.

Last night at 2:30 in the morning, here is what I said to an imaginary therapist:

I talked about samsara. "Life is suffering," I said. *The first noble truth. American society is so fake. Happy happy joy joy*.

The imaginary therapist asked me why I felt that way.

I gave her a lecture on Buddhism. *Life is suffering*, I said. *That's the way things are*.

I felt wise. I felt above it all.

Why can't you sleep? The imaginary therapist asked me.

I'm busy talking to people who aren't really there.

11:30 a.m.

In the mail room, my pile of envelopes has grown into a tower that teeters dangerously. I went out to the bathroom; Vicky was sitting there in a sleeveless shirt, her hair oiled in a curl around her ear, chatting away happily on the phone. Celeste says Vicky has come a long way. She says that Vicky hit bottom, and decided she had to turn her life around. I thought about that as I unlocked the door to the bathroom. How Vicky probably does not second guess everything she says, does not watch herself, warily, from three feet away.

How I have hit bottom, too, probably.

But I'm keeping it to myself.

Wednesday, 1 p.m.
South Street Seaport
The Red Notebook

From where I sit, the pink South Street Market Building juts out into the water, blue awnings over every window. Dark patches move around the end of the wharf: closer to me, the cobblestone street and the perennial ice cream man.

It is probably a bad sign that I have started taking the red notebook to work.

"Label-typer!" Calvin called to me that third time. It was after the fourth or fifth lecture; shy still, I was making my way swiftly to the door.

Someone had asked Calvin whether Buddhists believed there was a "core self."

His answer was immediate: There was no self at all.

There was a kind of stir in the audience when he said that—a ripple of surprise. "Anatman," he said. "No Self."

Immediately, a chorus of protest. How could that be? We felt ourselves ... we shouldn't trust our own *minds*?

"Where do you find it?" Calvin challenged us. "Is it in the brain? Is it in the leg?"

"But you know it's *there*," said one young woman in a Ramone's tee shirt.

"You *think* it's there," said Calvin. "But it's an illusion. So we see things and feel things ... but then this idea of the 'I' comes in—where does it come from? You paint something, and get lost in the experience—is there a self present then?"

Silence. People didn't like it.

"Anatman. Sunyata—all things are empty of essence," said Calvin. "We always take things so personally: *how could he do that to me? Why did she say that?* Guess what—you rid yourself of the illusion of self, you're going to be a lot happier, because it's going to be impossible to insult you!"

When the lecture was over, I wanted to get out of there, sift through the things he had said. I made for the door; that was when he called me. I turned. Then somehow he was in front of me, standing between me and the doorway.

"Walking to the subway?" he asked. "Like some company?"

The blood shot up my neck. I nodded then looked away, trying to cool down.

I had to wait for him to get his backpack, say goodbye to some of the people swarming around him. By then I knew that Calvin had "regulars" who stayed after the lectures to banter. I felt them looking at us as we left.

Since the second lecture, I had been thinking about the things he said, even having conversations in my head, but I hadn't bargained for having to talk to him alone. It was like I was going to have to take a test—my mind went blank, then scratched at the blankness, frantic.

When he returned to me, I felt him first; a cloud of heat. "Come." He touched my elbow. We clattered down the steps.

Outside, the astonishment of The City. We had just been inside looking at slides and hearing about anatman. Now cars and bicycles whizzed by in bright sunlight. Buses passed, lowing like giant rectangular cows. A woman with a suitcase struggled up bus steps.

I was aware of how we must look together: the young girl in the thrift store skirt and tennis shoes, the wild old wizard in the bright orange tee shirt and janitor pants. I warded the glances off, built a wall under my skin.

A small, shaggy dog sniffing tree roots. A giant clock on the side of a building that had stopped, its silver hands frozen in place.

"So," said Calvin. "What did you think of the lecture?"

"I don't understand how there cannot be a self."

He shrugged, looked off in the distance. "What we call a self maybe isn't as solid as we think."

"If you get hit by a car, are you going to think *I'm not a self*?"

"A body gets hit. Can we say that a self gets hit? Are you your body?"

"All I'm saying is that if someone hits me in their car, I'm not going to think it isn't personal."

"Did the driver try intentionally to hit you?"

"But what if he did? It would have been personal then."

"Yes and no," said Calvin.

"How could it be no?"

Everything was passing us. I looked up: red, white, and blue triangular banners flapped in the breeze to announce a super-market opening. But where I was didn't matter anymore.

"Let's say he has had a bad day. Decided that you, an innocent label-typer, are the reason. Is that really personal?"

"So then you're saying no one ever has to take responsibility for anything!"

Calvin shook his head. "I'm not saying that."

I didn't speak.

"Maybe it's more like having a different relationship to yourself."

"What does that even mean?" I asked.

He laughed. "It's an experience."

"Very mysterious."

"The secret of happiness—that's what you came for, isn't it? You ask a question, then you don't like the answer."

We were next to a store called "Gourmet Health." I looked up, searching for something to say to him.

14th Street and 6th Avenue: a woman with a dog. A sign in Spanish for a divorce lawyer: *divorcio barrato.*

"Tell me about your job," he said. "May I know the name of the company you work for?"

I told him, and he nodded sagely. "A nonprofit. Bettering the world. That's good."

He told me about his own job: he was a high school art teacher. He launched into a story about fighting with his principal. The principal wanted him to shave his beard. "Not losing the beard," he said, shaking his head, looking out into the distance. "I've *earned* the beard." He looked ahead determinedly, face fixed. I felt sorry for him suddenly. I wondered why he was telling me this, a person he hardly knew.

It was a long walk across 14th Street. We were at the part where there are rows and rows of discount stores with circular racks of cheap clothing set out on the sidewalk.

"So what does the label-typer do when she isn't typing labels?" he said.

"I don't know," I shrugged. "I read a lot." A lame answer, but I couldn't think of a better one.

"Write?"

I blushed. "Sometimes."

Calvin looked at me closely. "Very busy searching for happiness," he said. We were at the subway by then. I stood with my foot wedged between two bars that made up the gate around the steps, rocking back and forth.

He leaned close to me. "I wonder where you're going to find what you're looking for, label-typer," he said into my ear. "An ashram? The top of a mountain? A loft on 14th Street?"

I looked at him, blinked. "Was the Buddha happy?" I asked.

Calvin looked up, snapped his jaw shut. He was serious suddenly.

"The Buddha was beyond happiness," he said. "The Buddha got to *equanimity*."

I gazed at him. "Are you happy?"

Calvin gave a little, gulping laugh. His eyes grazed me. "I'm just older. Experienced." Near us, a man in a bandana with a fluorescent shirt opened the rear door of a white van. The moment dangled, faded away. He tapped my shoulder lightly. "Time to go," he said. He gave me a little wave and I hopped down the subway steps. He didn't look back.

Wednesday, 3 p.m.
The Center for Urban Research
The Blue Notebook

Notebook break. When I look at the clock, an hour has gone by. I have made good headway on my envelopes.

I think about what Calvin said: we all have soap operas in our heads. I am no different. I guess there is probably too much mental time for me at this job.

For the past hour, I've been staring at small, framed notices that have been hung on the pink wall, like office samplers:

Please do not place paper clips on the copying machine.

Please do not leave the paper tray empty.

People, please respect.

Vicky wrote them. They are directed less at me than at the research staff—people like Beth and Ed who rush in to get copies then rush out again, always under some deadline.

Twenty-seven and still at an entry-level job.

Fuck her. I don't *care* about that.

When I first started working, I was a temp at an ad agency. In the afternoon, we all had to crowd into an auditorium and watch a TV ad they had produced, and when it was over, everyone stood and gave it a standing ovation.

It was an ad.

That was when I knew that work was bullshit.

When Celeste and I first started to have lunch together, she kept talking about how I needed to move on; I wasn't going to want to be in this job forever. I always told her the same thing: that I didn't care.

"You're going to care later, Ellie," she'd say. "You need to start thinking forward a little. Build your résumè."

"I don't care about my résumè, Celeste."

When Calvin talked about résumès, he quoted Popeye: "'I yam what I yam ...'" What kind of résumé is that?

People, please respect.

Wednesday, 9 p.m.
107th Street
The Blue Notebook

I guess I'm lucky. Celeste came just as I was finishing up the mailing. I didn't want her there, but she came in the mailroom anyway, stood next to me, and watched. "Do you need something?" I asked.

"No." All of a sudden, she said, "Ellie, what are you doing?"

"I'm sending these out. They're done."

"You can't send these out like this."

"They're done, Celeste."

"The page numbers are mixed up."

"No they're not," I said.

"They are. Look." She picked up one of the reports, flipped through the pages. Pages 27 and 28 were backwards. So were 54 and 55.

"Oh, Christ," I said. "People can just look down at the page numbers and read them in the right order."

Celeste looked at me solemnly. "You know Amber would never go for that Ellie."

The anxiety crept through me, but I was angry too.

"Jesus Celeste it is NOT a big deal if two pages are switched."

"You know you can't do that, Ellie. You know Amber will have a fit." Celeste looked at me steadily, unblinking. *She's winning again*, I thought.

"Jesus. I've been working on this all day. I just want to finish."

"You can't send these out this way, Ellie. You can't send them out with the page numbers wrong. You can't do that."

"Celeste. It's *two* page numbers."

"You *know* what Amber would say if she saw this. Are you asking me to pretend I didn't see?"

"It's TWO page numbers, Celeste."

"Ellie I can't let you."

"Yes you can. Just say you never saw them."

"I can't do that, Ellie."

My throat closed. I walked toward the door, but she stopped me, stood in front of me.

"I'll help you. I'll get Vicky to help too. We'll get it done in no time."

"Jesus." It was a sob.

"It will be okay, Ellie."

Silence.

"Really."

Another gulping sob. "I'm so tired, Celeste."

"We'll get you some coffee and undo these and it will be done in no time."

She was right; it only took two hours with the three of us. Celeste kept making jokes, asking Vicky to do her Janet Jackson imitation. She was nice.

I stand here now looking down at the neighborhood. All the bad thoughts I've had about Celeste. All the times I told myself I didn't like her. I think about that Zen poem that Calvin had Judith recite at one of his lectures:

To divide what you like from what you dislike is a disease of the mind.

Better if I didn't have a mind at all.

Thursday, June 18, 7 p.m.
Alphabet City
The Blue Notebook

A lull in the salsa outside. I am sitting here in my frayed shorts on the lime green armchair contemplating my bare legs.

Well at least I did something.

Cass convinced me to come see The New Heights Group.

The meeting was in a hulking school building on East 11th Street; to enter we passed a painted metal barrier, through an asphalt courtyard, then up the cement steps to a giant hall that has seen better days. In the auditorium, we sat on metal folding chairs. Damp, but we were glad to get out of the sun.

An experience.

In the auditorium, we looked up at a wood stage. There were about ten of us there, mostly young, with a variety of "looks"—sweatpants, jeans, Indian sundresses with tiny mirrors sewn into them that you can buy on the street. Cass was wearing a pair of fringed denim shorts over her chalk-white legs, with black socks, combat boots, and a halter top. I leaned into her, wanting to be a part of her, and not a separate person.

Two men in jeans and tee shirts stalked the edge of the stage. The one she likes, Tommy, had a ponytail, a lank face, rock-carved cleft in his chin. The other was less attractive, with eyes buried between the mounds of his cheeks, a big, easy grin. His face said it all: he would not want to be doing anything else right now.

I still can't believe I went.

Cass was enraptured. She sat leaning forward, one leg crossed over the other, gripping the seat of her chair for stability. Ray (but we are to call him Buck Rogers) said this: "Before I went up that mountain, I wasn't the person I am now. The mountain changed me." Cass nodded slightly as if she were in silent conversation with Ray, just the two of them. I looked at her: the hollow of her white thigh; the blue veins beneath the surface of the skin, her hands with the bitten-down nails gripping the seat.

Tommy said we, too, should be taking the names of famous people for these meetings. Why? Because he-Mattie/Tommy—and his partner, Ray/Buck started this group for a Reason. The mountain blessed them with an experience—changed them—and now they want to help us have that same experience.

He kept shaking his head in near-disbelief at his own insight. "Pay it forward, folks," he kept saying. "Pay it forward."

They changed places on the stage often. Tommy would say something, then step back and Buck would come forward. Buck explained about the fame. It happened when he was at 24,000 feet, he said. "At that height, that is when you are really starting to feel it. Your thighs are pulsing and your muscles are grabbing for oxygen and they don't want to do this anymore. You are feeling the exhaustion and at the same time, you have to be hyper alert, because one single sound, one crack in the snow cover can mean a collapse—an avalanche or a fissure that someone can fall through.

"So at 24,000 feet, I'm starting to sag, and I'm looking up at the sky, wondering why I'm doing this, and guess what I realize?" He stopped and waited but none of us said anything.

"What I realized, I'm going to get up there, and it's going to be amazing, even though, with the cloud cover, I may not see much at all"—a polite titter from us on the metal folding chairs—"And when I come down, everything will be different. I'll be One of the Ones—you know? People will know me. They'll know my name. I'll be one of about 102 people who've summitted Everest. My claim to fame.

"So I'm standing there with my feet freezing in my boots, and I realize"—he looked around at us—"This is dumb." Appreciative laughter from the audience.

"So I have this choice—I can give it all or I can keep going. Now that I've realized this—now that I've seen through myself, y'know, what's the point?—and then I decide.

"I decide that I'm going to go, I decide that I'm going to summit, and I decide that the reason I'm going to summit is that when I come down from the mountain, I will take whatever I've gotten mentally—whatever the mountain has given me—and I will share it."

I remember looking over at Cass. When we were in college once, she insisted we go winter camping. My mother had that new boyfriend I couldn't stand, so I didn't want to go home for the break. Cass didn't want to go home either. So she said we should just camp in the woods behind the dorms.

It was horrible. So cold that even when we crawled into the same sleeping bag, we couldn't stop shivering. We needed to eat, but we couldn't make ourselves get up to build a fire. Cass wouldn't give in. She kept saying "I know how to do this." In the end, after two days and a night, I convinced her that we should sneak back into the dorms.

Today it was that same Cass, staring up raptly at Mr. I-Climbed-Everest.

"So that's why I'm here today, folks. That's why we're all here— because I have something I want to share with you. Here's something I decided that day at 24,000 feet: I needed to think of things differently. I needed to stop thinking in terms of deficit; I needed to start to think in terms of assets. I needed to stop feeling incomplete. I needed to think—and this is important, folks— as if I already have the thing that I want.

"What I want I already have." He nodded, agreeing with himself. His hair nodded with him.

That was when I heard it—clapping. First one guy then a few others. I looked over—Cass was clapping too. Christ. But I slapped my palms together, one of the crowd.

We all had to give ourselves famous names. At the end of our row, there was a guy with a short hair except for one long thin tail of hair in the back sitting with his legs splayed—he took Elvis Presley. A woman in a black thrift store skirt called herself Zsa Zsa Gabor.

"Zsa Zsa Gabor!" laughed Tommy. We all had to turn to the person on our right and tell them our fame-name. Cass's name was Sir Edmund Hilary.

"Sir Edmund Hilary," I said. "Jesus, Cass!" I guess I shouldn't be surprised. In college, Cass and I always had the same argument. She said I needed to *do things*. "You sound like my mother," I said. And then, "Don't you want to *think* before you do things?"

"All you do is think," Cass always said.

After the talk was over, we went out into the parking lot. Blinding in the full light: I could barely see the building across the street;

shapes emerging out of mirage. In profile, Cass's face looked even sharper, her cheekbones slanting toward her nose; the jet-black hair throwing off light.

"Didn't you *love* it?" said Cass? "Wasn't it *great*? Aren't you *psyched?*"

"It was interesting, yeah."

"Interesting! Ellie, it was fucking awesome. It was outrageous! Everest!" She turned her face to me; bliss.

"It's a big mountain, Cass."

"That's what I love about it!" she crowed.

"Cass. You were just in a fire tower and you didn't even like it."

"That was different. It was crowded. It wasn't wild. It wasn't a challenge." She stopped, dramatically and turned to me, her eyes round. "This is ... we are going to be talking our whole lives about this."

"I'm not sure I can do this, Cass."

Her face sagged slightly, disapproving. "You can't think that way, Ellie. You always do that."

"Do what?"

"You never take action. You're always waiting. You wait for your life to start."

"I don't do that."

"Yes you do."

"Seth left. I'm in mourning."

"You're always in mourning, Ellie."

"No I'm not."

"Yes you are. I went away for the summer and I came back and everything is the same."

"No it isn't," I said. I wanted to tell her then: Calvin and the apartment on Spring Street and what came after. But I had that feeling. My body was caving in.

Now I sit and listen to the ongoing carnival outside.

If I was like Cass.

If things didn't bother me.

If I was like anyone else.

Friday, June 19, 1 a.m.
107th Street
The Blue Notebook

Outside, the orange light sprays the hoods of cars like a kind of gelatin. When I look down, there are only two old men under the bodega's awning, as if in a stage light. Threads of discussions in Spanish float up from hidden doorways.

My mouth tastes of metal.

You're always in mourning, Ellie.

Screaming at Cass in my head the whole way home.

She can't say that to me. She's supposed to be my friend.

So ANGRY.

Thumbtacked to the wall above the desk in the other room, the Buddhist prayer:

May all sentient beings possess happiness and the causes of happiness.

May all sentient beings be free of suffering and the causes of suffering.

May all sentient beings never be separate from joy and free of suffering.

But people aren't good.

Friday, 2:30 a.m.
107ᵗʰ Street
The Red Notebook

If you can't sleep, tell the story.

I went to every one of Calvin's lectures that winter. It was always the same: the loft full of people who were young but older than me; the slides of Tibet and Nepal; Calvin ad-libbing about whatever came to his mind.

Sometimes he talked about societal brainwashing. We were programmed, he said. Buddhism was about undoing that programming. *Brainwashing* sounded paranoid to me, like the CIA talking about Communism. At the same time, when I thought about it, there was truth to it. Programming: do well in school, get a good job. For all his supposedly radical talk about capitalism, it seemed to me Seth didn't really question any of that.

Another big theme was *concepts*. Calvin had started one lecture by yelling at the top of his lungs: "Opinion ... is a disease!" I shook in my seat, but immediately I thought about Seth, with all of his blanket statements about capitalism and the Left.

Of course, at the same time, it was kind of mind-boggling. How could you not have concepts? By that time, Calvin was moving back and forth between Tibetan Buddhism and Zen. He talked about the book *Zen Mind, Beginner's Mind*. That was the best way to be, he said—open; a perpetual beginner. We rely on thinking too much. The truth couldn't really be contained in words, he said. What mattered was experience.

He had the woman Judith who always sat up front and recorded his lectures stand and recite a Zen poem for us:

The Great Way is not difficult
For those who have no preferences;
Only when freed from hate and love,
It reveals itself fully and without disguise;

A tenth of an inch is the difference
Between heaven and hell,
To set up what you like against what you dislike
is the disease of the mind:

The denial of a thing is the assertion of it
The more you think about it
The further you go from the truth ...

I remember him walking me to the subway after that lecture. "I don't really understand how you cannot have concepts," I said. "I mean—logic."

"How can you learn anything if you have fixed ideas about everything?"

I considered this. We passed a brushed steel hot dog cart with a red scalloped umbrella; a fire hydrant; a store selling cheap office clothes, the mannikins with their pointed plastic toes lined up in the window.

"You're lucky," he said. "You're just at the beginning."

"The beginning of what?" I asked.

He didn't answer.

He was walking me to the subway pretty regularly then. I always blushed deeply when he asked me. I saw his entourage look on jealously—the older woman with the gray curls who sat up front faithfully; the gargoyle-faced man.

Sometimes we walked straight to the subway; other times he led me to Union Square Park.

"I don't understand what you mean by not having concepts," I said. "I don't think that's possible. And besides," I looked at him flirtingly, "not thinking isn't a strength of mine."

"Well, what *are* your strengths? What are you good at?"

These were the questions I hated. When we were talking philosophy, it was one thing. I didn't like talking about myself.

"I don't have any," I said. I gave him an ironic look. He groaned.

"You have to be good at something."

"Um ... I was good at school."

"Teacher's pet."

"Teacher's pet; Daddy's girl, that was me."

"Ah, yes, a good way to hide." I blushed. That day we were at Union Square Park on a bench, even though it was still nippy out. I watched a homeless man in a huge overcoat trudge by with a shopping cart.

"How is being a teacher's pet hiding?"

He didn't answer.

"You do hide, y'know. You should see yourself during the lectures. Expressionless. Poker-faced."

"I'm not *hiding*."

"A statue."

We got up, walked along 14th Street, to my subway at 7th Avenue.

"How is being a teacher's pet a way of hiding?" I said again.

"Let's just say this, teacher's pet," he said. "I am not the kind of teacher you're used to." We were in the middle of the street, walking side by side, but then he turned to face me, up close: the wrinkles, the very blue eyes, the aquiline nose. "I teach about life."

I looked at him. After the lectures, people would swarm him, want to be close to him. I understood the impulse—Calvin was a person you wanted to be close to, you didn't know why.

I looked at him now: the ridiculous yellow tee shirt, the sagging pants.

"How can you be so happy?" I said in wonder.

He chuckled, pleased.

Then he leaned over to me.

"I'm a mirror," he said.

I was happy that day. A statue that glowed.

Saturday, June 20, 5 p.m.
107ᵗʰ Street
The Blue Notebook

Cass called and started leaving a message. I was still kind of mad, but I picked up. Her excited voice as soon as I said hello.

"Have you been reading Tommy's book?"

My eyes climbed the wall, hedging. "Not yet."

"It's *awesome*. I can't put it down."

"I can't wait."

"He says we should make Dream Statements."

"What's a Dream Statement?"

"You know … you think about what you really want, and then you set it. As a goal."

"Oh."

"You want to do it together?" Through my window, I watched people parading down Amsterdam Avenue, slightly astonished … As if the last time I saw her had never happened. As if she never said *you're always in mourning, Ellie*. But that's Cass isn't it?

"Let's meet at Veneto's."

I said yes. What else was I going to do?

Veneto's was crowded: éclairs on revolving trays in a glass case; the fans spinning overhead, stirring the air. The people behind the counter were all related. They did their jobs calmly. A long line of twenty-somethings in cargo pants, black mini-skirts with fishnets, hippies in Grateful Dead tee shirts, ballerina types in leotards. Cass and I sat at a red laminate table, looking out the storefront. On the street, a tableau of garbage cans, a gas station sign, a mural for Adidas sneakers.

First, she wanted to talk about the place where she's squatting; some studio on Avenue B with no hot water and junkies shooting up across the street.

"Isn't that dangerous?"

She flashed her eyes at me. She was wearing a leopard-print skirt, the red roots of her hair showing against the black.

"You just have to know the block. You have to watch yourself."

Outside the plate glass window, a group of tourists, looking back and forth up 2nd Avenue, lost.

On the flat of one hand, Cass expertly spun a spoon in a circle while we talked. This is something she's done since I've known her. The spoon rarely falls.

"So my mother wants me to come home," she said. She looked up at the ceiling, squinted. "I told her that if she wants me to visit, she has to find me another place to stay. A neighbor—something."

"Why?"

"I can't take it there. The claustrophobia. I grew up there, remember?"

"You can't stay in your own house?"

"I just can't. I can't breathe in there."

The pastries Cass got were the chocolate lace cookies—dark chocolate with dark brown lumps and craters of baked dough. She ate them by softly crumbling the chocolate with a fork, lifting the fork tines to her mouth, licking them.

"Have you heard from Seth?" asked Cass. We both had our notebooks out, but I noticed neither of us had opened them. I had checked the chapter called "Dare to Dream" in Tommy's book before I left the apartment. *Envision it and it will happen*—that was his slogan.

"Yeah, he called. Once."

"What an asshole."

In college, when I would cry over Seth, Cass would get all self-righteous. I shouldn't put up with that. "You should leave him," she'd say. "He doesn't deserve you."

"I love him." I'd shrug.

"You give him all the power."

"Love isn't about power," I'd say

"So what have you been doing while I was away?'

Not this again.

"Just—living, Cass."

"You sound irritable."

"I'm not."

"Still going to those Buddhist lectures?"

It was Cass who had pointed out that notice in the East West Bookstore, but she never came to a lecture with me. She had to work on Saturdays. And then, after about a month, she left for Oregon.

Today would have been the time to tell her about Calvin.

I didn't. I just sat there, watching her mince her cookie into tiny puzzle pieces on the plate.

"Not interested anymore." I said and shrugged.

"You were so into it. It was the first time I saw you really happy." I shrugged.

"When I was on that fire tower, I thought about that stuff you told me about the lectures. 'Life is suffering. The way to be happy is to be selfless.' Then I met Tommy. It all seemed so perfect. Like a sign, y'know?"

I looked at a man dressed entirely in black and with a little goatee point at a tray of cookies, jerking his finger to the left to show which exact cookie he wanted. "I don't think Tommy's ... philosophy ... is the same thing as Buddhism, Cass."

"Why not?"

"Buddhism is about recognizing the emptiness of everything."

"That doesn't make any sense."

"It's kind of ... you have to grok it. We don't have an inherent self. What we think of as the self is conditional."

"That's like Tommy wanting us to be selfless and climb for the orphans."

"It's not the same thing."

"How is it different?"

"Trust me Cass, it's not the same thing."

She sniffed—Cass's signature *I'm annoyed* sound. "So you understand it and I don't?"

I sighed. "It's not about who understands it. It's about what it is."

"Well *I* think Tommy's book *is* like Buddhism. It's about doing things for other people."

I shrugged. "Okay."

Outside our window, a man in socks and Birkenstocks sailed by on a bicycle; a woman in a blue dress bent over to pick up a dropped scarf.

"I'm on Chapter Seven already. It's the survival part and it's *great*." She looked at me, big eyes bulging. I kept my face blank. "You really have to be on top of that oxygen when you're up that high: that's obvious. Tommy says you can't stress that enough."

"It's a high mountain," I said.

Cass had to go—there seemed to be a lot of meetings with the other squatters in her building.

Saturday, 8 p.m.
107th Street
The Red Notebook

I stand looking out my living room window. A pigeon patrols a window ledge six floors up; a white plastic bag inflates, wobbles at the end of a tree branch.

"The power of saving," said Calvin. That was what bodhisattvas had.

In the beginning, the lectures were about mantras. People thought of them as prayers, but that wasn't correct. Mantras were sound vibrations—syllables that awaken various energies in our bodies.

He was still walking me to the subway after the lectures.

"So are mantras like magic spells?" I asked.

"They can be."

I did not really want to talk about mantras. I wanted to talk about the things that had happened to me; the things nobody could see.

Like my parents' divorce.

What it was like when my mother wept, fell on me.

How it was to see my father's studio, emptied of all the things that were him.

In the end, I decided to tell Calvin about the gun.

After the divorce, my mother had several boyfriends.

There was Sol Stein, always in Hawaiian shirts, who talked on the phone a lot. He and my mother would sit around the kitchen drinking wine out of coffee mugs and joking about their bad marriages. I liked him OK, but he didn't stay.

Then, a few months after, there was Travis, with his beefy face, long mustache, and the tattoo on his forearm that read "on the wagon," with a picture of a covered wagon. The first time I met him, he stepped into my mother's car and said, "You're late, *dear*," in a Texas drawl. My mother laughed gaily. In the back seat, I flinched.

Travis was from Texas. After a month of coming over, he decided that my mother's cooking was "blandola," and started cooking "Texas" for us—fried catfish, grits. My mother enthused about it: *a man who cooks! A miracle!* I started to go for long walks just before dinner time. I'd come home late, slip into the kitchen, eat peanut butter out of the jar.

It was Travis who bought my mother the gun—a pistol. I first saw it in her bedroom.

"What's *that* doing here?" I asked. My mother was standing in front of the mirror in her slip; when I spoke, she smiled at her reflection.

"Travis thinks we need protection," she said lightly. "Two women alone."

"A *gun*," I said. "We're not gun people, Mom. That's a good way to get someone killed."

"He wants to *protect* me." Her eyes touched mine for a moment, then looked away.

"You're a *people person*, remember? You're not someone who *shoots* people."

"I'm not going to shoot anyone, Ellie," said my mother. "But I don't think it's such a bad idea. Just in case."

When I went away to college, Travis moved in with her. I used to call my mother once every two weeks from the payphone in the laundry room, and that's how I found out that my mother and Travis were moving out West. They had gone there for a week, and my mother loved it.

"You should see the sky, Ellie," she said. "So big!"

"You're just *leaving*? I asked. "Your *job* is here. You have *friends* here."

"This is a great chance for me, Ellie," she said. "I can start again. I need that." *What about me?* I wanted to say, but I didn't. Instead

I told her all the things I hated about Travis: the way he called me *girl*; the way he called the addicts he worked with *losers*; the way he spoke to my mother when she talked about her ideas—*now don't get intellectual on me dear.*

"He acts like he's smarter than you," I said. "And he isn't. He isn't good for you."

"*I'll* decide that, Ellie."

I guess my mother told Travis some of what I said because when I came home for Thanksgiving, he was waiting in my room for me, sitting in an armchair. My mother had gone out.

I stood in the doorway. "This is my room," I said.

He raised his eyes to me. "Technically," he said, "it's your mother's. Sit down, El," he said. "I'd like to talk." I didn't. "You don't like me." He looked out the window and shrugged. "Understandable. I'm taking your mother away." He cleared his throat. I hated him. "What isn't okay with me is that you interfere with your mother's happiness." He looked at me. "I know you've been trying to talk your mother out of going out West and I need you to stop."

I blushed. "You listen to our phone conversations?"

He shrugged. "She tells me." A little streak of cold ran through me. The neighbor's yard, visible through the window, started to blur.

"I don't need you to like me," he said again, "but I *do* need you to get out of the way." His eyes flicked at me. "You're a third wheel, Ellie."

"She can make up her own mind," I said. Travis smiled at the air and shook his head.

"You don't get it," he said. "You're not old enough. She's a mother, and it's easy to make her feel guilty. Too easy."

We both stayed silent for a minute. I willed him to leave.

He put his hands on his knees that pushed himself up and walked toward me. "Here's the thing, Ellie," he said. "I know you're used to being Daddy's girl. You're used to getting things your way. I care for your mother—a lot—and from now on, I'm going to look out for her." He met my eyes, solemn. "You don't want to cross me, dear, because I fight for the people I love."

When he left, I closed the door, quietly, and sat on my bed, shaking. I started to lie down, and that was when I felt it: metal.

I pulled back the covers, and there was my mother's pistol, with a note tied to it with string. *I fight for the people I love.*

Before my mother got back, I was gone.

When I told that story to Calvin, he didn't speak for a minute or two. Then he looked over at me, his face kind. "We'll have to teach you the mantra for stopping bullets."

I laughed. "Oh yeah? There's a mantra for that?"

Calvin looked at me solemnly. "You don't believe me?"

I raised my eyebrows. "Tell me."

"Sox, pox, serox."

"Okay," I said. Humoring him.

But when I got home, I wrote it in my notebook.

Over and over, filling two pages.

Saturday, 11 p.m.
107th Street
The Blue Notebook

Try writing it as a fairy tale, said Sarah Hamsted.

A young, sensitive girl lives a privileged life; a princess in a castle. Then her parents get divorced, and everything falls apart.

Until she meets a magician in the East Village.

Until he sells her a bag of magic beans.

Sunday, June 21, 12:15 a.m.
107th Street
The Blue Notebook

Stories.

In love stories, they never give up on each other.

The high-born lord of the manor marries the servant even though people gossip.

The girl is captured by bad guys and the man leaves to get help. He says, "I *will* come for you." And he does.

The day Seth told me he was definitely going to California, we were in the kitchen. I was still temping then; the days I didn't work were balloons of relief, breathing space. I was making us a new recipe I'd seen in *The Times*—chicken dijonnaisse. As if Seth was some bourgeois husband in slippers and a cigar.

I stood at the counter, chopping onions; Seth sat at the kitchen table with his feet up on a chair.

"So I got it," he said. "The position."

"What position?"

"Christ Ellie have you been *listening* to my life? For Jerry Brown."

"But he's in California."

"I know."

"So you're going to California?"

"I have to."

"For how long?"

"A year. Something like that."

I put the knife down, walked out of the room.

"Ellie what are you doing?"

I went into the bedroom, locked the door, lay on the bed. "Jesus Ellie what are you *doing*?"

97

You can think a thing in words, but your body will reject it. Mine did. I said it over and over again: *I'm okay, I'm okay*, but my body did not hear it. Then three weeks later it was Cass, announcing she was going to Oregon. The answering machine picked up. I could have rescued the call, but when I heard *Oregon* I left the machine on, pretended I wasn't at home.

I do know this: love isn't leaving. How could it be?

Monday, June 22, 2 p.m.
The Center for Urban Research
The Blue Notebook

Celeste and I went to lunch today. We sat on our usual bench, looking at the cobblestone street that passes the South Street Seaport and the river. It was sunny; the crests of the brown wavelets flashed in the light.

Celeste wore a pair of plaid pants that tapered down to her tiny feet and flat sandals with a strap between her big toe and the rest of her toes. Sitting, her feet didn't touch the ground. She'd bought French fries again.

"You know that messing up those page numbers was not a good sign," she said.

"I know."

"Did you read the article I put on your desk?"

"Yes."

"Losing sleep ... losing concentration ... it's all part of the same package, Ellie."

I kept my eyes on the water and the figures moving through the heat.

I sighed. "It's a bad phase. I'll be all right."

"Depression is an illness, Ellie. Like cancer. You have a diagnosis. You get treatment. You take medicine."

"It's not the same thing," I said doggedly. I looked down at my feet. A pigeon leaned over the crack between two cobblestones, its iridescent neck popping back and forth.

"There's a new class of antidepressants that don't have side effects. I could get you the book about it—it's called *Listening to Prozac*. This is the eighties, Ellie. They're making a lot of strides when it comes to this kind of thing."

"No thank you."

"If you felt better, you'd be able to function better at work."

"It was just a couple of page numbers, Celeste. I'll be more careful next time."

"If I hadn't come—"

"You know it's possible no one would ever have noticed."

"They would absolutely have noticed, Ellie. And Amber would NOT have been happy when she found out."

The usual clusters of tourists gazing at the menu on the side of the ice cream truck. I was so hot I felt my scalp glow.

"You need a job you care about Ellie. Then you won't make these mistakes."

I thought about when I met Calvin. It wouldn't matter what my job was. I was going to be a bodhisattva—Beyond All This. The rest didn't matter.

"What I do to make money doesn't matter, Celeste. Who I am is what matters."

"I have news for you honey bunchkins. What you do matters quite a lot. You're not going to be willing to type labels all your life, Ellie. You need to move on. Don't you *want* something?"

Seagulls gathered around the tourists at the ice cream truck.

"Happiness doesn't come from wanting things, Celeste."

"So what does it come from?"

"I don't know, Celeste," I said irritably. "But I know it doesn't come from that."

"It's healthy to want things, Ellie. It's called joining the human race."

"I'm not interested in becoming a yuppie," I said.

"What do you want to be?" Celeste snickered. "A hermit? Go off into the wilderness with a loincloth?"

"Maybe," I said. "I might climb Everest."

Celeste spit out her French fry laughing. "In what universe?"

I watched figures walk by in the haze: a man in khaki with a briefcase; three men in business suits, heads twisted toward each other.

"My friend is," I said defensively. "She's part of a group that is climbing to raise awareness about Nepali orphans."

"What an utterly self-indulgent idea," said Celeste. "Why not just raise the money?"

I might have left, but she dropped it. Celeste wanted to talk about her idea.

There is a call for proposals, and all of the research associates at the Center have ideas. They are all very solicitous of them. In the last few days, they've all come to me, asking me to proofread or type their proposals. Sometimes they will anxiously ask me what I think.

Celeste's idea is about pornography. "It's an industry that employs far too many low-income women," she said. "Shut down Times Square, and re-train sex workers."

"Ambitious," I said.

"It's a *great* idea, Ellie," said Celeste.

"I thought it was supposed to be a research idea," I said. "That sounds more like a proposal."

"You do the research to support the proposal," said Celeste lightly. She was swinging her legs in the air now, pleased with herself.

"And I have an idea for *you*," she said.

"Oh yeah?"

"Are you ready?"

"Sure."

"I will write you in as co-facilitator of the project. You'll help brainstorm ideas, design the surveys ... this could be a real stepping-stone for you, Ellie." She turned her face to me, brown eyes flushed with earnestness. "But you'll have to step up to the plate." Her voice got lecture-y.

I knew what it meant: she and Amber will remind me that I have a *role* every time they pile on the work.

"If it's after five and we need something done, you're going to have to stay and get it done ... Can you do that?"

Two women in dresses and high heels passed, their haunches working under the fabric that slid over their hips. I could hear snatches of their conversation—where they went to get their nails done.

"Do you know how many young women end up in the sex trade?" said Celeste. "They're lives are *fucked* after that. It *matters*, Ellie."

As a mother watches over a child, so with a boundless heart should one cherish all beings.

I thought about my neighbor at home, Willie: seventy at least, and always with dried spit on the sides of his mouth. When Seth was still with me, Willie introduced a young woman to us. His niece, he said.

"Willie has a niece?" I said to Seth.

"No, Willie has a live-in prostitute who's a crack addict," said Seth.

"Seriously?"

"Jesus Ellie how can you be so naïve."

I see her in the hall regularly. She has black hair that hangs down straight, unwashed. She never meets my eyes.

"Of course it matters," I said to Celeste. And then, when that didn't seem strong enough, "It's horrible."

When we got back to the office, Celeste had me start the proposal—a real pain in the ass. She wanted a fancy layout with columns and different fonts. I tried to do it, but the words keep bouncing all over the screen; I couldn't contain them.

When I finally got it right, Celeste decided she wanted to change everything.

"How about we work on it tomorrow?" I asked.

Celeste looked at me steadily. "What did we just talk about at lunch, Ellie?"

So I stayed.

I sit here in my living room on the threadbare lime green armchair and listen to the windows rattle in their frames each time a truck goes by. The air itself is salsa. I suppose I am lucky that she is even my friend. I suppose she is right: I should do something.

I am nothing.

Why is this so? If, Subhuti, a bodhisattva holds on to the idea that a self, a person, a living being exists, that person is not a true bodhisattva.

Monday, 11 p.m.
107th Street
The Red Notebook

When I started going to Calvin's lectures, there were always book recommendations. *Zen Mind, Beginner's Mind, the Bhagavad Gita, the Diamond Sutra.* I went in search of every book that he mentioned.

Mostly, though, I didn't understand them.

It was months before he called me. I had attended his lectures every week until they stopped for the summer. Seth had a meeting he went to every Saturday, so I liked having Calvin's lecture to go to at that time. I had a notebook where I wrote down some of the more startling things Calvin said: "You're only on the Path when your feet are off the ground. A second has 17 parts."

In between, lots of doodles. "Jottings of the Demented," Seth called it, then cackled at his own joke.

When the phone rang that day, I thought it was my mother. Since she'd moved, she called every other weekend.

I picked up the phone and a voice I did not know spoke to me.

"Is this a statue?"

"Hello?"

"Hot enough for you?"

"Hot," I agreed. I wanted to ask *who is this*, but the voice seemed to be so familiar with me.

"You missed the lecture." Then it came to me who it was. "It was a good one."

"Oh. Yes. I couldn't. I was away." Thinking fast because in truth I had forgotten about it almost the day he announced it.

"Care for a re-run?"

"Excuse me?"

"A re-do. Would you like to meet me for a recapitulation?"

Blood rising up my neck. "Oh."

"Are you free on Tuesday?"

I can be, I thought. "Yes."

"Meet me at three. Village Bagel."

I did not think until later about how it was that he had my phone number. At the time, it seemed a bit of a miracle—one I shouldn't question.

I met him one week later. I dressed carefully: a new dress, sandals. The same stammering fluorescent light on the blond-wood tables. Calvin sat in his green janitor pants and a bright orange tee shirt, the white beard shooting out in all directions.

"Oh, ho! It's the girl in green!"

It was true. I had bought a dress with birthday money my mother sent me—a creamy lime green sheath that made my collar bones stand out elegantly. I looked ravishing in it. I knew that.

Except for the two of us and the man with the walrus mustache who worked behind the counter, the place was empty.

"What can I get you, milady?" asked the man with the walrus mustache when I stood in front of the register. I bought my tea, then sat down with Calvin.

Calvin was animated, talking about the lecture I had missed. He nodded his head knowingly. "I just started naming things." He looked at me solemnly and started. "This table is shit," he said. "The floor is shit. The register is shit. The food is shit. Your clothes are shit." His face was grave. I understood, I supposed: everything was the same. Nothing was special.

Then he began to complain about Judith. "Her tape recorder goes dead in the middle of the lecture and she wants me to *stop*." He looked at me with his bushy eyebrows raised, as if I would surely find this as outrageous as he did. I smiled back nervously. What to make of all this? From time to time, behind the counter, the man with the mustache broke into brief bits of song.

From the day Calvin had called, a conversation had been going on inside my head. In this conversation, Calvin asked me questions and I answered—brilliantly. He did not ask me how I had come to be so wise. It was a mystery; a miracle. That was what I had been carrying around with me for the past week but as Calvin continued to talk, I started to realize: he didn't have anything special to say to me. I began to wither a little as he went on about Judith, and people's poor understandings of Eastern religion, and the stupidity of the Chinese government.

At some point he must have noticed that I looked bored because he leaned forward.

"So how are you?"

I thought, ever so briefly, of telling him. Of describing Seth's leaving.

"I'm okay."

"How's work?" Still peering at me.

"Boring." I shrugged.

"We need to teach you some Xerox machine meditation practices."

I smiled thinly, didn't answer. Calvin described an encounter he'd had with the man who did the hiring at the New School. I smiled, waiting.

And then, suddenly, he stood, his chair legs scraping against the linoleum. "Come," he said. "I have something to show you."

The heat hit as soon as we went through the glass doors. It grabbed my body, which began to swell. We walked east, then turned right when we came to Broadway. There were a lot of people out; a guy with a Mohawk in a tee shirt with cutoff sleeves; a girl in clogs; a red-faced jogger in track shorts, shirtless; groups of young NYU students who looked at Calvin and me curiously as we passed. Cabs streamed past; I took in each store name.

We must have walked ten blocks before I asked him where we were going.

"It isn't far," he said, grabbing my hand. "A friend's place." I remember looking across Houston Street, seeing a gas station, remarking to myself. Calvin had been talking this whole time, but I wasn't really listening.

Three more blocks. I could feel the sweat trickling down the sides of my ribcage under the dress.

"Where?" I said again.

"Spring Street!" he said as we turned a corner.

It was a small brick building not far from the corner. Across the street was an Asian deli with clear plastic walls in front to keep in the air conditioning. I looked at it longingly but waited beside Calvin while he fumbled with some keys.

"The buzzer doesn't work?" I asked.

"No one home." Relief. I wouldn't have to meet anyone new.

There were five flights. By the end of the first I was sweating everywhere. The green dress clung to me, and I kept my arms apart from my body so the dress wouldn't get drenched. Calvin just kept going. I was winded but I followed the backpack. I wasn't going to let a man his age out-climb me. At the end, though, I sprawled against a wall, trying to draw breath. "Look at you," Calvin grinned. His face was tinted red also, as if we both had fevers.

He opened the apartment door and the reek hit immediately. In the tiny kitchen, a running faucet; two sick cats sprawled on a sheet of newspaper. A blazing little room with two tiny electric fans swaying from side to side. One of the cats croaked at us as we stepped in.

"Whose place is this?" I asked.

"Come." He pulled me into the bedroom—one lumpy bed, a gigantic bureau with some rolls of paper on top, a crack running along two entire walls. "Sit." He picked up an enormous book from the dresser and set it on my lap. It was a Tibetan art book—pictures of deities with rays of color emanating out from their bodies; mandalas. I turned the pages—the pictures didn't look any different from slides he had shown in class. Disappointment gnawed me. I had a headache from the climb. Soon, I promised myself, whatever this was, would be over.

"Try this one," Calvin flipped a page, then sat behind me on the bed. I could feel the bed dip, the heat of his body at my back.

The picture was a yab-yum—a couple, as the book described it, "in sexual embrace." He had shown slides of these in the lectures. The idea, he had said, was interpenetration—the unity of devotion and wisdom.

The figures themselves were all grimaces. They were locked in a kind of dance, both standing, the female facing the male. Both left legs were bent, swaying to the left a little. The male's right leg went off diagonally to the right, foot tipped up at the heel like a dance move. The female's right leg was wrapped around his waist.

There were lots of arms. Their two faces were close together, both with mouths open. They looked as if they had fangs.

"Why don't you try visualizing," Calvin said from behind me. His voice had dropped several octaves. "You are the female, in close embrace with your lover. Close your eyes while you are in ecstasy," he purred. "What do you see?"

He began to knead my shoulders. I moved forward on the edge of the bed, but his body followed, right up against me.

"I don't want this," I said.

"Sure you do," said Calvin. The kneading continued. "What kind of consciousness do you have when you are locked in yab-yum," he said in that low voice. "Where is the mind?"

"I think I should go."

Calvin's fingers were digging into my shoulders.

"Relax," he said. I stiffened, moved a little farther forward on the bed. There was now the barest sliver of mattress under my sitz bones.

"The yab-yum is the holiest of holies."

I stood up, faced him. "I think I should go now."

I couldn't look at him. I looked into a very particular section of air in front of my face; willed myself into it. I wasn't going to cry here.

"You don't want to know what satori is like?" said Calvin. I didn't answer. He stood too, but I didn't look at his face. I looked at parts of him—a sleeve; a wrist.

"That's what's at the center of the mandala you know. Yab-yum. The center and the doorway. You want to go somewhere, you have to take steps."

"I need to leave. Thank you. I need to leave."

"Suit yourself." Calvin shrugged. For one moment I looked him full in the face. Calvin looked back guilelessly. Before I left, he gave me a yellow flyer that described his next round of lectures. There was a Xeroxed picture of him on it—the beard, the proud nose. I ripped it into pieces and threw it in a garbage can when I got down to the street.

Tuesday, June 23, 12 a.m.
107th Street
The Red Notebook

Go toward what glows.

When I think back on Calvin, I wonder if I had hubris. I did have this: beauty. Milky face with dark hair. Small, virgin breasts, sculpted hip bones. "Hot," Seth used to say. Beauty is a thing that blinds people. And if you hear it about yourself too often, you get blinded too.

I remember the moment I decided. I was standing at my living room window, looking out at the building across Amsterdam Avenue; a faint reddish exterior with rows of windows that reflected the sky. There was a window with beige curtains. From time to time a figure would appear, inch past the curtains, and stand looking down Amsterdam Avenue, but I could not see the person clearly. I looked at that building, but what I was seeing was Calvin: the white beard, the belly hanging over the belt. How, when I undressed, I would be a wonder to him. It would be his luckiest day. At that moment, I turned, caught a flash of myself in the full-length mirror behind me. Liked what I saw.

1 a.m.

The first time.

The first time, it was a joke, a lark. Seth had left—fuck him—so I was going to meet Calvin, the Wild Teacher Man, 59 to my 25.

An escapade. Somewhere in the back of my head, Seth was watching. He was seeing that I was going on without him.

But I was also watching myself. I was my own audience, and I was enjoying what I was seeing ... Ellie Adkins has an adventure. Another one-night stand.

This one was going to be different, though: with his belly and his beard, Calvin was going to worship me. I looked out the window, smiled.

The first time, Calvin set the date and time a week before: same as the last time—Tuesday, 3 p.m.—but a different place: the corner of 8th Avenue and Spring Street. A week to imagine it. To look into the air and laugh. In that week, I went through the motions of my life, but the whole time, at the back of my mind, a movie was playing. In that movie, Calvin took my clothes off, layer by layer. Gasped at what he saw: the elegant rounds of my shoulders, arch of my collar bones, small, perfect breasts. He would be in awe because for men there is such a thing as church, and it is women's bodies. Especially if the women are young.

I imagined what he would look like: the belly, the wrinkles. I promised myself I would be kind; I would not laugh at him. I imagined his penis, then shied away from the image. That was not the part that I liked. The part that I liked was the way I enchanted him.

That first day, even though we were meeting in the afternoon, I took the whole day off from work. Stood in front of the full-length mirror in the small bedroom I had moved into when Seth left and preened. What should it be—the plain white tee shirt that clung to my breasts, with the jeans that sloped just the right way down my ass, my thighs? The thrift store frock? Carelessness—that's what I wanted to show him. I did not have to try to be beautiful. I couldn't help it.

I left my apartment hours before our appointment. Got off the subway at 23rd Street and walked down to Spring Street. Passed store window after store window and my own reflection; a young woman in dungaree shorts walked beside me, snapped away, came back. I would glance into the store windows and check: there I was. Smile at myself: what I was doing was secret and impossible. I lived in a glass world now. My own self was a series of sliding doors.

Ninety degrees. At Spring Street and 8th Avenue, the heat boiled up from the pavement. The light was an enemy lined up along the plains waiting to meet me. I stood there and waited, took each thing in: the white stucco side of the building across Spring Street. The woman who came out in a housedress, peered at me, went back inside. A bus lumbering by, a taxi, a man on a bike.

Time stopped.

Cars passed. A taxi door opened.

When he came, he rose from the ground like a miracle. Ridiculous, in a way, with the white ZZ Top beard, the hawk nose, the janitor pants. This pleased me. I was going to sleep with somebody who should not exist. I could do what I wanted. I didn't care.

As we walked east, Calvin chatted. How cold the air conditioning was on the bus. Inevitably, his rivalry with Eckerman. I didn't answer.

From Wooster Street to Greene. From Greene to Mercer. From Mercer to Crosby. The fiddle with the key at the front door. The five flights in the suffocated air. The new lock. The smell of the cat pee on the paper in the kitchen; the croaking meows. The room with the lumpy bedspread, the crack on the wall, the giant dresser with rolls of paintings lying across it.

The light.

It poured in.

We swam in it.

His breath smelled. His mouth, soft and edgeless, my own breath in rags soon. Now he is reaching under my shirt. Now I feel it; his palm passing lightly over nipples, my own startled breath. The curl of heat unfolding inside me, opening between my legs, my body straining towards him.

In the beginning I am faking my ecstasy and then it changes. He puts his finger in me. The pleasure whines and twists and mounts.

The world falls away: only this.

The light. My own cries.

Here is a moment I revolve around:

I am on top of him. The bed tips; Calvin's hair is spread out on the pillow below him. One leg on either side; his palms on my thighs. I have risen up, gasped; he is watching, puckers his lips, pleased.

"To think that you were trying to hide yourself," he says. "To think that you were going around in disguise."

"I was not in disguise."

Calvin raises his eyebrows in mock surprise. "A person disguised as a statue."

"I'm not a statue. That's just what *you* called me."

He puckers his lips, lifts his pelvis; the sensation pushes through me.

"Good thing I have the magic ability to see through disguises."

"Oh yes? What is behind the disguise?"

He says it smoothly, evenly: "What is behind the disguise is someone who has a good heart."

Later, at home, I will open this gift a hundred times. I will play it again and again like a music box. I will listen with everything I have.

Wednesday, June 24, 2:30 a.m.
107th Street
The Blue Notebook

Memoir is like fiction, said Sarah Hamsted. *The narrator has to have a problem.*

My problem: I am telling myself a story. I do not know if it is real.

Maybe I am the victim of unfortunate circumstances.

Maybe I am a spoiled girl who cannot handle everyday life.

Maybe I am on the verge of transcending all this.

Maybe none of those things.

At night, we are a ghost ecosystem. Chalky orange dark over everything; a few lights blinking rhythmically in the windows of stores. In the doorways of the buildings below me, ghouls sit and talk companionably; hell is a leisurely place. I cannot see them below me, leaning back in the doorways on my side of the street, but I hear their raspy laughter. Above them in my dark-and-light striped living room, I pace, the words to a Lou Reed song, "Waiting for the Man," in my head.

Earlier tonight I danced to that song, flinging my arms around, shaking my hips in tight circles. In the movie I was in, Calvin saw me, saw my rebellion: Yeah, yeah, yeah. I am an addict; nothing to lose. See-how-tough-I-am-I-don't-care.

But the clock sees; contradicts me. Taps out my life like a metronome.

Goodbye.

Goodbye.

Saturday, June 27, 3 p.m.
107th Street
The Blue Notebook

If I hate going to work, it is the weekends I hate more. Forty-eight hours of my apartment: the paneling that curves away from the walls in parts; the lumpy plaster underneath the kitchen wall. The sameness is a sick feeling.

This morning I chugged tequila at 6 a.m., woke to a car alarm bleating at nine. They're a form of hell, the car alarms; rhythmic, diabolic. There are three electric fans grouped around my mattress to try to drown out the noise. I go to sleep with earplugs in; a wet tee shirt on against the heat. When the light comes, everything in the apartment becomes hot to the touch.

Now I am in Riverside Park. I came here to get away from my own head, as if that is possible. Movemovemove, down the four flights with the stucco walls painted the color of French's mustard, unidentified bits of grime on the chocolate-brown floor; out to the noisy, fermenting streets where the heat transforms what I see; the laundromat is still the laundromat and the bodega is still the bodega, but we swim in an aquarium of watery air, our bodies swelled by the humidity. Out past the line of old men sitting on 107th Street; the Church of the Ascension with the statue of the Virgin Mary, her arms out in a gesture of benevolence. The cement hand that has fallen off and is just a metal rod.

Move.

I do not know what I am doing here except to join the parade: a good-looking doctor type with ruddy cheeks; a woman jogging with a fanny pack; a couple with a toddler in a stroller who reaches up to show them a toy in her hand.

Move.

A stone wall that overlooks the soccer field, where young boys move in lazy zigzags; a pigeon looking down from the branch of a sycamore; someone's lost shirt hanging from a metal fence.

That is why people like cities, I think. We are never truly alone.

When I was young, I would go into my father's studio and just lie down while he painted. I could close my eyes and the sun was two blue fists pressed against my shuttered eyeballs.

Once, I remember kids from the neighborhood teasing me. The teacher had asked me to read my essay in class. I had gotten an A. In the playground, they surrounded me, chanting it: Ellie-got-an-A-Ellie-got-an-A.

Friendsyourownage.

That day, I ran all the way home once school was out. I pushed right through the door of my father's studio, threw myself at his legs.

"Ellie what happened?"

I let the sobs out then. I could barely explain it with the breath I had left.

The light in the studio: golden. Falling through the windows at angles; interrupted by the jagged shadows of objects, but ready to wrap around me.

And the way Max hugged me, hard against his knees.

Ellie there is nothing wrong with you.

It was that day he told me that we were alike. I had calmed down and was lying on the floor listening to his brushstrokes.

I wasn't accepted either, y'know."

The world stopping.

"Really?"

"With boys it's all about sports."

Brushstroke.

"I was always the last chosen for any team. No good at football." He shook his head. "No good at baseball either. They used to call me Max the Mess."

Quiet: A tree branch swaying in the light outside his window; the swirls in the wood floor beneath me.

"Did you feel bad?"

The brush stopping. I can feel him looking at me.

"At first, but then I learned to enjoy my own company."

More brushstrokes. I watch the branch dip gracefully. Otherwise the world is still.

His face; his eyes caressing me.

"They're peasants, Ellie."

"What are peasants?"

"The common people. The mob."

Peasants. I think about it now: what an idea we had of ourselves, me and my father and mother. We were better, somehow; apart.

Now look at me. I am one in eight million. Nobody knows me. The trees with their legs in the air; the gray river; the cars pulling the light with them on the West Side Highway.

I don't understand how I got from that life to this one.

9 p.m.

Nine p.m. now; the light has dimmed and the air is breathable. It has been a long day; crying in Riverside Park, walking very fast through my tears to get some ice cream, as if that would change things; coming home to the empty apartment.

I am sitting on the floor near the white loveseat, a fan pointed at me. The wood pushes up into the back of my head.

The phone rings. For a minute I am sure that it is Calvin. He is overseas but has snuck away to call me.

It rings again; I look at it. *Do not pick up.*

"How can it be love if it doesn't stay?" I asked Calvin.

"You're asking something else," he said. "You're asking can you depend on people." Outside the salsa hits a high note, then slows down. From the floor I trace the slanted oblong shadow that leans against the wall over the plywood sideboard, the rug a stiff, dusty brush against my bare legs and arms.

Here's the good news, folks: If you don't have a self, no one can insult you.

The great way is not difficult for those who have no preferences.

No preferences: love me back or don't; it doesn't matter.

That was never what I was asking him.

Sunday, June 28, 3 a.m.
107th Street
The Blue Notebook

In the sea foam room, a kind of silence. I have not moved for two hours. In that time, Calvin has come to me countless times. Knocking on the front door of the apartment, magically appearing by my bed, pulling the sheet off to get to me.

Again and again. *He isn't coming*, I scream at myself.

But I can't believe. *The denial of a thing is the assertion of it.*

Monday, June 29, 9 a.m.
The Center for Urban Research
The Blue Notebook

On my desk, a note from Celeste: "Guess what, Amber liked the proposal! She *loved* it!"

Great. Celeste is going to be impossible now.

She just came in, one foot dragging along the carpet.

"So we got it!" she squealed joyfully.

"Congratulations," I said. "You did good."

"It's *ours*, Ellie." She shook her head; a few glossy curls bounced. "We're going to work on it together."

"This is *your* project, Celeste. I had nothing to do with it."

"No, but you're going to," she said. "I'm going to teach you." She lurched towards the extra desk, fell down in the chair. "We've got a LOT to do, Ellie," she said. She was breathless, like someone who has just won an Emmy.

Then she outlined the work:

"We're going to have to find ten interns or so to do the interviewing. That's about five hundred inquiries to send out."

"Five hundred!"

"Those are the proportions." She shook her head. "Fifty to one—if we want ten good candidates, we're going to have to reach out to about five hundred people."

I pictured the work: each letter will have to be printed, signed, folded. Five hundred labels to type. Just so Celeste can feel good about herself. Fuck.

"That's going to take a lot of time," I said. "At least a week."

"We've got two days," said Celeste, standing.

"Two days. I can't do that in two days."

"We *have* to, Ellie," said Celeste. She walked to my desk, leaned down, and put her face close to mine. "If this is going to be a success, Ellie," she said, "we're going to have to *work*."

She meant me, of course.

Fuck.

2 p.m.

I hate her. Seriously.

I always do this: I believe in people.

You only need one person. That is what I said to myself when I met Celeste. Seth was gone. Cass was gone. Then there was Celeste, sticking her face into my office.

She is *not* a good person.

At lunchtime, Celeste appeared in the door of my office. Vicky was beside her; they were both all smiles. "Vicky has agreed to help us," Celeste announced. "I'm taking you both to lunch."

I didn't want to. Celeste was going to be relentlessly cheerful, and I didn't want to be around that. I got up anyway and followed Celeste's tiny feet.

We went to a restaurant called Fred's and ordered sandwiches. It was packed; we were crammed together against a window that only showed people's feet walking by on the street outside.

I thought about how I would rather be by myself. When Celeste isn't here, I go to our bench and read.

"So, Vicky," said Celeste. "Knowing that this research is about the sex trade, tell us what your experience has been. What you know." She lifted her glass of water to her lips, a grand gesture.

Vicky closed one eye. One oiled curl looped around the back of her ear and ended on the side of her cheek. Her sleeveless dress showed shoulders covered with moles.

"I can tell you that tricks are the first thing you turn to if you're an addict," she said. "Plenty of girls I knew did that. I just got lucky." She smiled, embarrassed. "I was with the dealer."

"What happened to them? Your friends who became prostitutes."
She looked at us, direct. "AIDS mostly."

"Did you have friends that died?"

Vicky's face got sad. "A lot."

"That's terrible, Vicky," said Celeste.

"Thank you," said Vicky.

"It must take a lot of courage for you to talk about this," said
Celeste. Vicky closed one eye. "I've been in a lot of Twelve Steps,"
she said. "You get used to it. It's good to face it, y'know? It's good
you're doing a report like this. It's good."

"I think it's an important issue," said Celeste. "There's a lot of
focus on poverty at the agency, but not a lot of focus on low-income
women. Women are so much more vulnerable, wouldn't you say?"

"I guess," said Vicky. "I kind of take it on myself, y'know? If I had
finished school." She shrugged. "The family didn't help. My mom
was an addict and all."

Celeste turned to me. "That's tough," said Celeste. "That's a lot
to transcend, wouldn't you say, Ellie?"

The food came. I launched into my BLT. Why did she say that to
me?

"Ellie doesn't know what it's like to struggle with the kinds of
things you've struggled with," Celeste said to Vicky. "Ellie is blue
blood."

The blood rushed to my face. "I'm not *blue blood*. I'm middle
class."

"She thinks that I'm interested in the project because I'm ambitious, not because I really want to make change."

My face got even redder.

"Jesus Celeste. I never said that. I never said anything like that."

Vicky's eyes widened. I could tell she didn't want to get into this
fight.

If I wasn't penned in by Celeste, I would have gotten up and left.
Immediately.

"The key to good research," said Celeste, "is you really have to
listen to the people you're researching. You really have to put
yourself in their shoes. This project is going to be A LOT of work,"
said Celeste, "but it could really make a difference. I hope you're
ready to make a difference."

"Sure" said Vicky.

I didn't answer.

"Ellie?"

I wanted to knock Celeste's plate off the table, stick the fork in her upper arm. *I liked you.*

"Absolutely," I said.

Later, Celeste limped into my cubby to make it up to me.

"That was for Vicky, Ellie. She thinks that all people who are richer are happier. I wanted her to feel like she's part of this. As an equal."

"So you used me as your example? I'm your case study of a person who is fucked up in spite of advantages?"

"It's kind of true. In comparison to her."

I turned my back.

"I want this project to be a success, Ellie."

I didn't answer.

"Ellie?"

"Am I doing the work?"

Monday, 7 p.m.
107th Street
The Blue Notebook

It was a long afternoon. Typing labels isn't a great way to silence the angry voice in your head. By the time 3 p.m. rolled around, I couldn't stop cursing her out. I just decided—this shit was NOT getting done today. Let her wait. Let her have Vicky do it.

At four, I went to Amber, asked if I could talk to her. Amber looked up from her desk, surprised, her long braid coiled around one shoulder. "I wonder if I could go home a little earlier. I'm not feeling so well."

"Are you okay?"

"I think so. I just need to rest."

I managed to get out of the office before Celeste saw me. *Fuck her*, I kept thinking.

It's all such bullshit.

A long walk. I walked fast: a young woman my age walked by, also in office clothes; we stared at each other blankly. A store front filled with sequined evening dresses, wholesale only; fluorescent orange netting on the side of a building. One block I was angry, one block I was scared.

Monday, 10 p.m.
107th Street
The Red Notebook

"Wear that lacy thing," said Calvin the second time he called. It was at work; I blushed, deeply, then smirked at the pink wall, enjoying my own private joke: *he likes my Sears camisole.*

Once he said that to me on the phone, I couldn't stop smiling to myself. I pictured him taking it off me. He would lift the straps. I would raise my arms. He would slowly pull it upward. There would be the moment when my breasts shook out, small, perfect. He would be waiting for that smooth, outer arc of them.

In my fantasies, he does not speak; he is too overcome. He tugs at my clothes; I make him wait.

A scene: 4 p.m., a Saturday. Calvin will give a lecture in the loft on 14th Street in two hours.

In the kitchen, the miserable cats are silent; the pee smell wafts toward us into the bedroom. It does not matter.

Calvin lies beneath me, eyes closed. I am perched above. The light coming through drawn blinds stripes our bodies.

"If this were a painting, what do you think it would be called?"

He opens one eye. "Hmmm. A Sassy Statue Seduces a Magician."

"Is that how it is?" I hunch over him, pleased. The gray-blond hair swept back from the long forehead, cut with long horizontal ridges; the hook of the nose, the deep-set eyes. "I don't think so. You seduced me, not the other way around."

The eyelids open again; tiny doors to his attention. "You knew what you were doing."

I sit up straight. "I absolutely did not."

He gazes up. "All that blushing. You were sending signals."

"I'm self-conscious. I can't help it." His eyes close again. I lean down closer to his face. "I didn't have *intentions* towards you. I thought of you as my teacher."

"You didn't let yourself think it, but you wanted it, and your body let you know."

I sit back again: is he right? The light falls against the crack in the wall, which is the color of putty.

"So you knew me better than I knew myself?"

Calvin does not answer. His eyes fly open. He thrusts up into me and I gasp.

That is the kind of question and answer he likes; he gets the last word.

When I am away from him, I walk. From my apartment to the Metropolitan Museum to look at Asian art. From the office to the 42nd Street Library. I can't stop thinking; my mind can't stop getting over the surprise of it—why didn't I see the signs that he wanted me? How did I overlook them?

At work, I go through all the motions: standing at the copy machine, feeding the sheets in, pulling them out, checking the page numbers, stapling. All that time, an imaginary Calvin watches me, makes sexy comments. *Look at the statue, doing office work.*

A whole week to wait. Finally, The Day comes. Now time has slowed.

I dress in front of the mirror: put on one outfit then another. Turn to my side, toss my hair. Put it behind my ears. Shake it out again.

He cannot help but want me.

Out the door.

The subway ride to Union Square; the walk from Union Square to Spring Street, passing store windows, street signs, two slouchy art students with punk hair; a Mexican worker, a couple of working girls.

At Spring Street, the wait in the sun. The heat rises from the pavement.

When he comes, everything changes; he is here now. A cloud of Calvin, and I am swept up in him.

We walk past the Spring Street Bookstore, the Village Tavern, a small flea market in an empty lot.

Calvin is babbling; he feels like his brain is melting; a lady on the bus was wearing perfume, and it made him feel sick.

Let's get there—that's all I think.

Calvin keeps talking while we walk. He went to sit in on Eckerman's class last week; they were studying Tibetan conjugation. How the hell is anyone going to learn anything *that* way?" He laughs. "All that learning—a whole PhD and he doesn't know a thing." When he, Calvin, gets the phurbu, he will be able to take control of the monastery and run things the way they should be.

Pay attention to us. Here. Now, I want to say. I pull ahead, a dog straining its chain.

It has been a week since I last saw him.

It has been an eternity.

The front steps; the stairs up to the apartment; the lock on the door.

For the first hour, I am all breath. He brushes my nipples with his fingertips until the pleasure streams through me, a river of urgent tingling; plunges two fingers in, pulls me on top of him. He spreads my lips, places a thumb against the mound of my clitoris while I arch my back.

Time stops.

But then we grow tired, settle. This is my time, I think. I roll on my back.

"A question," I say.

Calvin is all attention.

"I still don't understand about concepts."

"Maybe you're trying too hard."

"I re-read *Zen Mind*. I get it intellectually, but I don't see how it actually works."

"So the statue is studious," says Calvin. His lips, red with the white beard around them, purse with amusement.

"Where did you *learn* everything?" I ask.

He makes that mock-groaning sound. "The void," he says.

"That's not an answer," I say. I am perched on top of him; he's gone soft, his hands on my thighs, but I like being perched up here.

"Maybe there is no answer," he says. "Maybe the answer is—the truth moves."

"I don't believe that," I say. "I think you know, but you're not telling me."

He laughs with pleasure. His hands twitch on my thighs. "That's right," he says. "I can't let you steal my secret knowledge," he says. "Then where would I be?"

Light stretches across the walls.

"I want to be like you," I say.

He widens his eyes.

Outside, a truck rumbles away.

"Be like yourself," he says. "You'd look funny with a beard." Smiles into my eyes. For a minute, the light is a string between us.

Tuesday, June 30, 10 p.m.
107ᵗʰ Street
The Blue Notebook

I did a good thing. I went to the East West Bookstore instead of the library. I met someone.

Luckily Celeste was in meetings most of the day. I did everything she wanted, then left before she could come in and find fault. Walking home, I remembered Cass talking about Everest in the Café Olana. *Remember—we used to go to the East West Bookstore?* So I decided to go.

I haven't been there in months.

A surprise: there is a Buddhist nun there, a Westerner, who helps customers. I saw her when I first came in: maroon robe over Birkenstock sandals; a kind of crew cut—dark hair that made a fuzz around the outline of her head.

I went to the Eastern Religion section. From there, I could peek out at the front desk. At the front counter, the nun sat with a hippie-looking guy. A window above spilled light onto them. She was one of those people who talks through a perpetual smile.

If I kept still, I could hear them. They were talking about pricing the books. "When I look at a new title, it's hard to put a price on it because of my opinion of it," she said. "I look at *The Secret*, so popular, and I want to put a price of $2.50 because I never found it at ALL illuminating. Then I look at the *Heart Sutra*, all of ten pages, and I want to charge $10,000 for it." Her rich laugh sailed out over the counter, threaded through the lines of shelves.

Still listening, I moved to the Mythology section. I turned a corner, and there she was; the face sticking out of the robe; narrow with baggy cheeks and small, dark, glistening eyes.

"Looking for something in particular?" she asked. Her ears flapped out from the shaven skull.

I found myself blushing.

"Just browsing," I said.

She turned away and then I blurted it out.

"I'm wondering," I said. "Romantic love, spiritual love. Is there a connection or are they totally opposed to each other? Do you know of any books about that?" I could feel my face burn. Stupidly.

She turned back. There were faint freckles sprinkled over her baggy cheeks.

"Wow," she said, blinking. "Best question of the day." She shook her head from side to side slightly. "This is why I like working here," she said to the air. "The questions people have." Her eyes traveled over me and she had an idea. She turned and started walking, her maroon robe swishing around her ankles, her stockinged heels peeking out with each step. I followed. She kept turning her head to say things as we walked.

"I guess the obvious choice is Rumi," she said. "Have you heard of him?"

"I've heard of him," I said. "I haven't actually read him."

"Rumi is *amazing*," she said. "Thirteenth century, and he really understood it all ..." She turned and walked the length of the shelf, her hands trailing along the spines.

We rounded a corner: she stopped, scanned the shelves, and pulled out a book with an Arabian man in a blue robe on the front. "*Divan-i Shams-i Tabrizi*," she said. "This is his masterpiece. This is what I started with."

She opened the book and read from it:

Only one who has been undressed by Love
Is free from defect and desire
O Gladness, O Love, our partner in trade,
healer of all our ills, our Plato and Galen,
remedy of our pride and our vanity.

I raised an eyebrow; my Mr. Spock look. "So spiritually, the purpose of romantic love is to bring you down?"

She smiled.

"I would say, to open you up."

Pause.

"Rumi was in love with his teacher, but his teacher left him." She shook her head. "Love and longing, right? And then"—she raised her arms to the sky—"All this transcendent poetry."

I wondered how someone became like her—ecstatic over hopeful ideas.

"I feel like longing kind of sucks," I said. She laughed.

"Of course it sucks." She looked at me. "You have to use it. Rumi has this quote. 'Let your teacher be Love itself.' My teacher, Lama Yuden, says something similar: 'everyone and everything is your teacher.'" Her face lit up. "In the Tibetan Buddhist tradition, students are supposed to look at their guru as the Buddha himself. It's really about the *attitude* love brings ... I feel like that's so *liberating*."

I looked at her, deadpan. "I'm not finding pain liberating."

"Isn't it good to be aware of *who we are*? Don't worry if it hurts, y'know? Use it?"

"That hasn't been my experience of pain," I said. "I'm just ... pain is horrible. It doesn't do anything for me. I feel like when you're in pain, you just want not to be."

She raised her eyebrows up to her bald skull. "Pain is growth," she said. "The student *should* be in love with the teacher. It's all about the *act* of loving, not the *object* of the love."

I looked at the floor. "I feel like that's an *idea*," I said. "That's an idea of how it is supposed to work, but it doesn't really work."

She blinked. "Stick with it," she said. Suddenly she beamed. "That's how the magic happens, right? Just ... persevering?" A delighted little laugh.

She seemed about to leave. I didn't want her to. I looked at the maroon robes, the crew cut, the earth sandals.

"So what's your name?" I asked.

"Pema." A Tibetan name. It couldn't be her original one.

"And yours?"

I told her and then asked, "When did you become a nun?"

She looked up. "When did I ordain? I guess ... three years ago."

"Is your ... nunnery here in New York?"

She shook her head. "I've been in Nepal for the last few years. My teacher is there—Lama Yuden."

"Oh."

Moment of silence.

"I have to get back to the front desk." She smiled gently.

"Okay."

I browsed a bit, went up to pay. I bought two of the books Pema recommended to me: *Buddhism in Action* and *The Buddha Said.*

"Let your teacher be Love itself, Ellie," she said, when she gave me my change.

Wednesday, July 1, 1 a.m.
107th Street
The Red Notebook

Dear Calvin,

I am reading Rumi now.

It is not just you who said it. It is also Rumi: humility; give up your self.

I am trying. I walk through The City, anonymous.

I am following directions, but something is wrong. It does not feel the way it should.

Wednesday, 2 a.m.
107ᵗʰ Street
The Blue Notebook

"Madhyamaka; Mind-Only School," said Calvin. "Everything is mind."

I sit, the shadows crisscrossing my body as cars move up Amsterdam Avenue. I'm in a night aquarium. I have my aquarium toys: my electric typewriter, an old Girl Scout badge, rows of books. My landscape of mind ripples out the window, down Amsterdam, all the way to the end of the island.

On the wall that faces the street, one of my father's paintings; a brown background with a huge fountain of colors coming out of it: blue, yellow, red, each one a smooth, bold stroke. When my father left, I took it off the wall of his studio and put it in my bedroom. Everything that my father left behind, I took for my own. Seth made fun of me for it. "Oh, look," he said. "The Ellie Adkins Museum of Personal Loss."

There is before the divorce, and there is after.

Before the divorce, my mother believed in love; goodness.

That was why, even though she and my father had met in art school, she had gone to work to support us—he was the better artist, and she believed in him.

It was why we had to do certain things. We had to visit Aunt Greta, who lived in an apartment that smelled like used band-aids and said the same uninteresting things over and over again. "Because," my mother said, "when you love someone, that is what you do."

My father never went.

I was twelve when I began to read my mother's romances. I found the first one on her nightstand: *The Shivering Sands*. Midnight blue cover, with a picture of a rocky coast, and a solitary figure, the misty silhouette of a woman.

In the book, a young woman comes to stay at an estate; she is trying to find out what happened to her sister, who disappeared. There are two men in the story. Man #1 is unctuously kind; Man #2 fights with her all the time. There are many encounters between them as she gets closer to solving the mystery. At the end, an astonishing discovery: Man #1, who has been so kind, leads her to a cave and tricks her into stepping in quicksand, then leaves. It is Man #2, the one she has always fought with, who comes just in time to save her.

After that, I read them all: *The Hunter's Moon; Mistress of Mellyn; The Pride of the Peacock*. I couldn't get over the surprise: the person who was nice to you wasn't always the person who loved you.

A MEMORY.

A scene:

I am standing with my mother in my parents' bedroom. Twin beds pushed together; quilted blue-and-white bedspreads; windows overlooking the backyard, which stretches out to the row of lilac bushes that border our yard from others. My mother is in Bermuda shorts. We are folding laundry. She smells of lemons.

We have just been at the dinner table. An hour of silence; my father had received a rejection for a grant proposal, and every time my mother said anything, he looked past her at the wall, as if he had not heard anything. It was her face I could not stand; with each thing she said into the silence, it became more drawn, the bones pushed upward through the skin.

It had happened before; there is a rejection, and my father will not speak to us. Those times, my mother and I stuck together, busied ourselves with house chores. If we kept acting like it, everything would be fine.

But this day, I am inflamed with the injustice of it. "Dad shouldn't not talk to us," I say. I say this importantly. I know she will agree; my mother who is all about goodness.

But she doesn't seem to know what I'm talking about. She looks at me, her face far away.

"He's just upset honey."

"But he shouldn't treat us this way." This is what my mother believes—people should be friendly—so I know I'm on safe ground. "You don't deserve it."

My mother has just finished folding the arms of a shirt back, placing it on the pile. She smiles absently.

"Welllll," she says finally. "When you love someone, you have to accept them the way they are."

I don't understand it. For my entire life, my mother has been talking about the obligations of goodness.

"Shouldn't he love us back?" I ask hotly. "Shouldn't he treat us better?"

My mother is looking out the window. She doesn't answer. When she looks back at me, I see that she understands something I don't.

"Love isn't about what you *get*, honey," she says. "Love is just ..." she shrugs. "You just love." She is looking out the window, but she is not seeing what's there. My mother has a vision of a better world.

Maybe it was that, the thing I couldn't see, that I have been going toward all this time.

Wednesday, 3 a.m.
107th Street
The Red Notebook

It took two more calls from Calvin at work before I understood: this wasn't a one-night stand.

He called once a week.

Each time he called, he said my name to me: *Ellie Adkins*.

My face glowed hot. Everything around me fell away.

All week his desire for me was a movie that played in my mind. Now he was admiring my thigh. Now he was reaching for the buckle of my belt. In the movie, I heard my own intake of breath, a hiss.

Luckily there wasn't much to do at work: a few mailings, some filing. When there was an errand to do outside the office, I volunteered, took my time. I carried my head that was full of Calvin out to City Hall Park, sat on a bench among the patchwork London plane trees, watched people walk by.

That month, the lectures were all about Vajrayana Buddhism. "Enlightenment in one lifetime," said Calvin. "How do you get there? Not by books," said Calvin, shaking his head. "Not by logic. Not by words."

"How then?" someone else called.

"It's not knowledge that comes from *thinking*," said Calvin.

One lecture, he just told us a bunch of Tibetan trickster tales. A clever rabbit who tricked a tiger into sticking her head through the hole in a stone wall. She couldn't get it out again, and the rabbit taunted her. The rabbit and the turtle; Calvin claimed it was Tibetan in origin—that got a few people laughing. "So what's the real moral of the race between the rabbit and the turtle, folks?" said Calvin. "They always say 'slow and steady wins the race.'" He stopped, looked around the room, slowly shook his head from side to side. "Maybe it isn't your strengths that are gonna get you there," he said.

"So that's why we need tricksters, folks," Calvin shouted at us. "The trickster is going to pull away those puffed-up ideas you have of yourself and show you who you really are. Vajrayana knowledge," he then said. "Experience. Not thinking."

All that week, I mulled it over. When we were back in the bedroom, I asked.

"Buddhism is about getting tricked?" I asked.

He smiled. "Don't try to learn it, then you will learn it."

"Why is everything in Buddhism riddles?"

"That's good," he said. "Short-circuit the thinking."

"Isn't that kind of dangerous? Let's forget about logic?"

I am pouting, but it is a kind of play: *come and shake me out of it.*

He does. He overturns me on the bed, puts two fingers in me.

"How about this," he says, as I cry out. "Do you have words for this?"

The same every week—he calls, everything falls away from me. Walking through the days: a week of fantasy: what I will say, how he will want me.

The second lecture about Vajrayana Buddhism is about the guru. We are all sitting in a semi-circle. Calvin begins by railing about the Chinese government. How they had no right to invade. "China was never part of Tibet," he says vehemently. We have heard this before. We are waiting for him to get somewhere new. Sometimes it takes a while.

A young punk rocker walks in; purple hair in a mohawk, ripped jeans, dyed sneakers. He is late. Calvin stops talking, watches him walk to the back of the room and sit down on one of the folding chairs. We are quiet also. The punk rocker doesn't know we are all watching him.

"Hello ... Spike," says Calvin.

Laughter erupts.

That starts it. "You know what they say, don't you?" Calvin raises his voice. "When the teacher is in the room, it should be as if a *tiger* is in the room. That is the kind of attention you should bring."

There are many stories about students and gurus, after that: Bodhidharma who cut his ear off to get the teachings. Marpa who searched for his teacher all over India. And then Milarepa, who came to Marpa, asked to be his student, and had to work for him for eight years building towers of stones that Marpa made him dismantle and rebuild a few feet away. Just as Milarepa gave up, Marpa finally gave him the teachings.

All week I think about it. I walk through Central Park, watching people jog, play tennis. Why is the teacher mean to the student? Shouldn't there be trust?

There are moments I ask myself if it is a good idea for me to sleep with this man. One night at midnight I go into the bathroom, turn on the light, and look at my face in the wood-framed mirror that is propped against a pipe. *What are you doing with him?* I ask silently.

But then I remember:
What do you see when you look at me?
A person with a very good heart.

4 a.m.

From Rumi:
This is love: to fly toward a secret sky, to cause a hundred veils to fall each moment. First to let go of life. Finally, to take a step without feet.

Thursday, July 2, 8 p.m.
107th Street
The Red Notebook

A memory:

I am on top of Calvin. It is always this way. "This is the tantric position," Calvin says.

I look down on the bare chest with its white curlicues of hair.

"So, when you look at me," I start, "what do you see?"

His head turns on the pillow. He makes the mock-groaning sound—this is one of those questions he does not like.

"A nymph," he says. I set my face.

"No," I say firmly. And then: "Seriously."

A thread of light, reflection from a car hood in the street below us, throbs on the wall in front of me.

"So what are we doing here? What are we to each other?"

"Isn't it obvious what we are doing?"

I don't speak. *He knows what I mean*, I think.

"As to what we are doing here ... Sukhavati."

"What's Sukhavati?"

He raises a hand from my thigh.

"Sukkha, opposite of dukkha. Joy. Bliss."

I sit up straight, look down at him.

"You can't live life from an armchair, statue."

He starts to thrust, but I just sit there, don't push back.

"I'm worried," I say.

He stops. "About what?"

I look at him steadily. "I'm worried about my heart."

He watches me. Finally, he speaks. "We'll have to be careful," he says solemnly. "Hearts are delicate things."

All that week I am happy.

But then, two days before I meet him, it comes to me. I am crossing Broadway. There is a young couple sitting on the bench in the island and I realize: *Calvin and I don't know each other.* When I was with Seth, I knew his parents—Ralph and Sadie. And knowing them—Sadie with her droopy face and whiny voice, Ralph with his red-faced disapproval—I knew things about Seth. But I don't know any of those things about Calvin, and he doesn't know any of those things about me.

I must change that, I realize. As soon as possible. I decide I will tell him about my father.

Friday, July 3, 9 p.m.
107th Street
The Blue Notebook

A bad day at work. Cass called me at work and invited me to another meeting of the New Heights Group. I needed to do something, so I went.

We were back in that school auditorium again. This time we watched a movie, *Ten Against the Mountain*. The leader of the climb just made the fatal mistake of bringing his client to the summit, even though he knew a storm was coming. When the storm came, the two men crouched in the snow, faces leaning toward the ground. One man shouted to the other: there was no more oxygen canisters left. "That's impossible," the second man screamed.

After that, Tommy Hilfiger came onto the stage to talk to us, lean and energetic in a jean jacket and hiking boots. "So what are you getting from this?" he asked us. "I hope what you're getting is: climbing this high is dangerous. You get up this high, you don't have oxygen—" He shook his head from side to side—"brain of a reptile ... And what does this tell us?" he continued. "That the worst thing we can do is to care more about summitting than the cause—what we are there to do."

Beside me, Cass looked up raptly.

After the film, Tommy Hilfiger gave a little lecture. He hoped that the film taught us a bit about what we would be up against when we climbed. How the mountain would test us. He'd read our dream statements, and they were inspiring.

"Some of you spoke of giving back," he said. "Wanting to aspire to something bigger. So beautiful." He shook his head. "Y'know?" His face was a gilded mask under the light. "A wise man once said,

139

'aspire to small things, then big things.'" Tommy nodded, surveyed us. "At the end of our lives, we are going to look back at what we've done, our accomplishments. I can't think of any bigger accomplishment than a project like this.

"So ..." He clapped his hands, prowled the edge of the stage. Cass followed him with her eyes, basking. "We have a lot of work to do," he said. "Physical work, mental work, but also financial work." He opened his eyes wide. "You know how much it costs to climb Everest? A *lot*. Each of you is going to need to raise that money," he said. "Each of you needs to have a goal of two thousand dollars or so. I have a list here; I'm going to give it out. Some phone calls to make, pledges to get ... Because we are trying to do some good here." He swept his eyes over us. "All of us celebrities." He smiled winningly.

Pledges. No way. There is no way I am going to do that.

When the meeting was over, Cass and I went out to the cement courtyard. It was nine at night and the street outside the courtyard was crowded. The heat had gone and a few people sat out on their stoops; one or two in plastic lawn chairs. Cass looked great in her dungaree shorts and little magenta top. She looked up at the sky, sighed with pleasure.

"Great, huh?" she said. She shook her head back and forth. "Can't believe how lucky I was to run into him."

"You didn't tell me we had to raise all that money, Cass."

Cass raised her eyebrows ostentatiously. "You thought it was free?"

"That was one of the first things you said to me," I said. "I said it was going to cost a lot of money and you said you were going to be able to go low cost." She blinked, flexed a slender arm and looked at it.

"I am. Tommy has a sponsor for me."

"So what am *I* supposed to do? I'm not the kind of person who can call people up and ask them for money. You know that."

Her brows came together.

"Even for a good cause?"

So irritating. As if she doesn't know who I am.

"How about those Buddhist lectures you went to? Couldn't someone from that crowd sponsor you?"

"Someone who has an extra 2K?" I pictured myself writing Calvin, even if I thought he would get the letter, wherever he is. Telling him I want to go to Tibet, get him the Ralung phurbu. *I only need $2,000.*

"For Nepali orphans!"

"They weren't rich people, Cass."

Cass looked around distractedly. "Who else do you know?"

"I don't know anyone. You know that."

She gazed out toward the street. "Well Tommy has a list of people you can call."

"I don't think I'm going to be able to do this."

She turned her face to me, earnest in the dim light. "Why do you say things like that? Why do you let everything be a barrier to you?"

"Why do you even care if I come? You didn't ask me to come to the fire tower with you."

"You were with Seth then."

"I don't think this is for me, Cass. I'm not hardy. And there's no way I'm going to be able to get people to pledge money to me."

"I want you with me." Doggedly. "I want you to do this with me."

"Why?"

"I realized something on the fire tower, Ellie." Her eyes were roving around the courtyard, but then they came to rest on me. "At school you helped me. You helped me so much."

I looked at her: the half-red, half-black hair, the bitten-down nails. "You're really smart, you know that, Ellie? I don't think I would have graduated without you. Those papers you wrote for me ..."

We were both embarrassed. I looked at the cement arch over the school doorway: Public School 32. "That's what's easy for me—school. The thing that isn't easy for me is life."

"That's why I want you to do this with me. Her eyes pulled at me. "I want to pay you back. I want to help you not be scared."

I blushed a little.

"I see that you're afraid, Ellie. I don't want you to be."

She's right, I realized. Fear. Calvin has hurt me. He has made me afraid.

"Besides, you were the one who got me into this in the first place."

Surprise through my body. "No I didn't."

"All that talk about Buddhism. It got me interested."

We stood there in the half-dark. Cass took a step toward me, her arm flashing white in a streetlight.

"I want you *with* me, Ellie." Then I wanted to cry. Right then.

"Okay," I said. "Okay, yes I want to go."

"Good!" she said and hugged me. Gripped in her arms, I looked across the street at a fat-armed woman sitting on a lawn chair. I wondered what I was saying yes to.

But the hug felt good.

Monday, July 6, 9:30 a.m.
The Center for Urban Research
The Blue Notebook

Here's something that just happened:

In the pink mailroom, I was working on another mailing. Swiping the sticky backs of envelopes against the porcelain wheel that wets them for me, pressing the flaps to the backs of the envelopes. Celeste couldn't say anything about me leaving the other day because I got the labels done. Today I had to work on mailing the 500 envelopes for the "inquiries" Celeste wants to make.

Ed came in, a bunch of stuffed manila envelopes in his arms. His hair was slicked back from his handsome face.

"Ellie!" he exclaimed. "How are you?"

"I'm okay."

"They really have you working lately."

I smiled wanly, nodded my head.

"Mom isn't letting you get out much." I smiled down at my hands. "Mom" is what Ed called Amber when I first arrived here—*I see Mom's really piling it on*, he'd say, when he saw me hard at work. "And now there are two moms!"

I laughed. "Yeah. They pulled a fast one on me," I said. "Celeste says I am her partner with the project now. So I shouldn't complain when there are even more mailings." I set another envelope on top of the towering stack. "She says I can rise in the agency."

Ed was fitting his own envelopes into a white plastic box that I will take down to the building mailroom.

"You could y'know," he agreed.

"I don't have the right degree."

"Beth didn't have a degree at first." He stopped and looked at me while I worked. "I think you could do anything you want, Ellie," he said. I blushed.

Now he is gone, the shame stays with me; an actual substance that travels through my body. How pathetic I must seem. How clearly I must need the kindness.

Friday, July 10, 9 p.m.
107th Street
The Blue Notebook

A message from Cass on my answering machine: "Ellie—we have a *lot* of work to do. I am going to take you rock-climbing."

I'm meeting her tomorrow.

I don't want to.

I listen, sit, and look out at the lighted windows across the street; people living other lives. Pledges. Fuck. How can I even do that … call up random people I don't know and ask them for money to climb Mt. Everest? Ellie Adkins, who can barely make it to her secretary job each day.

Who doesn't even know how to sleep.

Saturday, July 11, 1 a.m.
107th Street
The Red Notebook

. In my head, I never stopped talking to Calvin: how much my father had loved me. How I had won an award for my essay, *An Artist's Daughter*.

When we met, at Spring Street, I did not say it right away; I waited.

The corner at Spring Street and Eighth Avenue.

The walk across.

My cries.

Then when we were dressing, the light dwindling through the two rooms, I started.

Back to him, head turned over my shoulder.

"You know ... I used to be a golden girl."

Calvin was standing, buckling his belt. His belt was so old that inside it was a series of parallel cracks. He used it anyway. "A golden girl, eh? You look very much ... flesh and blood to me."

"I was ... an achiever."

"Oh yeah?" Head down again, finding the right hole.

"Straight As. I won an essay contest."

No answer.

"People said I was *brilliant*. My father did anyway."

Calvin had walked into the kitchen.

"I'm talking to you," I said, hurt.

"I hear you."

"I'm telling you this because I want you to understand me."

Calvin bent over, picked up a sock, looked at me.

"You think I need a story to understand you?"

I stood, slender and becoming in my underpants and camisole. Blinked.

"It's not just a story," I said. "It's where I come from."

"So you think that's who you are?"

"It's part of who I am. An important part."

He looked at the wall, a half-smile on his face.

"It's how I came to be this way," I said.

He turned to me, his face soft. "Soap opera," he said.

"What?"

"A story you tell yourself," he said gently. I was standing halfway into my dungarees in the room with the cracks on the wall and the big tilting bed.

Now everything had changed.

11:30 p.m.

It was that summer Calvin announced a new lecture series: *Magic and Mystery in the East*. Last summer, actually. But now it seems like another land.

There were fewer of us coming then; people were on vacation. There were the regulars: Judith, with the gray curls framing her wide, friendly face, always dressed in a long skirt that swayed over her ample hips; Edwin with his troll face, comically solemn; soft-spoken Dacy. Now and then a new face would show up: an older woman in a pleated skirt, skeptical but interested.

The first lecture on magic was wild. Calvin talked about Tibetan lamas who could walk through the air, traveling across the country in days; hermits who could meditate naked in the snow.

"So how did people learn to do these things?" he asked rhetorically. "Focus." He gave us a little training: we had to stare into our open palms and visualize a young girl in a bikini swimming in the pool below a waterfall. Then we had to visualize her visualization; she was visualizing the same girl, in a bikini, swimming in the pool below a waterfall. And on and on. "One-pointedness of mind," said Calvin.

All that week, walking from work to home, I practiced. I imagined myself flirting with him: *I want to know your magic*. When the day finally came to meet him, I was ready.

A scene:

The rumpled bed, Calvin's hair spread like a fan around his head as he looks up at me.

I mount him, ease down on him, hold myself still.

"So that was quite a lecture last week." He smiles. "Are you a magician? Is there something I should know?"

"Of course I am."

"Really?" He arches his back slightly; laughs, pleased.

"I turned a statue into a living woman, didn't I?"

"No. You *said* I was a statue. That is not the same thing." I look down on him, smug.

"And look at this. I have created a room where time stops."

I smiled.

"True."

That night the lecture was about magic again. Calvin talked about airplanes. "Isn't that a kind of magic?" he asked. "A big metal thing full of people lifts off the ground?" He said that magic was just a matter of seeing past conventional reality. "We see a chair, we think it's solid," he said. "But what is it mostly? Empty space." That was how ninjas were able to dodge bullets, he said. They could see what was really there.

After the lecture, Calvin liked to go out to a nearby coffee shop with his Faithful—Judith, Edwin, Dacy, and then Special Guests. There were always a few students who had come to his lectures regularly in earlier years who liked to drop in and see him.

In July, it stayed light till about nine at night, but the coffee shop's plate-glass window was turned to the east, so the light came from banks of fluorescent lights hanging from the fake tin ceiling. We would line up along the glass counter full of croissants, muffins, and turnovers, and order our tea and coffee from the man with the walrus mustache. He could see what a weird crowd we were and amused himself by serving our paper cups with extravagant flourishes.

Once we were seated with our tea, the Calvin Show began. He told jokes, talked about the other students who had come to the lecture that night, sipped tea and sucked the excess liquid off his mustache with noisy relish. Then the testing started: asking questions about the lecture, shaking his head, "Didn't get it, Judith. Not even close." He never tested me.

If a former student came around, it was a minor celebration. Once there was a woman named Jill, stout and middle-aged, with a little mat of brown hair behind her head, two round cheeks that curved out like a valentine. Grouchy. Calvin gazed at her across the table, a little smile playing on his lips. "You should have seen Jill when she first came to me," he told us. She sat there, embarrassed, while he talked about her. "How angry you were," he said to her. "Remember that? And then I taught you to write haikus and chant mantras and then that was all you did," he said, laughing. "Every haiku was a mantra. The SAME mantra." Calvin's laughter built slowly, a wave that started in the belly, then worked its way up his body. By the time it got to his face, his mouth would be open, teeth showing. I was scared, sitting there: glad he hadn't turned his attention to me. *But his eyes are kind*, I told myself.

The Calvin Show always came around again to the subject of Eckerman, and how Calvin was going to beat him to Tibet to get the Ralung phurbu. Judith and Edwin seemed to be constantly on the look-out for opportunities. Judith had met a woman who was thinking of going to China. Edwin knew of a school group going. Then the scheming would begin. How could we get them to come to one of Calvin's lectures? How enlist them to the cause?

And then there was the question of whether the border between Nepal and China would open. Judith always seemed to bring hints that it was just about to happen. Calvin always retorted that she had been saying that ever since he got back from China, and it was just wishful thinking.

Sometimes Calvin would make jokes about us, sitting there. He called us the Eastern Asian Studies Society. He gave us different roles: Judith was Vice President; Edwin was Treasurer. "And you," he looked at me. His nostrils flared with amusement. "You're the antiquarian."

My smile was a grimace, just to show that I got the joke.

Sunday, July 12, 4 p.m.
107th Street
The Blue Notebook

Okay that was something to write about: Cass took me rock climbing ... off the side of a building.

It was on the roof of an apartment building in Long Island City—somehow, she knew the super. Cass wore overalls that had been cut off to make shorts. Her sturdy legs were bare except for black calf-high socks and work boots; black ends of hair stuck out from under her helmet. She wore a rock-climbing harness, with a coil of rope attached that spread out over the roof like an umbilical cord. My job was to make sure she didn't fall by holding the other end.

"What if I can't?" I asked.

"You'll hold me," she said. She told me to use the low wall that ran the perimeter of the roof as a brace. Then she leaned backward and began to inch down the side of the building.

I stood there holding her while I watched the elevated 7 train appear, the sun glinting off its silver edge. It tilted slightly on top of the elevated track. For a minute, I thought it would fall into the street below.

At college, someone painted a mural on the painted cement blocks that led to the gym. There was a slogan there that read "Do whatever you do intensely." I used to tease Cass that she had taken that slogan too seriously.

"So this is rappelling," she yelled up. "You would do it to come down an ice wall or a ledge."

"Are there a lot of those?" I yelled down.

"Some."

150

While Cass rappelled, I watched the sky. Last night at 3 a.m. I was still awake, imagining Calvin coming to me, magically knocking on the door to my apartment. Coming to meet Cass, I promised myself I would tell her about Calvin. But then I saw her. She was so ... sturdy.

She's always been that way. Even climbing down the side of the building, she was able to talk.

"I don't know how I'm going to get these pledges, Cass," I called down to her. It's not the kind of thing I can do."

"Don't think about it so much," she yelled up. "Just do it."

From the roof of the building we were on, Long Island City in panorama: the scaffolding behind a giant billboard; the side of a building where someone had painted, in white and magenta letters, *Goodbye New York*.

"Can't *you* try?"

A short silence. The sound of her grunting breath. "Tommy says the pledge part is important. Overcoming fear is important."

"How come *you* don't have to do it?"

From the rope I could tell she had gotten as far down as she was going to go and was coming back up. Her voice flew up.

"He thinks I'm not at the stage most people are. I'm more fearless."

More fearless. I looked down into the street where heads moved along; a fire hydrant threw a short, fat shadow.

"What's there to be afraid of, Ellie? If people say no, you just move on."

"It's hard for me now, Cass. I feel bad almost all the time."

"Why?"

"I don't know. I just do."

I could feel the tug of Cass's weight on the rope around my waist. A few minutes later, she appeared again, stepping on top of the roof edge like a miracle; black hair stuck to her forehead with sweat.

"Now your turn," she said.

"Oh no."

"Oh yes."

It took a while to get me into the harness. There were straps that went around my waist and the tops of my thighs: buckles, adjustments. I looked toward the door that led back down into the building, longing for it.

"You get up here," said Cass.

I didn't want to. I stalled.

"How do you do that?"

"What?"

"Just move on all the time."

Shrug. "I don't know. Because I can't let things stop me."

"I don't have confidence, Cass."

"So do things that build it."

"You sound like Celeste."

"Who?

"My co-worker. Actually she's more like a boss."

"Your boss talks to you like that? That's weird."

"She used to be a therapist. She gives me advice."

"Why do you let her do that?"

"Do you think friends should...confront each other? About their weaknesses?" I was looking at the edge of the opposite side of the roof, the roofs beyond it, just a step away.

"I think friends should be good to each other. So are we doing this or what?"

"Okay."

"Stand on the edge," she said.

I did. My stomach was dead set against it.

"It's scary at first," she said. "You have to remember," she looked at me steadily. "I've got you."

"Just lean back," she said. "You'll feel the rope holding you."

"I'm scared." Cass pursed her lips.

"Just lean back, Ellie. It's not that bad."

I did, slightly. It wasn't enough.

"More," she said. "The rope will hold you. Just step. Feel the wall with your foot."

"It's perpendicular!"

"Just trust the rope."

I looked at my hands on the rope. I did not want to look down.

"Stop thinking about the height," said Cass. "Ignore the fear."

"I can't."

"*Relax*. Just lean back; that's all you have to do."

I did. I leaned back farther and farther. The sky was over me. The top corner of the building came into view. The street hovered below. I kept leaning.

"That's it!' shouted Cass. "You're doing it! See? The rope has you! Now step."

But my body couldn't figure out how to do that. I was leaning, holding on to the rope.

"Just take a step," she called.

The world pivoted: my back hit something hard, and I was looking at the building across the street, but from the wrong perspective.

"Ellie," laughed Cass. "You're upside down."

"I know that," I said to the air.

"You leaned too far back."

"Obviously."

"But the rope held you," she said. "Right?"

"Yes," I said wearily.

She laughed again. "Ellie Ellie Ellie."

Sunday, 9 p.m.
107th Street
The Red Notebook

Dear Calvin,

Yet another letter you will never write back to.

Sunyata, you said. Nothing has an inherent self.

I sit here looking out of my living room window. I try not to be an inherent self. Not possible.

You can't hide, you said. But you saw me, then you turned away.

Monday, July 13, 9:30 a.m.
The Center for Urban Research
The Blue Notebook

On my desk, there are three pages of accounts by former prostitutes.

I imagine Celeste has left them for me. I pick one up and read.

There is the woman who was pushed out of a car while it was moving. Her dress caught on the door and she was dragged six blocks, the skin on the side of her face scraped off.

The woman who almost died of an overdose when a John kept shoving cocaine into her vagina.

The woman who was trapped in an elevator with a man who raped her repeatedly for two nights and days.

The young woman who loved the pimp who hit her "because he loved her," who kept telling her that after the prostitution would be the good part, but the good part never came.

It's like the animal rights pamphlets I used to read: the way they cut the tails off the pigs; de-beak the chickens, keep them in tiny wood boxes.

This morning, when I was finished reading all those accounts of prostitutes, Celeste appeared in my office. "So you see why we're doing the work," she said.

"Yes," I said.

But the work, quite frankly, sucked. I had to create a chart with all sorts of percentages and decimal points in it. There were seventeen columns. Celeste stood over me while I typed. "I think there has to be another column," she said. Each time she said that, I had to start all over again. I could tell she wasn't good at this because she kept lurching back and forth from my cubby to Amber's office, then coming back again with corrections. I could hear her softly cursing Amber under her breath. I pretended not to notice.

After three hours, my patience was ebbing.

"Who is going to even read this thing, anyway?"

"We *need* it, Ellie. And it has to be accurate."

"But seriously—who? One person? Five? It's just a *report*."

"Reports change things, Ellie."

"Really?"

Celeste slumped down in the chair beside me.

"It's not your name that's going to be on this."

"Yeah, I know," I said.

That stimulated a lecture: That's my problem; I don't want to commit to anything. I have to learn to invest in something. I could rise if I just put my mind to it.

I turned around and start typing, but the lecture continued. Do I really think it will just come to me. Do I really think I don't have to work for it.

I didn't say anything, but I told her I had to go to the bathroom. I left from the front door, took the elevator down to the street, and just stood there.

Fuck her, I thought. Fuck her, fuck her, fuck her.

When I went back up, Celeste was in the reception area, bending over Vicky's desk. She had Vicky working on the chart now. I could see Vicky looking unhappy, even though she gave me that friendly smile she gives everyone who walks through the door.

"Since you can't do your work, Vicky is doing it for you," said Celeste as I walked by.

On my desk, there were labels for me to type—another two hundred. I threaded the sheet of labels into my typewriter, felt the gush of despair rise up.

On the way home, I walked as quickly as possible.

I told myself how much worse it could be:

I could be locked into an elevator with a man who rapes me repeatedly.

I could lose the skin on the side of my face.

Everything's on fire, said Calvin. *And if you think there's water, the water is on fire too.*

All that summer the lectures are about magic. After, we go out to the coffee shop and Calvin holds court. One day a former student, Daniel, comes.

He is obviously one of Calvin's favorites. Tall with the face and fine blond hair of a baby, Daniel dresses simply: khakis and a worn tee shirt, looks at Calvin placidly, unafraid.

"So," says Daniel, "it's all magic this summer, eh? Calvin the Wizard."

Calvin loves it. He throws his head back and roars. The rest of us laugh along, a studio audience.

"Merlin," Calvin jokes. "That's how old I am. I appear out of the mists …" He laughs into his right eye, gazing around at us. Judith wobbles with merriment. Edwin blinks.

This becomes the running joke for the night: Calvin gives us all nicknames associated with the round table: Edwin is Galahad; Judith is—Calvin pauses for effect—"Morgan le Fay."

It's later that week that it happens. I am walking home from work, replaying our afternoon in the apartment on Spring Street in my mind.

I remember him, two weeks ago, assigning us roles for the Society. *Antiquarian.* A bit of mockery, I knew even then. And then I see what he was trying to tell me: I am too young.

The panic starts at the bottom of my belly, curls up, sending everything sideways, sliding. I push it down, but it just keeps spreading. Soon even my hands feel shaky.

It's the age difference.

Of course.

I am not his equal.

I look up. I push the panic away; it rises again, jiggles my insides.

I need to walk, walk, walk.

Up to Times Square, keep walking.

Up to 72nd Street, keep walking.

Calm down. It's not true. He chose you.

At 66th Street, I picture Calvin: the cold blue eyes, hawk nose, white beard. Who am I to you? I ask.

At 80th Street: *He's a Buddhist. Buddhists don't go around exploiting people.*

But then I think of us in the room on Spring Street. I remember how, when I ask a question, he will open one eye, patient, but wishing I hadn't spoken.

For a week it is all I think about. I fill the paper tray of the Xerox machine, clean up the mailroom.

In my fantasies, he reassures me. He strokes the side of my face.

Are you bored with me?

Of course not.

The next time we meet, I bring it up.

We lie on our backs, naked, our heads on the pillow, and look up at the plaster ceiling.

"So if you are Merlin," I say, "who am I?"

"Who are you?"

"Am I ... a plaything?"

The mock-groaning sound.

"You are ... my lovely assistant." He looks at me, humor twitching at the corners of his mouth. I stare back.

"Like Vanna White?"

His eyes wash over me. "I have taken you as my apprentice." He rolls on his back, the smile still on his face. "Although you are sometimes rather troublesome." The weight on my chest lifts. Look at that. So easy.

"You aren't bored with me?"

He raises an eyebrow.

"Bored?"

"I'm young," I say in a pained voice. "I don't know things."

"That's for sure."

"I don't want to be just another pretty face," I say. I can feel the blush begin as I say this.

Calvin mock-groans again. I like it—it always sounds like he is in genuine pain for me when he does that.

"Maybe I'm pretty," I say. "But not smart."

"Maybe you're just insecure," says Calvin sarcastically.

"I'm not really sure what you see in me, actually," I say. "You never said what interested you."

"Yes I did," says Calvin. "I said I saw you scowling when I gave the lectures. That was how I knew you were paying attention."

"But that's not why you *like* me."

Calvin sighs, and this time there is exasperation in it.

"Maybe you are just playing a trick on me, Merlin," I say.

"Maybe you are just playing a trick on yourself," says Calvin.

But I won't let go of it—I can't. I've been spinning around this all week.

"I don't even understand how this can be Buddhist, what we are doing," I say. "I thought Buddhism was against desire." I can hear my voice, rising, whiny. Soon I will be in tears.

Calvin has been silent. *I am making it worse*, I think.

Finally he flops over on his side to look at me.

"Don't you know the story of Merlin and Nimue?" he says.

"No." I am slightly sullen. "Who is Nimue?"

"Nimue is a young girl Merlin met toward the end of his life. She asked to be his apprentice, because she wanted his magic. Merlin taught her all his magic except one thing."

"What was that?"

"The spell to imprison him. If she imprisoned him, she would steal all his magic and she could be the master. So she asked, she cried—as women are wont to do—" added Calvin, giving me an ironic look—"She cajoled ... what do you think happened?"

"I don't know this story."

"Merlin gave her the spell. When he woke up, Nimue had created a cave he couldn't leave."

"Why?"

"What do you think an old man wants at the end of his life?" says Calvin. He looks at me, raises an eyebrow.

"I don't know."

"To be locked up in a cave with a beautiful young woman for the rest of time." His eyes hold mine.

A small dot of joy lets loose, expands into my body.

Soon it's a ticker tape parade.

Wednesday, July 15, 10 p.m.
107th Street
The Blue Notebook

Cass got me to go rock-climbing after work today. I sucked.

Afterwards, we got sandwiches at a deli and sat on a bench in the island between the uptown and downtown sides of Broadway. Cass's hair is red again on top; she's let the black dye grow out. She was relatively kind about my abysmal performance.

I was already feeling bad after the climb. Then she started in about all the stuff she's doing with Tommy. Recruiting "members," getting the word out about Tommy's "message."

"You need to get those pledges in, Ellie. Have you made any calls?"

"I will, I will." A bus pulled up to a light on Thomson Avenue. The fountain gushed. I thought how I didn't want to be alone, but alone is the only place that is safe.

"When?" said Cass.

"I'll *do* it," I said. "I'm not up to it right now." A homeless woman crossed at the light, pulling a shopping cart with an umbrella on it.

Change the subject, Ellie. "So what have *you* been up to?" I asked.

"Me?" Cass raised her eyebrows. She looked up Broadway, followed a taxi with her eyes. "A *lot*. Dumpster diving." She grinned at me. "A bunch of us in the building do it together. You'd be amazed what you find. On the Upper East Side? You can pawn that stuff and have enough money to eat."

I gazed out at the street: a guy in a beret walking a small dog,

I've been here two years now and no new friends; Cass has been back a month and already has a pack of them.

"You're good at taking care of yourself," I said.

162

"I've had to be," she said. A bus lumbered by. "I've been spending a lot of time with Tommy, too," she said.

"Oh yeah? What do you do with him?"

Cass opened her eyes wide.

"There's a lot to running an expedition like this, Ellie. Visas, permissions ..." She waved a half-eaten sandwich in the air. "He's writing a book, you know?"

"Another one?"

She shook her head. "He's an amazing person. Visionary."

"Don't you find it hard to believe in people?"

"What do you mean?"

"I mean ... I don't think most people are good, do you?"

Cass knitted her brows, raised an athletic arm to push back at her red-black hair. "I don't think about that. I just depend on myself, and then I don't have to worry about other people."

"But don't you *want* it to be a better world?"

Cass looked at me, eyes frank.

"The world is going to be what it is, Ellie. I'm not going to let other people's failings keep me down."

I looked across Broadway at the metal box of a newsstand, wondering how she does it.

"It's just a decision you make, you know? To be happy. You just *decide* and that's it." She raised her arms in the air. "So simple."

"Is that something Tommy says?"

"Yes. But I already thought it."

After that, she wanted to talk about *thinking big*. She's been reading guidebooks—after the expedition, we could just go *anywhere*. Have I thought about that? *Anywhere*. How amazing the Himalayas are—did I know in the Himalayas, people consider each mountain to have its own god or goddess?

"To climb mountains is to aspire to the divine, Ellie."

"Is that a quote?

She nodded. "From Tommy."

Jesus.

Of course, I don't have anything better. A stupid job that I hate. I cannot hold on to a man more than twice my age.

I walked home; thirty blocks. A young mother pushing a stroller. She looked like she wished she could leave the baby behind.

A man coming toward me with the walk of a broken marionette.

Thursday, July 16, 9 p.m.
107th Street
The Red Notebook

Soap opera, he says. He does not want to hear my story, but if he sees who I really am, he will want to know everything about me. This is what I think. This is why, at the end of July, I decide to create some magic of my own.

I go to the East West Bookstore, the "Occult" section. I get a book about Merlin and two books of folktales. One of the books mentions Scheherazade telling a story to the Caliph each night to save her own life. An idea comes: each time I meet Calvin, I will tell him a story. I like the idea of this; I am performing for him. He won't be able to stop watching.

I make up a story about a young girl who meets a man in the research room of the New York Public Library on 42nd Street, and he turns out to be a wizard. He asks her to meet him in the park. The girl is clever and figures out that she can stop time by taking off the wizard's wristwatch.

All week, I practice in my head.

The fantasies are delicious: we are in the light, and I am barely undressed. I take off my shoes and tell him the beginning. I take my socks off and tell him the middle.

The day comes and I dress carefully, which means that I try on a few outfits before I end up with one that looks windswept, as if I am tousled model from the cover of a fashion magazine whose beauty is so overwhelming that she takes breaths away even in the most ordinary clothes.

I take the train to Union Square, walk down. The sides of car doors flashing in the light; a basketball game inside a giant cage; a dark green newsstand; a disembodied spray-painted MLK head on a metal store front; rows of puffy black graffiti like Mayan glyphs. At 8th Avenue and Spring Street I lean against the brick wall of the Library for the Blind. It has been baking in the unbearable sun, but its heat against my back is an elixir. Everything is sensation: sound, movement, heat.

When Calvin comes, I dip my head to hide the sly smile on my face.

The familiar journey east. Calvin is talking about Eckerman again; he may have someone who is going to Tibet, will get the Ralung phurbu. I barely listen. I am thinking of how it will be. Now he will see what I am, what's inside me.

The stairs; the airless hallways. The sickly cats.

When the door opens, Calvin goes to the bathroom as usual, and I wait on the bed for him. He returns, sits down beside me. The mattress dips.

"So I've decided," I say. "Nimue is going to tell Merlin a story."

"Oh-ho."

"Since he's all cooped up in her magical cave," I say.

He laughs. "Going to entertain me in our—" his nose twitches with amusement—"afternoon repose?"

"Yes."

He pulls me toward him.

"Not yet!" I say. "I have to tell my story."

"You can tell me after," he says.

"I want to tell it now," I say. "I'll undress while I tell it. You too." This is what I have fantasized. I smile at my own sexiness.

"Okay." He sits on the bed. It dips.

When I get to the part about the library, he lays down, closes his eyes.

"I'm listening," he says.

When I get to the part about the wristwatch, his eyes close. Then the snoring begins.

I look at him. The punchline is yet to come, but if I want to tell it, I will have to tell it to myself.

I stop talking. I watch his chest rise and fall. The bad feeling enters me just between my breasts.

I get up, begin to get dressed. *He can't do this to me.*

I am going. I pull the camisole back over my head; the white tee shirt. *Fuck him; I'm a person.*

It is when I have one shoe tied that his eyes fly open.

"What happened?" he asks.

I don't answer.

He sits up. "Where are you going?"

"Home."

"No, you're not." He grabs me, pulls me to him. I don't want to let him, but I do.

I am lying next to him on the bed, side by side, face by face, but I won't look at him. My body is heavy, now. The place between my breasts still hurts.

"I've hurt the statue's feelings," he says.

"Why did you do that?"

"I'm sorry," he whispers in my ear. And then, in a sensible voice: "I was tired."

"I don't think I matter to you," I say in a small voice.

Another mock-groan.

"You want to be an enchanter," he says. He waits. "But I'm just an old man. You have better things to do."

He runs a thumb over a nipple and I gasp. He continues, and my mind fills with it. *The other one*, I think. *Now keep going.* This is not what I want; I want him to talk with me, see me. But I want this too ... the hand on my breasts and between my legs. Soon I am crying out, my hips rising in the air.

"You want to be an enchanter," he says again. "Why aren't you good enough the way you are?"

When we're finished, we wash up quietly, clatter back down the steps.

It is when we are walking uptown to the lecture that he says it: "You were passionate today."

"Not more than usual."

"Yes more than usual." We pass a store window full of antique clocks. "See that?" he says. "Now that you're not a little girl anymore, you know what you want."

When he says this, I go rigid. He has not said that. I keep walking, but faster. The anger starts in my arms.

"I'm not a little girl," I say sullenly. "I don't know why you said that."

"You act like one sometimes," he says, sensibly. "You play games."

"No I don't," I say.

A guy with green hair on a skateboard; two girls in jelly sandals and denim shorts, their buttocks rotating as they walk.

Now my happiness is gone.

That week I do not sleep very well. I walk a lot: from my house down to Columbus Circle to watch the tourists gather around the giant stone fountain at the edge of the park; over to the East Village to linger in front of shop windows full of objects from the East—candlesticks made from tin; wood puppets.

My head is full of conversation. *I'm not a little girl*, I tell the imaginary Calvin. *I don't play games.*

One day I walk across home from Times Square, every step a whirlwind of thought. *You shouldn't say that; you don't even know me.*

At 50th Street, the marquee for *Late Night with David Letterman*. Fury. *How dare you? Maybe we should stop meeting, actually.*

Then despair: *You obviously don't think much of me.* In my mind, he protests. *Of course I admire you*, he says. *I chose you, didn't I?*

But by the time I have walked ten more blocks, I've begun to falter. I stop in front of a public school on Amsterdam Avenue: there is a hulking ancient brick building, a concrete playground with a basketball hoop at one end, and a seven-foot wire fence all around it. Maybe he's right. Maybe I *am* a little girl.

I walk fifteen more blocks. The despair mounts in my chest, builds, sharpens, sears.

I am nothing; worthless.

Tell me Oh Lord, how should a daughter or son of good family ... how subdue their hearts, how control their thoughts?

Monday, July 20, 12 p.m.
The Center for Urban Research
The Blue Notebook

Don't let her in. Don't let her in. Don't let her in.

Today Celeste came into my office with another article in her hand.

I had been typing. Another mailing: this one for Amber.

She stepped in, closed the door, fell with all her weight into the extra chair.

"I thought we should talk."

I kept my face bland. I knew it wasn't going to be good.

Big intake of breath. Fat, shaky hand pushing a giant curl behind an ear.

"You have ... issues, Ellie. I'm sympathetic, but we have a project to do here."

I waited.

"You're not invested."

I raised my eyebrows. *Don't let her in.*

"I'm doing the work, Celeste."

Her face: the big cheeks; the slightly trembly lips. "I've tried to be sympathetic. I've *tried* to help. Did you even look at the articles I brought you?"

"I did look, Celeste."

"And?"

My own voice, high. "I'm just not sure I want to do that right now. Go to therapy. Take a drug." Rolled into my typewriter, a sheet of labels and the first "H" names. I looked at it, asking for rescue.

"So you're making the choice to be sad."

"I'm not making a *choice* to be sad, Celeste. I just *am* sad. There's a difference."

She leaned forward. Her lips juddered. "You *are* making a choice, Ellie. And now it's not just affecting you—it's affecting *me*. I've given you a chance to rise and you're not just screwing yourself, you're screwing *me*."

"Celeste, I'm doing the work."

"Barely. You sleaze out of the office every chance you get."

"I didn't feel well!"

"It's passive aggressive. It's passive aggressive and it needs to stop."

Keep the tears down, Ellie. Look at the wall. Don't let her in, don't let her in, don't let her in.

A hard look at me, then she struggled up.

May all sentient beings possess happiness and the causes of happiness.

May all sentient beings be free of suffering and the causes of suffering.

May all sentient beings never be separate from joy and free of suffering.

I fucking hate her.

Monday, 9 p.m.
107th Street
The Blue Notebook

Write about what you know, said Sarah Hamsted. *They say that for a reason.*

Here are things I knew about Laurel:

The way the light fell on the rhododendron leaves at the corner near the deli on Main Street.

The way the pines on the other side of the street stood mysteriously far away, a jagged green wall, the border to an entirely other world.

The dust on the side of the road, mixed with pebbles and beer can tabs, on the way to the supermarket on Main Street.

The lopsided merry-go-round in the playground.

When I look back, I can see the moment when it started to end: my father did not get the NEA award.

I was fourteen.

When the letter came, he stayed in his studio for five days without leaving. He must have come to get food while I was at school and my mother was working. I watched my mother go out to the door and knock on it, then, after a while, come back to the house.

At the dinner table one night, a family conference. My mother did the talking: "Your father needs some time alone. He's going out to an art colony in California for a while." Careful words. Averted eyes.

The next day we gathered solemnly to say goodbye to him: same flannel shirt and jeans as always; one compact black suitcase. "I'm not leaving you," my father said to me pointedly. Which seemed strange.

The first month it was cozy. It was summer, and after dinner my mother and I would go out and sit on the trellis with glasses of iced tea. I liked the feel of the cold glass against my cheek; watching the dissolved sugar rise up from the bottom and sink back down when I jiggled the glass.

It was one of those nights that she told me my father might not come back. I remember the astonishment: everything was the same—the sprawling back porch, the careening green lawn, the border of stones around the peonies—but everything was changed.

"Not ever?" I asked.

"He said this life isn't working for him anymore," she said, looking ahead. "He said he can't do it." I looked at her face: papery.

"He said that to you?"

Her eyes flicked over me. "Before he left."

In the nights that followed, more news came out. My father had left once before, when I was a baby.

"Where did he go?"

"There was another woman he was interested in." She made a face. "Another artist."

"How long was he gone?"

She shrugged. "About a month. He called from time to time. I'd tell him what you were doing ..." She glanced at me, haunted. "There were other times too ... some artist who does photorealism ..."

My body divided in half; each half moving away from the other: Avery Snow.

It didn't make any sense: my father teasing me in his studio; *I think you're going to be the famous one, Ellie.*

This.

I guess that's when I started to talk to my father in my head. *You can't do that. That's not right. What kind of person are you.* I'd go into his studio, read the poems typed on his index cards:

What possesses me possesses you—

She did everything for you. She gave up her own art for you.

I thought of my mother and me trooping out of the house to visit Aunt Greta; my father standing there. *Because it's the right thing,* my mother had said. *Because when you love someone, that is what you do.*

In the weeks that followed, two postcards came for me. Both were blank with one of my father's scribbled cartoon drawings on the front. One showed a man working on various paintings at once. On the back it said, "Art Man!" The other had a drawing of various artists working on project. "The crew at Dorland," he had written on the back.

There was nothing for my mother, and when I saw her face looking at the postcard I had gotten, I didn't want it anymore. Something had scooped her out, made her hollow.

So I understand, looking back, why I wrote him that letter. I couldn't let him get away with what he'd done to her and not say anything.

When I was young, I remember fighting with my mother. She wanted me to make friends with the class scapegoat; walk her home from school. I wasn't popular at school myself, and I was angry that she told me to do it. "Why?" I kept asking. "Why do I have to?"

"We have to choose, Ellie," my mother had said. "We have to choose between right and wrong."

My father did come back. There were gifts; precious ones. Silver and enamel earrings in the shape of butterflies; a necklace made of feathers for me. For my mother, a shawl so soft it was like it had been woven from colorful cobwebs. Three days of celebration: cookouts, outings to the park. Then my father found the letter I'd left for him in his studio, and then he really did leave.

Right and wrong. I wish I hadn't chosen.

Tuesday, July 21, 1 a.m.
107th Street
The Red Notebook

By the middle of August, something has changed. No more happiness: now there is nothing but thinking and walking. I try to keep my mind on each separate minute. When I walk, I tell myself to notice things: a delivery boy in a long white apron sweeping the street; the edges of his uniform like long golden lines released to the air; a young man who walks next to a stone wall, his shadow following him.

A scene:

In the bedroom, the heat has not stopped us. Our moist bodies slip past each other, his with the pot belly that hangs over his spindly thighs; me white, elegant, wan.

Outside, there is the banging of a delivery truck door, a part of the Asian market that can be seen from our small window. Inside, time crawls through the air. I lie next to Calvin. Calvin places his hand on my thigh, moves it up, looks pleased when I gasp.

I think about the past week and all the imagined conversations I have had with him.

"It's so long," I say. "It's so long to wait."

"One week," he says. And then: "Besides—it's always long when you're waiting."

I search his face. "Is it long for you?"

He laughs. "I'm an old man. I'm used to it."

Pain moves into my chest.

"I wonder why you don't want to be with me as much as I want to be with you."

Calvin makes his mock groan. "Just because I can't doesn't mean I don't want to."

173

"Well why can't you?" I ask and stare at the wall angrily.

"Do you want to spend this time pouting?"

The next week I ask the same question, get the same answer. "Do you think about me?" I ask.

"Sometimes," he says.

Each time I meet Calvin, it's the same: the hour getting dressed in front of the mirror, trying on outfits; the journey to Spring Street. Each time, Calvin and I stop at the bookstore window so he can look at the new titles. I look behind us, at the reflections of the cars passing on Spring Street; they lengthen and snap together again as they go by.

Greene Street, Broome Street, Calvin's chatter and faces passing: a punk with green hair; a young couple in sagging, tattered jeans and tee shirts who stare at us, curious. A tavern, an Asian grocery store with chrome-lined shelves for the fruit; a vendor selling cotton dresses from India. My eyes linger on everything, even the faces of the dogs on the ends of their leashes. The dogs' eyes and mine meet and hold on, as if we would like to break away and go off together.

The climb up the wood stairs, the heat lying heavily on the sides of our faces. Fiddling with the lock. When he opens the door, the wave of stink from the cats; they meow at us—the tabby and the little gray—and I answer them, pushing them forward with my ankles.

When we get inside, Calvin throws open the windows—that is the first thing. He has already begun to undress, and I look away from him. I stand at the window and look into the street, where a truck stops, and a man gets out of it. Now it as if the end is already present in the beginning.

A scene: A Friday in late July.

In the room where we meet, there is no shower to wash up. When we are done, we stand at the kitchen sink. Calvin grabs a kitchen towel and wets the end of it, soaps it up, washes his crotch, then hands it to me. This is my time to talk to him, tell him all the things I have been thinking to him all week in the letter I never stop writing in my mind. Sometimes, when this time comes, it is so urgent that my mind goes blank.

Today, I say I don't understand the difference between love and desire. "I thought the Buddha said that desire is the root of samsara," I said. "Isn't this desire?"

"The root of samsara isn't desire," says Calvin. "It's attachment."

"I don't see the difference," I say.

"It's all the difference in the world."

"How can you not be attached to someone if you love them?"

"Love and attachment?" Calvin asks in mock amazement. He widens his eyes. "Not in the same room. Not comfortably."

I stand there naked and look at him. This is not what I expected—not at all. I have crawled inside myself. My voice has a hard time coming out.

"What is this I want to know what this is."

Calvin bends down to wipe the inside of his thigh, then stands and hands the washcloth to me. "Why do you have to call it something?" he asks reasonably. "Why do you have to define it? Maybe it's just like Spring—it comes and goes."

That day, in the loft on 14th Street, Calvin gives the tantra lecture. Outside, everything is flesh: women wear halter tops, tiny skirts, tank tops that don't cover their bellies; men wear shorts and sweat through their undershirts; in Union Square groups gather around chess matches played on chessboards that are balanced on tops of overturned cardboard boxes. The sweat collects under the roots of our hair.

In the loft, we have dwindled to ten of us. We come in exclaiming about the heat, and sink down gratefully in our seats, out of the sun. Electric fans ruffle the edges of the thangkas; we must raise our voices over the noise. Hot as it is, we lean into each other a bit with the camaraderie.

Calvin stands in front of us in his blazing blue shirt. "We have heard of tantra in connection with tantric sex, "and sex is part of it, but tantra is much more than that. Tantra means"—and he stops for effect—"Everything in the service of enlightenment.

"We are used to dividing things," he says. "Good from bad; pure from impure. Tantra means you use it all—the mud and the sweat and the tears. All of it is energy." He throws up a slide: it is a picture of an emaciated figure with a turban sitting cross-legged with fires all around. "So you have yogis who meditate in charnel grounds to meditate on death and decay. You have monks who have sex with prostitutes.

"Nothing is sacred, folks," yells Calvin. Even though I'm used to it, his yelling jolts me. "Nothing is sacred and everything is sacred. In the West, sex and holiness are separate," he continues. "We have the Virgin birth. In the East, sexuality is celebrated; it's part of life. Take a look at our goddesses." A slide pops up: a wooden Virgin Mary from a medieval cathedral: blonde hair, pale face, blue robe. Next to it, a bronze sculpture of Tara, the mother goddess with breasts like giant balloons and a tiny waist; her entire body a giant Valentine.

"People think the second noble truth means desire is the root of suffering. It's not desire, folks—it's attachment. *I gotta have it.*"

The next slide shows the bronze statue of a female figure; just as voluptuous as Tara. She is dancing with one leg on the ground, knee bent, and the other leg off the ground, bent like someone side-stepping off a stage. "A dakini," Calvin says. "A spiritual being; sort of like a spiritual muse." He laughs. "Playboy pinups for monks."

The next slide shows a yab-yum: two bronze figures in flagrante delicto.

"So you say, 'what's this?' Monks and women having sex? What kind of religion is this? So is it just symbolic, or did it really happen? Consort practice. You ask a Tibetan monk in the West whether this ever happened, and he will deny it up and down," Calvin shook his head. "But those stories don't come out of nowhere, folks."

All week I talk to Calvin in my head. Consort practice—is that what this is?

It isn't. It can't be.

I walk diagonally through neighborhoods, past blocks I've never been before.

It isn't. It can't be. Maybe it is. I'm being used.

I do not sleep well.

At work, everyone is on vacation, so there is nothing for me to do but think. I am so busy doing this that I barely know where I am. My mind is a Rubik's cube now. Each time I turn a square, it turns into its opposite. Three days go by of nonstop ruminating. Then I get an idea.

There is only one way to get him to pay attention to me, to show him I am his equal: logic.

I wait until we are at the Bagel Café to say it. Calvin is busying himself with his tea.

"So," I say, swiping a hand in the air. "What is the place of love in Buddhism?"

I wait, watching the door for Judith to arrive.

Calvin does not even look up.

"Love is a fixation," he says.

"What!"

He looks at me. "Obsession."

I laugh, ostentatiously. "Really," I say. "That's the message of Buddhism, eh? There is no such thing as love and compassion?"

"Compassion, yes. What you are talking about is something else."

"Love," I say.

"Addiction."

I laugh again.

But when I see his face, I stop. His eyes are grave. He is not smiling.

He makes the mock-groaning sound. "The statue doesn't like *that* one," he says.

Another long week.

This has to stop.

He does not love me.

Something is terribly wrong.

But then I start imagining.

Calvin does not mean it. He comes to my door. That is how much he longs for me.

For a week, walking and thinking. By turns, I yell at Calvin, plead with him, reason, turn away in disgust. By Friday, I have written him a letter: *I don't understand.*

Wednesday, July 22, 9 p.m.
107th Street
The Blue Notebook

Tonight, three phone calls, all from Cass.

The first time, when I heard her voice, I could have run to rescue her from the answering machine, but I didn't. I let her speak into the tape.

"Great meeting tonight—where were you?"

The second call half an hour later. This time I sat in the living room, watched the answering machine lights go on: first red, then green.

"I think I have some leads for you. For pledges. Call me."

Still sitting there when she called at 10: "Ellie pick up."

But I need to be away from Cass tonight. I need to be away from can-do-ness.

I need rest.

Thursday, July 23, 7:30 p.m.
107th Street
The Blue Notebook

Almost dusk. Below on Amsterdam Avenue, a family walks by with giant duffel bags of laundry that look like big stuffed worms.

I went back to the East West Bookstore today. I needed to see that Buddhist nun, Pema.

She was there; same goofy smile, too-small eyes, and ears sticking out from her head, and of course the same crimson robe.

She recognized me.

"Can I talk to you?" I asked.

She led me to the back. "This is the Philosophy section," she smiled conspiratorially. "The section where no one comes."

"I want to know about magic," I said.

Pema raised her eyebrows.

"I was going to lectures by this teacher," I said. "He was Buddhist. He talked about magic a lot."

She smiled. "Magic was a big topic at Zhiba," she said. "But not from Rinpoche. It was the tourists who wanted to hear about magic. They read stuff in guidebooks, and they wanted to know about it. They would ask Rinpoche about that. He said, 'it's the Westerners that have magic powers. They arrive in silver birds that can fly over oceans carrying hundreds of people. They can look into a box, press a button, and capture the world.'" She looked up at the corner of the room. "He said that when Westerners come here, they don't really want magic. They want wisdom. They want peace." She looked at me. "I think that's true, don't you?"

I was blushing. I nodded.

She took a little breath. "I'll tell you something. When you want to ordain as a monk or nun, you have to start by doing 10,000 full length prostrations while chanting mantras," she said.

I looked at the bristly hairs on top of her head. "That's a lot of commitment."

"Here's what Rinpoche said to me one day when I was complaining. I was saying that I had been there at the monastery for six months, and I still didn't know anything more. He laughed at me. He said, 'Pema—you believe in magic. I believe in work. Go do your 10,000 prostrations.'" She looked at me. Her face creased into two giant dimples when she smiled. "'*You believe in magic. I believe in work.*' I wrote that on a piece of paper and tacked it to the wall so I wouldn't forget."

Someone moved one bookshelf over. I didn't want them to hear us. I looked at her saggy cheeks.

"Did you choose your teacher, or did he choose you?" I asked.

She nodded. "I chose him. Definitely."

"Did you feel like a ... pull? In some of the books I've read, disciples feel all these ... sensations. Like your hair stands on end and stuff like that."

She gazed toward the front of the store. "Some of the tourists who came to visit us at Zhiba were looking for that kind of experience. I did choose Rinpoche, but I didn't have any out-of-body experience or anything. I chose Rinpoche because I saw how he treated people. He was kind to everyone." She kept her eyes on the front of the store. "He was kind to everyone differently, that was the thing. He was kind to the Nepali villagers who came in one way, and he was kind to us Westerners in another."

I walked up Broadway: A church with a cement saint in a niche five stories up, clasping her hands and looking skyward; a double-parked truck with red taillights blinking rhythmically. I thought about Calvin. He wasn't really kind, was he?

No.

He was shiny.

Friday, July 24, 3 a.m.
107th Street
The Red Notebook

It was in the fall that things changed. There were a lot more people coming to Calvin's lectures—during the summer there had been about ten of us; in the fall, at least double. Nothing pleased Calvin more than that. He talked more than ever about the Ralung phurbu; how, once he got it, he would be dharma heir. He talked about other things too: Fall was the best season, he said. And why was that? The "blue light of fall," he said. Magic light. "Best light for painting. Best light for seeing what is there."

It was that month Calvin told me he couldn't see me as often. "Why not?" I asked. Inside me, everything grinding to a halt.

"I have a wife."

"You've never talked about her before."

"Before was before."

Now it is all unbearable: the room full of light, the sagging bed, the crack that runs up the wall.

His announcement comes after we have made love. Out on the street, I am angry and walk very fast up Broadway, away from him. I tell myself I will not go to the lecture.

I tell myself that all the way to 14th Street, where I will have to turn right if I want to go to the 1st Avenue L station to go home. Instead I turn to the left, creep into the loft after everyone else is already sitting in their seats.

In the lecture, Calvin talks about tantra again. "Tantra, everything in the service of enlightenment. Even grief," he says. "Even rage." He tells the story of trekking in Nepal. He brought a group of students, among them a woman who wanted to go more than anything. She had saved her money for a year, trained for the trek they were going to make.

"Two days before we start, she falls asleep in the sun. Second-degree burns." Calvin raises his eyebrows, surveys us. Shakes his head back and forth. "Can't go trekking with second degree burns." He makes a face. "So much drama." Calvin shrugged, looking at the wall behind us. "Can't go." He has that guilty-but-defiant look on his face, as if he's reliving it, but in front of us. "You can think of it as a calamity," he said, looking at us. "Or you can think of it as an opportunity."

What an asshole, I think, afterwards. I shoot up Broadway. I keep thinking it, through midtown, *asshole, asshole, asshole*. I'm done with him. At 50th Street, I can't walk anymore: I jump down into the subway. *Fuck-him-he-can't-do-this. He doesn't know what love is. Why did I follow him? Why did I trust him?*

All that week I am a walking argument.

On Tuesday, he calls me at work, says my name to me.

"I didn't like that story," I say.

"Which one?"

"The one about the girl with the sunburn."

"Can't go trekking with a second-degree burn," he says.

"You could have stayed with her."

"And jeopardize the whole trip?"

"I thought it was a religion of compassion," I say.

"Does compassion always mean getting everything you want?"

"I don't think we should meet," I say.

"Suit yourself," he says. Fear in my chest. "Come to the lecture, though."

And even though I tell myself that I won't, I do.

The lecture is familiar. Milarepa, but other students eventually became enlightened too. If you really want the teachings, you're going to have to sacrifice—that is the message.

Afterwards, when everyone is leaving Village Bagel to disperse, he pulls me by the arm. "You're coming with me," he says. Inside, I smile. I tell myself I am still angry, but I have to work to stay with it. He wants me. He has taken me by the arm.

We go to Port Authority: the walk down 14th Street all the way to 8th Avenue, then the A train.

"I hate that story," I say as we walk.

"Which?"

"Milarepa and Marpa. A teacher is supposed to be *trustworthy*," I say. "What that story teaches is that you shouldn't trust."

"Tantra," said Calvin mildly. "Whatever happens, use it. Opportunity."

"Oh, so hope for the worst, eh?"

He laughs. "The statue is getting sarcastic."

"The teacher is making the statue sarcastic," I say. Just before he gets on the bus to go back to New Jersey, I agree to meet him the next time.

Friday, 7 p.m.
107th Street
The Blue Notebook

Things are only getting worse at work. Today Celeste had me working on the questionnaire that they will give the prostitutes ... although they don't call them prostitutes, they call them sex workers.

Amber must have sent Celeste back ten or fifteen times to change the questions she was asking. Each time I had to retype the entire thing because of the formatting. I was patient in the beginning, then I started to get pissed off. I took a long time to type the later versions. What difference did it make—they were going to change them anyway, and I was going to have to retype them. Sometimes it was changing a word. ONE word.

I kind of hated them both—Celeste lurching around, thinking she's so sophisticated, and Amber with her long braid and that pretentious way she holds her hands when she's about to sign something; she makes a tent with them, lays the pen between her first and second finger.

Then in the afternoon, Celeste said I was taking too long to type the new versions. I said "you're just going to re-do them anyway," and she said, "that's not your business, Ellie," and then she called me passive aggressive again. Fuck her. I was typing but I was all shaky inside.

I guess she must have complained to Amber because just as I was getting ready to leave, Amber called me on my phone and asked me to come in to see her. When I sat down, she asked me if I was happy here. I remember looking down at my hands, pushing the blush away.

"Everything's fine," I said and looked at her. "Is there a problem with my work?"

Amber sighed.

"You know we're a team here, Ellie. Every role is important. You were hired to make our documents look ... *perfect*. To *shine*. You understand that, right?"

"It's kind of hard to make them shine and get them out fast at the same time," I said.

"Yes," she said. "I realize that. But it *is* your job. It is what you signed up for."

We both sat there; a little silence in the calamine-lotion room.

"Do you think you can commit to that?"

I fucking hate her, I thought.

"I'll certainly try."

I got up.

"That's all I'm asking, Ellie."

I wanted to cry. I practically ran to get out of there.

The worst thing was later. The phone rang and I picked it up and it was Vicky. She said she got my number from my resume that was on file. She said she was sorry to disturb me, but she wanted me to know. "I think Celeste is starting a paper trail on you, Ellie. I had to type it. I just wanted you to know. I'm not supposed to tell you, but I wanted you to know."

I thanked her. I was calm, but as soon as I hung up, I wasn't.

Saturday, July 25, 1 a.m.
107th Street
The Blue Notebook

She isn't my friend. She never was.

1:20 a.m.

She is probably right. I need to commit myself. I don't commit myself.

1:31 a.m.

That isn't friendship, though. I can't stop screaming that in my head. That she is a liar.

1:45 a.m.

I can't do anything. I can't be loved. I can't keep a secretarial job.

3 a.m.

I need tequila.

3:15 a.m.

In the all-night liquor store, there was plenty of action. A couple walked up from the direction of Central Park: a woman in a halter top with hair all over the place, a man in a fishnet shirt. We all had to wait for the man behind a wall of Plexiglas. He asked for what we wanted, took our money through the tiny slot. I was lucky I was ahead of the couple; I could see they didn't have much money and were going to take a long time to figure out what to get. After, I walked the three blocks back to my apartment; passed couples in doorways talking softly, a corridor of whispers.

I like it there. When I am in the all-night liquor store, I feel I am close to hitting bottom.

That there won't be much farther to go.

I called in sick to work. I shouldn't have, but I did. When I woke up, my head was a stone slab. I wouldn't have been able to work anyway, but I know it looks bad.

Fuck it.

8 p.m.

Well, I guess I'm going now. I have to.

Cass called. I was home, so I picked up.

Of course she wanted to know how the pledges were going.

"Cass," I said. Then I started to cry.

"EllieEllieEllieEllieEllie," she cooed on the other side. "It's okay. What happened. Don't worry; we'll deal with it."

I told her everything. Calvin and not sleeping and work. *Jesus,* she kept saying.

"Are you mad at me?" I asked at the end.

"No," she said. "I'm mad at *other people*. Especially that old man teacher of yours." Silence. I waited. "We are going to get you through this, Ellie," said Cass. "We are going to get you onto that mountain and get you healed."

"We are?"

"Yes," she said decisively.

I didn't want to hang up after that. I didn't want to be alone again. I don't want to be alone anymore ever.

There has to be help.

10 p.m.

**I still haven't done anything about going to Everest.
No pledges
No visa.
No climbing equipment.
Fuck.
How am I going to get those pledges?**

Sunday, July 26, 12 a.m.
107th Street
The Red Notebook

October was like this: the days began to shorten.

A scene: Upstairs in my apartment with no curtains on the windows, I dance to the Lou Reed son "I'm Waiting for the Man." After all, I am an addict.

In the full-length mirror I admire myself flashing by: *He doesn't even know these songs*, I think. *He's just an old man*, I think. *He can't have me; I won't let him*, I think. But when he calls, I always say yes.

In the fall, it is rarely the two of us anymore; it is usually at a lecture and then at Village Bagel with the rest of his entourage.

A scene: Village Bagel. The fluorescent lights make everything look sick.

There weren't many at the lecture that night—Calvin isn't happy about it, blames it on Judith. It's because of Judith that he doesn't have the Ralung phurbu; when they were in Tibet two summers ago, she got altitude sickness and they had to go back.

"Ever hear of Diamox, Judith?" Calvin asks loudly. "Ever hear of preparing for a trip?"

This starts a general beat-down on Judith.

"Guess who calls my house last night right as we're sitting down to dinner?" Calvin continues.

None of us answer. We know what is coming.

"Judith," he says. "Wants to read me something she's written about me." Calvin rolls his eyes, looks up to the ceiling and shakes

189

his head *what I have to put up with*. "My perfect teacher," he says in a dreamy, mocking voice. Judith's face clamps tight. She tries to smile but one crooked tooth sticks out. "Always at dinner," says Calvin. "Invariably at dinner. Family sits down, phone rings. My son says, 'must be Judith.'" He shakes his head. "Well, Judith," he drawls. "Someday you'll write something that will be worth answering the phone for at dinner time." She laughs but her face looks terrible.

I think about that now: how none of us said anything. If we had said something, he would have turned on us. All of us bodhisattvas of compassion who didn't say a word.

I see Calvin again in early November. Everything brown; bare trees like upside down broken umbrellas with their spokes up to the white-gray sky. Calvin wears his orange sweater; I wear a magnificent white coat that I bought at Macy's. He smiles at me from across Spring Street when he arrives, grabs my hand when he is close enough, then chats away while we walk east. At the bookstore, he stops to look into the window. There's an art book. "Look," he says, "a book by a statue. Did you write that?"

We have so little time and it is the last time I am going to see him for a month, but he keeps stopping. When we get to Mercer, he sees something on the ground and bends over and to pick it up, holding it up to see what it is. It's one of those tiny metal keys that go with a diary that locks—the $6 kind you get at the drugstore. I had one when I was eight years old.

"Look," he says, "a key."

"The key to my heart," I say.

"The key to knowledge and understanding," he says. And then he gives it to me.

We keep walking. Sullivan Street, Thompson, Wooster. I don't speak; I think about what has just happened. I have offered my heart and he has stepped aside.

I should stop, I think. *Right now, I should stop.*

But I don't. I let him lead me to the apartment. I follow him up the steps.

Monday, July 27, 8 p.m.
107th Street
The Blue Notebook

He said he was going out of the country. He said it.

I need to write things down.

I am still reverberating.

I do not believe it, but I do. I was in The Village, walking back from work, and I ran into Judith. I passed a Tibetan gift shop on 6th Street; someone called my name. When I looked up, there she was with the gray curls framing her face.

"Ellie Adkins."

I did not want to see her, and I did.

"Where have you been?" she boomed. I stood there, not wanting to look up. To the left of us, the scarred sidewalk, one cement square tilting up, a small tree with a tiny cage around its base.

"Just ... being," I said evasively.

"We haven't seen you," she said. She leaned forward, jolly. "Calvin said you were away on a trip. Very mysterious."

"He did?"

"You've been missing some good ones," she said. "I've been recording them."

"Good what?"

"Lectures!"

"Calvin has been giving lectures in The City?" I am blushing. There is knowledge flooding in. I don't want it. No. Keep it out. I see Judith watching me, surprised.

Judith's eyebrows pull together, go up.

"Like always," she says.

191

Ah. When I hear it, I think *of course*. I think *how obvious*. At the same time I know I have been poisoned.

Now I just want to be away.

"I wasn't on a trip, but I'm going to be," I said.

"Oh yeah?"

"Yes," I say. "Tibet."

"Does Calvin know that?"

"Calvin doesn't know anything." I feel it now, brewing in me. I hug her, wrapping my arms around her wide torso. Once I turn the corner, I run.

So many hours before I go to sleep, and so many more hours before it's morning again.

Tuesday, July 28, 2 a.m.
107th Street
The Blue Notebook

I need to write it down. *See it*: he does not love you.
Do you understand now, Ellie? He does not love you.
Why can't you *fucking understand*?
It won't change anything.

Tuesday, 3 a.m.
107th Street
The Red Notebook

The end. The end happened day by day. I did not live in time anymore, just an eternal present tense.

November: a hard month.

I do not sleep. In my head, I write a thousand letters a day. In actuality, I write a letter a day, tear it up, write another.

Finally, I send one. In the letter, I write that I think he's bored with me. That I am his concubine.

He calls. "You're not my concubine," he says. "Concubines were slaves."

"That's how it is," I say. "You call, I come."

He laughs.

"Why do you think I call?"

"You have compassion for me."

He laughs again. "Compassion. Co-passion," he says. And I feel better for a short time.

Even when we aren't meeting for sex, I go to every lecture. In the lectures, he tells stories and I hang on to them. There is a purpose to this. It's like Marpa and Milarepa; he has a reason for treating me this way. If I listen to the stories I will understand.

A week before Christmas, I meet him. During the walk across Spring Street, he talks; I don't. When we get there, I sit on the edge of the bed. "Don't turn the lights on," I say in a small voice. "I don't want them on."

The bed sinks when he sits beside me. When he touches me I cry out and launch into him. I need him. He hurts me and I need him, all at the same time.

"You are tired of me now," I say when we are dressed again. My throat is on fire.

"Not tired," he says. But wearily.

"How long until I see you again?" I ask.

"Well," he takes my hand. "It's Christmas. You know what that means." I don't want to see his face, the terrible kindness.

I don't speak. This is impossible impossible impossible.

That month, I call in sick to work for a week. I lie in bed, face to the wall. I eat what is in the apartment. Pickles. Pasta with olive oil. Canned peas.

It isn't until February that he calls again. I am at work, typing address labels. The phone rings and there is his voice.

"Ellie Adkins"

I stop what I am doing. My face is hot.

"What are you doing?"

Silence.

"Filing?"

"Typing."

"Typing the akashic record?"

Silence.

"Typing statue stories?"

Silence.

"Just typing."

"I am wondering if you would like to meet for tea."

Silence.

"I haven't seen you for two months," I say finally. "I thought we were finished."

"We're far from finished."

"It's so hard for me this way," I say. "It's too hard."

"Just because it isn't what you want it to be, it isn't worth having at all?"

So sensible sounding.

"Do you want to meet or not?"

Silence.

"When?"

The stories we tell ourselves:

It's just this one time.

I can say yes and still not go.

My not-going will really say something to him.

Let him stand there and wait.

Not going. Not going.

Love is an addiction.

I write him at least a letter a week. In one I say that he has destroyed me. In another, I tell him how grateful I am to him for showing me what non-attachment looks like. In a third I say I do not understand, it never makes sense, never comes together.

March

Calvin comes up from the subway. I am standing with my back to the Library of the Blind in an old down coat. I do not dress for our meetings anymore. I don't pretend.

Three weeks and this was the first time I am seeing him.

He approaches, leans forward, kisses my forehead.

"You look green," he says.

"We don't have very much time," I say.

"Maybe we just have tea," he says. I look at him in a panic.

"I don't want that." He chuckles.

"You just want me for my body," he says. His eyes sparkle with the joke.

We walk east fast. I practically gallop.

In the apartment, I start to take off my clothes and he stops me. "Whoa, Nellie," he says. "Whoa, Ellie." He smiles, inviting me to laugh, but I don't.

"It's getting heavy," he says. "You need to lose weight." He pats my leg. "And I don't mean physically."

"What does that mean?" My voice is small, awful.

"Heavy," he says. "You're too heavy. Too much *gravity*. Do you still want to make love?" I do. Now I need the light in the room. The crack in the wall. Those are the only true things I knew.

After, we go to the lecture in the loft on 14th Street. It's cold so we take the subway.

In the subway station, I ask him, "What's the opposite of gravity?"

He thinks for a minute before he answers: "Grace."

April

I have been going to every lecture. Mainly, they are re-mixes of things Calvin has said before.

Tantra: we all have negative emotions. You have to learn to *use* them. Angry? Focus it; do something constructive with it.

Think of others, not yourself.

Thinking isn't going to get you there.

Our once-a-month rendezvous: the wait at Spring Street with my toes freezing in my sneakers, the walk across Spring Street, climbing the stairs.

Inside I fall on him. He holds me off, laughing.

In the middle of lovemaking, when I am on top of him, he stops me.

"You're bleeding," he says. "I can see it; running all over the walls."

I start to cry and he strokes my hair. "You should write poetry now," he says. "This is the time." He wrinkles his nose, amused.

May, June, July

Now I know that it doesn't make any difference whether I am with him or not. He will still fill my mind.

Then it is the summer. The world is on fire, and we are walking to Union Square Park.

Tuesday, 7 p.m.
107th Street
The Blue Notebook

Everything has changed. Calvin has called.

I had been lying on the green rug when the phone rang. The stiff bristles pushed into the back of my head and let me know the world was real. The flat roofs of apartment buildings and small parts of the sky appeared in the tops of the windowpanes.

When I picked up: *Ellie Adkins*. There is always that moment when I have to place his voice.

I do not speak for a full two minutes. I look into the phonespace: a shadowy tunnel where nothing is.

"Hot enough for you?"

I don't answer.

"Out of the country," I say. "You lied."

Mock-groan.

"I lied for *you*. The best thing for you," he says. "You needed a ... vacation."

"*You* decided?" I am in a room, but it is sliding away from me. Maybe he's right.

"Best thing for an addiction," he says. "Cold turkey."

He can't. He can't say that.

"I'm in a lot of pain." I say.

Pause.

"Don't identify with it," he chirps.

My throat is rough. The world has fallen away and it's him and me, but he is stepping backward, away from me.

"It's just the thing that's yelling the loudest," he says.

From then on, I barely hear him. What a hot summer it's been. Judith has been buying up Tibetan goods; she is going to start a small shop on Third Street. There is a lecture tomorrow; they have been good ones lately. This one will be at 6:30, the loft on 14th Street. I should come.

When it's over I bury my face in the rug. I inhale dust, dig my face into the bristles.

9 p.m.

Three times I have tried to leave the apartment. *Do something.*

Last time I got as far as the kitchen, then something brought me back to bed; just a little lie-down.

Gravity.

I lie on my left side, look at the white wall. I trace the quarter-wave of the scroll at the top of the paneling. Above it, smudges of dirt; tiny gray flecks where the paint has aged.

How could he do it to me.

"Where do we find the sense of self?" Calvin roared at us during that lecture. He answered his own question: "In our sense of self-injury. *How could you do that to me?*"

He looked at Judith, his perennial scapegoat. "After all I've done for you," he said, mockingly.

It's just the thing that's yelling the loudest.

10 p.m.

I should eat something.

Outside a siren keens somewhere to the east. Just below my window, a jangle of voices.

I should eat. There are strawberries at the market of 106th and Broadway. I picture them: red, sweet, with little yellow dots on them, lined up in their clear plastic carton, rows of them on the green AstroTurf that lines the chrome shelves wheeled out on the sidewalk. You can smell them when you walk by.

Two blocks away. That is something that is obtainable: strawberries.

Something that beckons.
There has to be something that beckons.
You shouldn't have. I hate you.
Why did you. Why would you.
He has seen me and turned away.

11 p.m.

I am up. Just when it's time to sleep.

In the living room, with all the lights on, I blast Joan Armatrading as loud as it goes. I want her voice to drown out my mind.

I can see myself in the living room mirror: jeans, white tee shirt, wide hips, long brown hair.

Behind me the blank white wall with the piece of paneling that has come loose.

Out the window, the same scene: old men seated on upside-down white buckets, under bodega stage lights.

I am young, young. *Fuck you old man. Fuck you.*

Wednesday, July 29, 12:30 a.m.
107th Street
The Blue Notebook

Time to lay down now. I have taken my Benadryl.
  I can do something. I can change, and he will love me.

1:45 a.m.

In my room, diamonds of orange light from the gate on the window that faces the fire escape.
  There must be someone to help me.

2:30 a.m.

You are sick with him.
  He is the sun and you are the earth. You revolve around him. He pulls you to him. You can't stop your own pointlessness.
  He does not love you, does not love you, does not love you.

Wednesday, 3:15 a.m.
107ᵗʰ Street
The Red Notebook

"Tantra," said Calvin: everything in the service of enlightenment.

Passion. The afflictive emotions.

He threw that slide of Mahakala up on the wall. "Take a look at this guy, folks: fangs, bloody claws, the skulls of the dead hanging around his waist ... this is what your father looks like when you've wrecked the family car."

Laughter. Frightened laughter.

Another slide: a mandala with a buddha in the center; at the edges, snarling guardian deities on the corners. They look like Mahakala: same fangs, skulls.

Everyone wants to be a sweet, serene Buddha ... well you're going to have to get past this guy first!

Exciting, a challenge, I thought when he first said it.

Maybe everything that Calvin said will come to pass.

He still does not love me.

Wednesday, 4 a.m.
107th Street
The Blue Notebook

It has been four hours. I am not asleep. I get up, stalk through the apartment to the bathroom. Orange light stripes my naked body.

There is no time anymore.

When I return and look out the living room window, the world has stopped.

Stick trees in the orange darkness. Orange light on the hoods of cars below my window. The Don't Walk signs flash on an empty block.

Inside, I sit cross-legged in front of the mirror. I must understand.

There are the narrow shoulders, the fluted collarbones, the tea-cup shaped breasts, the smooth sweep to the hips. There is the milky face with the dark eyes, ski-jump nose.

I do not know this person who looks at me. 238,000 miles to the moon; things fall away in that kind of distance. Things are never heard from again.

I look at myself; a face in a crowd that I will never see again.

The clock ticks. The floor breathes.

Do not think that time merely flies away.

7 a.m.

I know one thing: I am not going to that lecture. On the subway, workers in their humiliating office clothes: synthetic blouses, plaid skirts.

72nd Street, 42nd, 34th, 14th, Chambers, Park Place.

Not going to that lecture.

He doesn't want me; well, he can't have me.

Fuck him.

My rage is a black cloud that surrounds me.

I am a wrathful deity.

I am a female Mahakala: fangs, claws, a skirt of decapitated heads.

A goddess.

Wednesday, 10 a.m.
The Center for Urban Research
The Blue Notebook

It is not that hard to type labels, except when you haven't slept.
I slide the label sheet into the typewriter cartridge. I bang away.
Victoria Yello comes out Victoria Uello.
Della Traglio comes out Della Tagli.
My throat closes.
I have to get out of here.

2 p.m.

At lunch, I walked to the East River and back again. My legs ached. I was thankful for the reality of it, the physical pain. When I returned, Amber had been looking for me. Even with that bland look she always has, I could tell she was angry.
She needed me to work on something.
Fuck.
A chart.
Seven columns. When I brought it to her, she wanted the numbers aligned. I tried, but there is something wrong with WordPerfect; I can't figure it out.
"I can't send it like this," she said testily.
"I don't know what to do," I said.
"Re-do it?"
I tried. Really. But then I just didn't want to anymore. I went into Amber's office.
"I'm afraid I'm not feeling well," I said.

"Again?" said Amber.

"I'm sorry."

"Jesus."

"I'm so sorry," I said. "I'll go to the doctor ..."

"Seems like there's an emergency every time we really need you," said Amber. "Do you have a fever?"

"Maybe."

"I'm really going to need you to stay."

"Okay." I shrugged.

But when I come back in again and the chart is wrong, she was disgusted. "Go ahead," she said in a tight voice. "Go home."

It's 5:00 anyway.

I am not going to that lecture.

When the words come, stop and write them down, said Sarah Hamsted.

City Hall Park is crowded: a woman with short brown hair in plaid pants; two men with their suit jackets held over their shoulders.

I don't see much. I am Lhamo, the female counterpart of Mahakala, and I stalk the land.

If he thinks he can treat me that way, he can fuck himself.

Fucker. Asshole.

What you have put me through. You are so fucked up.

At Canal Street, an empty store window full of copper tubing. Markets that sell cheap fake Cartier watches; Chinese paper lanterns; sets of toy plastic rollercoasters that tiny penguins climb then shoot down.

Not going to that lecture.

I walk north: food trucks with moving electronic neon signs: steak burrito sandwich, beef sausage, BLT. Green plywood walls around a construction site; Post No Bills. *You can't do this to me, can't do this to me, can't do this to me.*

At Lafayette, a half-finished building with black netting over the top floors like a widow's veil. I am not going to that lecture.

But I will go near.

Here is what I will do:

Turn the corner.

Walk west along 14th Street.

The doorway that I am not going to enter will appear: 214.

I will pass it, feel it go through me. I just want to be near.

The numbers go by: count them ...

216.

At 214, I keep going. At 212, 210, 200. At 180, I turn around, retrace my steps.

Stand outside the door at 214, looking at the buzzer.

I can buzz, but not enter.

I buzz.

I can go up the steps part of the way, but not into the loft.

I start to climb.

The door at the top opens.

Love is an addiction.

"Well, hellooooo," booms Judith when I enter. I do not answer; I smile wanly.

"Not feeling that well," I say.

"Too hot," says Calvin loudly. I do not look at him. I sit in the last metal folding chair. Dacy says hello, then Edwin. They look sympathetic. I wonder if everybody knows. I do not look at the front of the room, where Calvin stands. I look at my lap.

The lecture is about wrathful deities. "What do we really mean by no-self?" says Calvin. He throws a slide of Mahakala up, uses a laser pointer to point out the gory parts: the bowl of brains, the bowl of eyeballs.

"So what's going on? Sacrifice. What are we sacrificing? Our minds, our outlooks. Our concepts of ourselves, going up in smoke. What did you think people?" he thunders at us. "Transformation was going to be painless?"

He talks about chod. It's a Buddhist meditation practice—monks go into year-long retreats in total darkness. They imagine offering their body parts to demons to eat. Enlightenment isn't a game, says Calvin. Or if it is, you're betting everything.

When it's over I lean forward, put my face in my hands. I feel a hand on my shoulder, hear a gentle voice. "Are you okay?" It's the quiet girl with circles under her eyes, whatever her name is: Heather?

I twist my face up to look at her: the slightly baggy cheeks, eyes outlined with black.

"Not feeling well," I say. "I think I should go." By the time I have moved to the edge of the row of seats, Calvin is there.

Hand on my arm. "I want to talk to you."

I still don't look at him. I have mastered the art of staring into space as if there is something fascinating that only I can see.

"Come," he says. He pulls me toward the door. "I'll be back," he calls to the others. He lets go of me when we get to the stairs, but I follow him down.

Out on the street.

"We're not going to the park again," I say.

"No."

We walk west, along 14th Street.

The blinding whiteness of his beard. The red of his lips. Green janitor pants, sagging belly. But he's still a god to me, I think.

I have thought of this moment so often that when it comes, it is not real. I have to hold on by my fingernails to keep from sliding off of it.

"Judith tells me you are going to Tibet?"

So that's what he wants.

Keep him away; all he does is hurt you.

We pass storefronts: Gourmet Garage, Hardware: Keys Made. People pass us, and I look down the street: twigs at the ends of dwarfed street trees fend off the light.

"Oh *that's* why you invited me."

"I invited you because I wanted to see you."

"Why?" I ask. He doesn't answer. We walk: a brick-fronted building that sells television sets.

"I was invited, but I'm not going. You have to get people to pledge money to the organization if you want to go, and I haven't raised any."

"Well there happens to be some money in the treasury of the Eastern Asian Studies Society."

Something moves through me; stops my organs.

"So you can get rid of me."

Mock-groan.

"You've got quite the interpretive powers. An offer of help becomes ... oh, how Machiavellian."

"Yes. I should be more trusting," I glare at him. "All promises fulfilled. The Secret of Happiness! I'm so happy now! Jubilant. One big party." I look ahead, furiously. I am furious with everything. I am furious with Union Square.

"Journey's not over yet," says Calvin, shaking his head.

"Oh, so you're still making promises?"

"I never made any promises."

I should walk faster. I should shoot ahead of him. Fuck this.

I don't.

"How much does a pledge need to be?"

"Two thousand dollars."

"And what are these pledges going toward?"

"I don't know. Nepali ... starving ... children," I shrug.

"Good cause," says Calvin mildly.

"They're climbing Everest, Calvin. I'm not going to climb Everest. I'm not a climber."

"You don't have to go up the mountain once you get there," says Calvin. "Use the visa to get into Tibet. Make a pilgrimage. Go to Ralung."

"I'm not getting the Ralung phurbu," I say. "I know it would be convenient for you, but I am not going."

We are at the subway. I stop.

"I wish I never met you," I say.

I turn my back on him, sprint down the steps.

You don't matter, I tell myself. *You don't matter, you don't matter.*

If, Subhuti, a bodhisattva holds on to the idea that a self, a person, a living being exists, that person is not a true bodhisattva.

When I left Calvin, I went down into the subway and just stood there. Then, five minutes later, I went up the staircase on the other side. I knew where I needed to go.

It was nine at night; the bookstore was closing and they were just starting to pull down that metal gate that covers the store window at night so no one can break in. The woman did not want to let me in, but I said, "Is Pema here?" and I guess Pema heard me. She came out with her smiling, ugly face framed by the dark fuzz all around her head and said my name.

All the reasons I needed her were there somehow in the air between us. "I'm going to have an austere dinner now," she said. "Would you like to join me?"

She took me up in a cramped elevator to the fourth floor and opened the door to a small room with just a single bed in it and a shrine: a cardboard box turned upside down, covered with a shimmery yellow cloth, and with a picture of her teacher propped against the wall on top of it.

"I have to go back down to finish closing up, but I'll be back soon," she said.

I studied the shrine: a photograph of a Tibetan monk in mustard-colored robes, beaming, with a semi-rectangular face. He had his palms together, a necklace of wood beads strung across them. His awkwardness made him look even more kind.

I wondered where the bathroom was. I thought about what I wanted to ask her—how is she able to be so happy inside.

She came up the stairs, slowly. When she appeared, she had two plain, white, diner-style plates with food on them. "Rice and dal. I learned to like it in Nepal. Reliable. And very cheap."

She handed me my plate and sat cross-legged next to me on the floor. I looked down: chalky white rice, yellow lentils. I tasted it. Salty; comforting.

"Isn't it kind of hard to stick with this when you know you can get any kind of food you want in New York City?"

She leaned back a bit, eyes half closed. "Well, I treat myself to pizza every once in a while," she said. "I've been thinking about you. How are you? I thought of how I gave you Rumi, and then I started wondering if maybe that wasn't a little too intense for you right now, with how you are feeling. Books are a big responsibility!" She widened her eyes and laughed.

"I'm falling apart," I said. I gave her a bleak smile. "I came here because I was hoping you could glue me back together."

She looked down at her plate, embarrassed. When she looked up, her eyes were very bright. "Maybe the best thing would be just to accept that you're falling apart," she said. "Maybe what's making it so difficult is that you are resisting it."

"I need to keep it together to live," I said.

Her eyes traveled over me. She put her fork down. "I did not tell you why I became a nun."

"No."

"I became a nun because I lost someone I could not live without."

"Oh?"

"A friend. A very old friend." Her face hurt to look at. I didn't speak.

Her eyes flickered up, above my head.

"She killed herself." Angry smile. "Threw herself off a highway overpass."

"Oh Jesus. That's bad."

She looked at her hands in her lap.

"I had just started to attend lectures by Lama Yuden," she said. "I went to him and told him what had happened, and he said, 'Now you have the experience of Siddhartha.' I said I did not understand, and he said, 'Life is a catastrophe.'" She looked into the air, nodding.

"It's true," she said. "Life is a catastrophe." She looked at me. "So maybe now you are having your catastrophe."

"What if I don't come back from it?"

"You'll come back. You were brave enough to let it happen in the first place."

"I was an idiot," I said.

She looked down, smiling.

She shook her head to the side. "Maybe it's the same thing."

It wasn't a nice room. The walls had lumps of plaster under the coat of paint, and the color, a garish yellow, looked like something that would keep you up at night.

I looked at the shrine. The picture of Lama Yuden looked a bit weather-beaten. "Do you pray here?" I asked.

She smiled. "I do full-length prostrations," she said. "It's part of the practice. I did my 10K, but then I kept going."

"Jesus. How far are you?"

"I stopped counting. I just think it's a good thing to do."

She got up to put her plate on the windowsill, then sat back down.

"I've been thinking about a book that would be good for you right now," she said. "It's by a Christian saint—St. John of the Cross. I found it in the Mysticism Section. He's the one who first used this term: dark night of the soul. You think you're falling apart, but maybe this is just part of the process. Maybe this is your dark night of the soul."

I sat looking at her ugly yellow wall.

"I want to be like you," I said. "When I first started going to my teacher's lectures, he told us that Buddha consciousness is a consciousness you can keep even in a slaughterhouse. I wanted that. I think you have it."

"You should see me when a customer gets me mad," she said.

I didn't laugh.

"So here is something else Lama Yuden said to me. He said, 'the dark things are just as important as the light things.'" I looked up. "I can't tell you how surprised I was by that," she said. "I can't tell you how it has kept me going."

"I kind of wonder if I should do what you did—go to Nepal and become Lama Yuden's student like you did and become a nun."

"Do you want to?"

"I have the chance to go to Nepal. My friend is part of this movement called The New Heights Group and they are going to climb Everest to raise money for Nepali orphans."

"Is that what you *want* to do?"

"I don't know what I want to do. I want to stop falling apart."

"Staying or going, that always seems to be the question. I'm not sure if it really matters that much. When I was in Nepal, some things changed for me, but it wasn't as much change as I thought it would be. One thing that did happen—I got to see a lot of tourists. They would come to Zhiba for meditation classes, and I would see how instead of really becoming *like* this new place they were in and adapting to it, they brought themselves along and tried to get the place to adapt to *them*. That's why you can get spaghetti and banana pancakes in Thamel. You know that old saying, right—wherever you go, there you are."

"Yeah." For a minute we sat there in silence. "Do you trust Lama Yuden?"

"Completely."

"I don't think I should have trusted my teacher."

"Everyone is your teacher," she said. I looked up: she was smiling that calm, rueful smile of hers. "The world is a generous place when it comes to people who will test you."

"I think I should stay here and be your student," I said.

She closed one eye. "That's not an option right now," she said. "I'm not taking students. I'm definitely not ready for that."

"When will you be?"

She laughed. "I think you're ready to be your own teacher, Ellie."

I felt ready to cry. I didn't want to.

"Remember the first time I saw you?" she asked. "I said love is a good teacher."

I nodded. My throat was closing and I couldn't talk.

"Now that I told you about my friend and how I became a nun, maybe you understand it more. I'm not sure anyone would ever stretch for enlightenment if life was easy."

I said, "Love is a good teacher because it has us by the balls."

She got up. "I need to go to bed now. I get up at four to do prostrations. Let's get you a few books."

Thursday, July 30, 6 p.m.
Chinatown
The Blue Notebook

At the corner of Duane and Broadway, a black plastic bag twirls in the air on the other side of the street, curls itself around the slender metal neck of a streetlight, rocks in the breeze.

They can't do this.

Fuck them.

I have never walked faster. Every time I want to write, I sit down, then I walk again.

I was polite.

We need to see a lot of improvement, Ellie. Celeste and Amber sitting there next to each other on one side of a small, round conference table. Amber with the long white braid, big face, elegant fingers. Celeste looking at me solemnly with her puffy cheeks, giant brown curls, her big legs in plaid pants tapering down to the tiny feet.

Me.

It seems like I'm not invested in my work. *We are a team—we need all our members on board, Ellie.*

Invested in my work? I type FUCKING LABELS.

I didn't say that.

They pretend to be so fucking liberal.

You need help, Ellie. This from Celeste. *Can we agree that you will seek it? Otherwise we may have to think about next steps.*

Both with those solemn faces.

Next steps. Whatever the fuck that means. I told them I was thinking of going into therapy.

"That's good, Ellie," said Amber. "That's a great step."

Fuck them, fuck them, fuck them.

And Celeste? I would like to cut up everything she owns into little strips.

Angry? Use it, said Calvin.

Yeah, right.

Walking and stopping to write, then walking again.

At the courthouses, giant stone staircases ripple up to ten-foot-high metal doors. A chain link fence guarding a parking lot with a little shed for the guard. Empty here except for a few bicycle messengers. A woman in a business suit with a briefcase clopping along in high heels.

Move.

The little park is crammed with people. Men sit in their undershirts playing chess on cement tables. Old women in black cloth shoes play mahjong. People walk along tugging blue plastic bags, portaging bags of laundry in shopping carts.

Then Mott Street. The hole-in-the-wall shops brimming with souvenirs: wood backscratchers, whizzing, neon-colored toys, mugs with the NYC skyline, boxes of caps, confetti, plastic turtles with batteries that swim in small tubs of water, fake Gucci wallets and Cartier watches.

I don't have to put up with this. I can go.

I remember the day Calvin talked about bodhisattvas. Buddhas were too remote, he said. You needed a being who was here in the muck with the rest of us—the Bodhisattva.

The Bodhisattva is just about to Get There, but vows to help everyone else get there before him.

On the west side of Mott Street, the fish market. Men and women in black Wellingtons come and go with buckets of ice. There are the pink trout with unseeing eyes; the crabs that scratch against the sides of their plastic tubs, the headless shrimp. Worst are the conches; knocked out of their shells with hammers, they slurp onto the ice, shining white slabs of flesh, exposed to the air.

In American supermarkets, it's all behind closed doors, hygienic. Here it is out in the open: what we humans do to the world. All of this dying. All of this indifference.

"We're going to consider you on probation," said Amber. Her elegant fingers grasping a shiny pen, writing something on a form.

The Urban Poverty Research Center. What a bunch of bullshit, I think.

Noodle Village, Peking Duck House.

In the bakery, little cakes, yellow-white domes.

At the corner of Pell and Mott, the small, dark shop that I realize I've been looking for. I go in and comfort myself: wood puzzle boxes, paper dragons that pull out like accordions, tiny tea sets, fans. Go for the magic; isn't that just me.

But I'm not comforted.

It's getting dark. I want to walk and walk and walk. Uptown to Times Square and keep going. Punish my body: *you will do what I say.*

When I step out of the shop, an ice cream shop with a line, a seafood restaurant. That is where I go, drawn to the plate glass window with the fish tank. The orange bodies slither past each other, their mouths opening helplessly. There is no space. Large, flat bodies travel in long figure eights, brush against each other. They come to the edge of the tank, lock eyes with me, swirl away. How can there be enough oxygen in there with so many of them? Above the tank, I can see families seated around large tables, great platters of food in the middle.

"Who is the greatest bodhisattva?" Calvin asked us. Then he shouted: "The great bodhisattva of hell!"

Angry? Focus it, use it. I picture myself, moving through this city like a strong breeze, stopping the slaughter.

I do not think about fucking memos.

The orange fish pace their glass cage, come to the edge, one by one. Look at me. I know what they're trying to tell me:

I need breath, I need breath, I need breath.

Sunday, August 2, 4 p.m.
107th Street
The Blue Notebook

This is my third day in bed. Celeste has called eight times. I haven't answered. I hear the messages. On Thursday night: *It's not personal, Ellie. It had to be done.*

On Friday: *You can still save this.*

Yesterday: *I thought you were a little more mature than this, Ellie.*

6 p.m.

I called Cass today and left a message. I said I would be able to get a pledge for $2,000. I said I wanted to come.

When she called back, she was jubilant.

"You're *coming*? This is gonna be *so great* Ellie. You are gonna be *so* glad you came."

Then a flurry of instructions.

"Thank you, Cass," I said. I must have said that eight or nine times.

Sunday, 8 p.m.
107th Street
The Red Notebook

Dear Calvin,

I have a notebook just for letters to you. It's red. This letter I am sending.

"Sacrifice," you said. "You have to let go of the old things to make way for the new things. In the Mahakala thangka, people gave up their bodies, their senses, their minds."

Maybe I have done the same.

Things could not be worse for me. I do not have a job anymore.

The Buddhist nun who works at the East West Bookstore is named Pema. Here is what she said to me yesterday: *everyone is your teacher.*

Here is what else she said:

That I must find my own way.

Do you remember that first lecture about Vajrayana? "You are on the path when your feet are off the ground," you said. "That is when you are wearing your off-the-ground socks."

I want to say that I am going to Nepal because you do not want me, but I am going to say it like this instead: I am going to Nepal because I need to stop orbiting you. I am doing it for myself.

I am going to a place I do not know, and I am on the path now. I am wearing my Vajrayana socks.

If you still want me to go to Ralung, I am going to need pledge money–at least $2,000. Send it to

The New Heights Group
293 West 28th Street
New York, NY 10001

Make sure you put my name on the check or I will not be able to go.
As for the map I'll need, you will figure out how to get it to me.
No doubt it will become Judith's job.

I am not a statue anymore.

Monday, August 11, 7 a.m.
Over the Atlantic Ocean

This is my new notebook.

I am thinking of Sarah Hamsted.

Don't expect success any time soon, she said. *Expect success in geologic time. How long does it take a glacier to move ten feet?*

Here is what I said to myself when I bought it:

I'm a mess, but I can be a new person.

Here is what I said: Do one thing.

So I did things: passport, plane ticket, sublet.

I am a failure at being loved. I am a failure at work. But I still have to live.

Remember: you can get on a plane and fly someplace.

We are seven hours into the flight. Cass is sleeping. Most everyone is: bodies twist uncomfortably under airline blankets, heads jutted to the side, while *Ghostbusters* flickers silently on the long row of monitors that hang above our seats.

The Void, that is what mountaineer said in one of those films Tommy Hilfiger showed us. Now we are going into it. It will obliterate us, peacefully.

In the airport, there was a distinct hour when I was happy. Everything took place out of time: a child in a jumper looking up at me from her seat, enquiringly; a blonde-haired hippie girl with a backpack; the swish of a woman's sari—we were already starting to enter a different world. A thought came: *I have saved myself.*

But it's not true.

Cass has saved me.

Fairly amazing that I am here now. Ten days ago, I couldn't get out of bed. Then it all happened: Seth called; coming back from California, needs a place to stay. "It's yours," I said. "The whole place."

A pouch around my neck with my passport and $5,000 in traveler's checks. In my backpack, books Pema gave me, several changes of clothes.

I had to get out of New York. I could not walk around that apartment at three a.m. anymore, a ghost staring out at a ghost bodega. And I don't know if I will ever be far enough away from Celeste.

On the monitors, a news break; the same news as an hour ago; the same serious talking heads. Someone walks unsteadily along the trail of dim lights that lights up the corridor to the bathrooms. The dull roar of the turbos continues ... how crazy we all are, getting into this metal tube that lifts above the earth, a thing humans were never meant to do.

In the dark oblong of the plane window, my own face, a ghost at 31,000 feet. Behind it, the reflection of Cass's sleeping profile. What comes to me is the wonder of it: a year ago I walked into a loft, saw a crazy man talking about an impossible quest. And now I am here.

Probably because I am stupid. But I needed the money, and Calvin gave it. He wants the phurbu that much. When I met Judith to get the money and the map from her, there was a postcard with a picture of a Buddhist monastery on it: a few sentences:

Vite, vite! Eckerman is sending a group for the phurbu. You've got a month.

Fuck him.

But I'll go. I know that. Just like I kept meeting him on Spring Street week after week.

I think of that postcard in my backpack. I haven't told Cass yet about my ulterior motive for coming.

Bad.

She's been asleep an hour. For the first three, she was practically bouncing in her seat. She opened the *Lonely Planet* guidebook and read entries to me. "There are *tigers*, Ellie," she gloated. "There are *rope bridges*." For the trip, she has completely changed her look. The red hair is back, and she's not goth anymore: special climbing pants that unzip under the knees to become shorts, a tee shirt that says Upward, hiking boots.

Once she fell out, I slipped the book from her hand; I wanted to look myself. *Go anywhere*, said Cass. It all sounds so easy: places to eat, places to stay. Just follow the map and go there.

I'm frightened, but I'm going.

Maybe I was always on my way to doing this. As soon as I saw that sign in the East West Bookstore. As soon as I walked up the stairs to that loft.

Monday, 5 p.m.
Kathmandu

I was HAPPY again!

We landed mid-afternoon. In the airport, a long walk along an almost empty corridor, stopping at the counter with a line of thin, grim-looking soldiers in khaki and then we were outside in the heat, like stepping into a giant laundromat.

Crazy getting a taxi—they all honked at us at once. Cass chose one, bargained him down. Then we were moving, and everything was a wonder. The narrow streets with ancient wood buildings; the hundreds of balconies; the carved wood window frames with dragons, warriors, goddesses curling over the arches; the stone street shrines, deities in lotus position draped with garlands of marigolds. At Durbar Square, the giant statue of King Malla kneeling on a thirty-foot-high pedestal, and the roofs of the temples—pagodas.

I remembered something Calvin once said: there were times in our lives when time stopped; when everything seemed perfect. *Everything happening in slow motion and at exactly the right time.*

The bicycle rickshaws are everywhere; shabby, ridiculous chariots with tassels on the hoods, driven by men wrapped in short, white skirts. On the street everything mingles together.

Funny about the things that are supposed to be luxurious. Our taxi, for instance ... the seats were fraying, mended with duct tape. Burning when we put our bare thighs on them: we had to sit on our bags. So many colors: orange and pink saris; dull greys and blues of men's lunghis; the buildings are all wood.

Once we got to the center of the city, the road was so crowded with pedestrians that we crawled, going the same pace as the people around us. Alongside the car a family walked—a slender mother in pink pajama pants, a man in Western pants and Nehru hat, a little boy in shorts—so close I could have stuck my arm out the window and held hands with them.

Just before we reached the tourist section, we passed through an outdoor market. There was a man riding a bicycle with a tower of birdcages on the back—it must have been five feet high—all filled with chirping birds.

Our room at the Potala Hotel is fairly basic: two beds and a window that looks out on Mandala Street, in Thamel, which is the tourist district. Nothing like an American hotel—there's bare wood floor, no mini-fridge. But I like the balconies. And it's cheap: one thousand rupees a night, which translates to about fifteen dollars. I guess I don't have to worry about my funds running out

"Don't sleep," said Cass. "You have to get into the new schedule." So we went for tea.

7 p.m.

If I was worried about being a lone tourist in a foreign place, I didn't need to be. The Bakery Café was filled with Western tourists, mostly our age. A big range—there were California-girl types with tattoos in pastel cotton dresses; serious hippies in yoga pants and halter tops, and a few older Lands-End types in sensible walking shoes. It's perpetual summer here; when we walked into the restaurant, the screen door slapped behind us.

Tea is called chai here—it is scalding hot, milky, and so sweet your mouth puckers. After tea, Cass and I wandered around in Thamel: Dylan and The Doors playing on rooftops, restaurants with names like Third Eye and Yin Yang Restaurant. It's as if the 1960s came here from the West and stayed.

The only thing that's bad about it is the thing I was looking forward to: Cass. I thought it was going to be me and her. Instead, everything is about Tommy. She can't stop talking about him.

9 p.m.

In our hotel room, we're on the top floor. The ceiling slopes up at a diagonal. My bed creaks when I sit.

Maybe it isn't going to be as easy to get Cass to go with me to Tibet as I thought it would be. Tonight, after our walk around Thamel, we sat on the deck of a restaurant and ordered milk tea. I mentioned Tibet just to see how she reacted. Not well. She said Tommy would know if the border was open because he knows about *everything* here. (I doubt that). When I said that maybe we could go to Tibet after Everest, she said "I'm not going to think about *after* Everest, Ellie. If we're going to summit, we need to think about *only* summiting. Tommy was pretty clear about that. We have to be *focused*."

Which is bullshit because on the plane she was talking about the other places we could go.

Cass said I should try to stay up till 10 p.m. to get on the new time schedule, but I can't take it anymore. I'm going to bed.

2 p.m.

Off to the side of the square, a cluster of bicycle rickshaws. A man in a plaid skirt sleeps in the back of one of them; others stand around and talk. Mid-square another cluster of men in white pajama pants, dark vests and Nehru hats. An emaciated dog noses around a waist-high street shrine to Ganesha, hoping for something to eat.

I am sitting at a small table at a restaurant called Thakali Kitchen. They have something called "hot lemon" here: lemon juice with hot water and honey served in a glass with teeny pieces of lemon floating on the top. Delicious.

Well let's face it, I'm upset.

This morning, Cass and I went to Durbar Square. Spectacular: stone towers with multiple trapezoidal roofs that get smaller as they reach the top; wood temples with painted dancing figures on the front; a towering stupa with concentric rings; there are banners on each ring that ripple continuously in the breeze, one continuous wave. The buildings are wood, built up from the street, ancient-looking and sagging but with flourishes. The corners of the roofs curve up as if they're dancing.

I was so happy, then Cass told me she was leaving—going to meet Tommy at the airport.

"What?" I asked. "He can't get to town from the airport by himself?"

Cass lit into me—we aren't here just to be *tourists*; we have a *mission*; did I *understand* that? I did what I always do when I'm upset—I walked.

I guess I should have realized it would be like this. That's how Cass is—whatever she's into, that's what she's into. *Do whatever you do intensely*.

It still hurts.

Walking was a good thing to do. I like it here: so alive. The gaunt cows, the armies of bicycles, the reds and oranges of the women's saris, the street shrines that rise from the ground. In the tourist section, the signs grow out of buildings like square elephant ears—a sea of opportunities: "Everest Trek," "Laundry 5 Rupees" "Visit Kashmir," "Shree Lal Pure Veg Restaurant," "Hillcake Water Tank." It's like New York with the busy-ness, but so much more human. Everything is lopsided, falling down, but people keep living and moving, going about their business.

Tuesday, August 12, 5 p.m.
Kathmandu

Back at the hotel. I can look down from our balcony and see other Westerners on Mandala Street: groups of purposeful trekkers with ski poles; partyers in an array of local clothing: harem pants, multi-colored traditional Nepali jackets that are strung on hangers in front of the shops.

Cass isn't here. Am I going to be alone all the time? It isn't rational for me to be mad at Cass. It isn't like I've been entirely honest about my motives for coming. But doesn't she want to be with me?

Wherever you go, there you are.

7 p.m.

I had a realization. I saw Cass talking to Tommy in the hallway of our hotel just now. The way she was standing, looking up at him, and then the way she put her hand on his arm, it came to me: she is in love with him.

Of course. Duh.

I fell in love with Calvin. She fell in love with Tommy.

How ridiculous we are.

9 p.m.

Well, we all had dinner together tonight at the Bakery Café, sitting around a rickety card table, ordering Western food from a menu written out longhand and slipped into a laminated plastic envelope. The menu items are dishes like pizza, spaghetti and meatballs, and raclette that are dim approximations of what they would be back home.

Only a few people made it here from the crowd that used to come to Tommy's lectures in the East Village. There's Dilly Jenkins, the yoga instructor; she arrived for dinner in harem pants and a tee shirt that had a big Sanskrit *Om* on it; Kelly the former school-teacher whose boyfriend died and has etched dark circles under her eyes. Other than that, our "expedition members" are people Tommy knows from earlier travels: James and Courtney, who go around in khaki shorts and sturdy shoes; they've been on a training regime for months. Finn the surfer dude with this stringy white-blond hair. Jorge the Argentinian who used to be a Rajneesh follower. Tommy. Tommy's partner Ray, who is big and not very good looking and funny because not-very-good-looking people have nothing to lose.

Tommy looks completely different here. He's in his mountaineer get-up: khaki shorts and a giant red bandana around his neck; hiking boots even though it's at least 80 degrees during the day. All through dinner, he talked about how *exciting* it was that we were here; that we were the ones with the *real fire to change ourselves and the world in the process.* Now that we'd gotten here, we could see the poverty for ourselves. "And it means something," he said, "that you are here with me, that you want to fight it. That's what you have to do, right?" he asked, shaking his head. "Fight."

Dilly said how she was so grateful Tommy had "raised our consciousness to it," and Joe, his partner, said "All I can say, Tommy, is that I am behind this 200 percent." The whole time, Cass sat beside him, nodding with an ultra-serious face. I didn't say anything. When I told Cass I was going back to the room, she creased her eyebrows.

Now I am sitting here with the blank wall in front of me and I feel the unhappiness. I don't fit.

They're wholesome. I don't know how to explain it any better.

Passive aggressive, said Celeste.

But if I don't feel it, I don't want to do it.

And I don't.

Eckerman's people are ... you've got a month.

What will I do if she doesn't want to come to Tibet with me?

I guess there is no way around it. I have to go with them to Everest.

Fuck.

Wednesday, August 13, 1 p.m.
Kathmandu

I thought it would be different. I thought I wouldn't be alone all the time. I get that she's in love with him, but ... what about me? What about *being here*?

This morning when I asked Cass if she wanted to go to Patan, she said she couldn't; she had to help Tommy look for crampons.

"You don't want to see *Patan*?" I asked. And then: "He can't do that without you?"

She looks good, here. The heat makes her less pale, and the khaki shorts and New Heights Group tee shirts she wears show how sturdy she is.

"We have a purpose here, Ellie." She frowned my way while looking at a page in the guidebook. When she looked up, I guess my face must have looked bad, because she tried to be friendly.

"Why don't you hang out with some of the others? Dilly, or that guy Finn? We're a team, you know."

Patan was even more spectacular than Durbar Square. I was feeling all woebegone and then I saw it, and everything changed. Crowded with temples: single square towers with a series of pyramidal roofs, one on top of the other; vertical wedding cakes. In front of the Mahadev temple, lions with braided manes, brutish mouths. And the wood carved doorway lintels: whole worlds blossoming out of themselves: buddhas blossoming out of dancing girls blossoming out of dragons.

I am a person who used to go to the 42nd Street Library to look up sorcerers.

Now I am in a magic place.

Two boys in white tunics sat on a balcony; one smoothed a half-inflated balloon across his cheek, smiling; on the street a man in a closet worked on an ancient sewing machine. I was happy again. Things are cheap, here. I could stay for a while.

6 p.m.

A good thing happened. Well, first a bad thing happened: I got lost. I thought I was going to Brahma Tole. I followed the map: Chikamugal, then Heyamat. I guess I was going the opposite way of where I thought I was ... I got pretty far away from the center of town. Everyone staring at me.

My legs started to ache, and I was getting upset. Ready to cry actually ... how the fuck am I going to go to Tibet if I get lost in a city with a good map?

But it turned out well. I found a café.

That was when it happened. It was called the Snowman Restaurant; mostly empty with a Nepali girl in shalwar kameez chatting with a friend. I noticed there was one other Western couple sitting there—a girl with black curls all around her face wearing a pale cotton skirt from an Indian bazaar and tennis shoes, and a tall guy in jeans and Birkenstocks with a head like a light bulb.

I kept hearing the woman say, "Oh my God, oh my God," and laughing. There was something about her laughing—shocked. Then I heard them throwing names around—Gyantse, Shigatse— and I realized they were talking about Tibet.

I did something very un-Ellie-like: I went up to their table. They were sitting there over plates of scrambled eggs, little clay cups of chai.

"I hope you don't mind if I overheard you. Are you coming from Tibet?"

"Oh yeah," said the woman. "We've *survived* Tibet." She looked over at her boyfriend and laughed. "Barely, right?"

Australians, from their accent.

He shook his head from side to side. "Just have to live to tell the tale."

He looked up at me. "Take a seat," said the man. "We'll tell you alllll about it."

I found out a lot. The Nepali border is open—they came through Hong Kong, flew from Chengdu to Lhasa, then took buses and trucks down to the border. The town on the Nepali side is called Kodari. "Definitely some backpackers there," said the man. "The word is out."

"Why did you say you *survived* it?" I asked.

"Bloody Jesus," said the woman. "Let me count the ways. By the way, I'm Giselle—this is Conrad." She extended her hand. "Well, first of all it's not very hygienic. You won't wash for a week or so—no running water in the guesthouses. At least the Tibetan ones."

"Which was where we stayed," said Conrad. "Not going to fund the bloody Chinese government if we can help it."

"You stop liking the Chinese when you're there," said Giselle. "It's settlers and soldiers."

"There are Chinese soldiers everywhere," said Conrad. "Everywhere."

"And they're bloody wankers. We're sitting at some café minding our own business and the soldiers decide to have a bottle fight ... they're chucking glass bottles at each other ... barely missed Gizzy's *head*. Real wankers," said Conrad, shaking his head.

"Get used to eating a lot of ramen noodles; that's pretty much all they have there," said Giselle. "We finally found some places to get stir fry—go into the kitchen and point to what you want them to cook up and then have yourself a plate!" said Conrad.

Giselle looked at Conrad. "Tell her about the flies."

Conrad threw his head back and laughed theatrically. "We find ourselves in this little village? Get ourselves something to eat? So we go into this shack? Plate of dead flies in the middle of the table."

They both laughed, looking at each other. "Tibetan centerpiece," Conrad squeezed out.

"Ew," I said.

Giselle leaned over and put her hand on my knee. "But the Tibetans are great people," she said. "Don't get me wrong. *Really* friendly. *Really* happy to see Westerners. And the monasteries— brilliant. Absolutely worth the trip."

"The dogs not so much," said Conrad. Conrad and Giselle locked eyes again; she was vibrating with silent laughter.

"Oh my god," Giselle gasped. "The dogs."

"Me and Gizzie went trekking to some lake?"

"Nam Tso."

"Right. You start out on this path that goes out to the lake, all grass, all nice and even. All of a sudden—"

Giselle was still vibrating with laughter. "Hound of hell!" she gasped. "Bloody Tibetan mastiff almost took my leg off." They both shook their heads, laughing, looking at each other.

Conrad nodded. "Yeah we *survived* Tibet."

"Seriously," Giselle recovered herself. "You should go. It's brilliant."

"Seriously," said Conrad. "Pristine. The views ... and it's so untouched. Place has been closed to Westerners for the last twenty-five years. And Tibetans are lovely. Truly."

"Are there a lot of other Westerners there?" I asked.

"In the beginning not so many, but there are a lot coming up from the Nepali border. Word is out." They eyed each other.

"Gizzie ran into someone who knew her first-grade friend," he said.

She laughed. "Always happens when you're on the road," she said. "You're out in the middle of fucking nowhere and you run into someone who knew your first-grade best friend."

The road. "Have you two been traveling for a long time?"

Conrad shrugged. "A year. Bound to go back soon."

"In Tibet, did you hear of a place called Ralung?" They looked at each other, shook their heads. "It's near Tingri ... near Everest."

Giselle shook her head. "We missed that place. Is that some monastery or something?" They both shook their heads, blank-faced. I brought out the map Calvin had sent. "Oh yeah," Giselle traced her finger. "That's the road up from Zhangmu to the border."

"You need a better map than this if you're going to Tibet, love," said Conrad. He raised his eyebrows. "Wait a minute." He rummaged in his daypack. "Let me give you this one. We're definitely not going to be needing it anymore."

He handed it to me.

"Thank you."

"Pleasure to pass it on." He looked over at me. "This place Ralung—is it a trek?"

"A short one, yeah."

"If you're going to Tibet alone, I wouldn't do *that* alone," he said. He stood up. "Going back to town? Share a rickshaw?"

So I had my first bicycle rickshaw ride too.

I'm sitting ... and here's what I'm thinking: They're *living*. Like Cass. Like Calvin. I want to be like that.

Maybe I want to go to Tibet. For *myself*.

Thursday, August 14, 4 p.m.
Kathmandu

I started talking to Calvin in my head again. I can't help it.

Everything I see here reminds me of him. On the way back to the hotel, I passed a large market. Giant thermoses and multi-colored plastic containers from China; enameled metal basins; heaps of vermillion, green, pink spices. On the edge, one family camped out on a blanket with piles of fruit: bananas, melons, yellow mangos. An old man with withered hands, a mother with her scarf over her head, a young woman in pink and white shalwar kameez. Bustle all around them: bicycle rickshaws, trotting dogs, shoppers. In the center of it all, the young woman gazed out into space.

Sunyata, said Calvin. *At the center of every mandala is a vanishing point.*

9 p.m.

Well it was quite the evening. At dinner, Tommy told us he had a surprise for us—it turned out to be a movie. He had a projector set up in a back room to the restaurant and we all sat on the floor and watched. It was called *The Way,* and it was about some woman from Germany who made it her mission to teach blind kids in Nepal. She decided they needed something to boost their confidence so she organized a trek up one of the nearby mountains, Nangba, and made a film about it.

It seemed like a weird thing to show us. In the film, the experienced mountaineers that the woman had recruited to help her were very insistent that the kids had to reach the summit, but it was clear the kids themselves didn't want to. The German woman kept arguing with the mountaineers about it. The mountaineers kept insisting that the kids needed to summit. In the end most of them didn't. They went off to some ice field and spent their time running their hands all over it. I mean—they were kids.

After the film, Cass led a discussion about it. She'd been out in the sun all day—her face was red. She looked as fit and outdoorsy as Tommy, although I noticed she'd bought herself a multi-colored Nepali jacket and was wearing that over the tee shirt.

She said she loved the film because it showed *how much difference you can really make*, and she asked if anyone else felt that way. Kelly, the woman with the dark circles, said "Well, this film resonated for me. Those kids in the movie have had a big loss, being blind, and I've had a big loss too." Dilly, Tommy, and Joe nodded understandingly. I don't think Finn the surfer dude was really into it; he just sat there drumming out the rhythm to some song against his leg.

"What did *you* think, Ellie?" Cass asked. I beamed at her.

"I thought it was good," I said. "I kind of liked that the German woman understood that the kids didn't care that much about summiting. It's like what's important isn't the goal; it's the journey, right?" I gave Cass an ironic look, but I guess she didn't like my answer; she frowned and looked away.

That made me mad I guess. I said I was tired and came back to the room.

She came back into the room after about an hour and didn't say hello. Finally she said, "I thought you were tired—why aren't you asleep?"

"I don't know." I shrugged. Then it started: why did I leave early? Why was I the only person in the group who wasn't a team player? Everyone else had been out practicing while I was galivanting around Kathmandu.

"And then that comment about the film," she said. "Could you *try* to be positive for once, Ellie?"

"How was that negative?" I asked. "How am I not a team player?" I could feel my face heating up.

"You're out there being a *tourist* all day," she said. "You're not getting ready. Everest is a *big deal*, Ellie. The others went up Champadevi today to acclimatize—where were you?"

"Nobody told me."

"Because you're always *off by yourself*."

"Nobody told me, Cass. Was I supposed to read minds?"

"*I* spent all day with Tommy looking for ice axes. For the *group*."

"You invited me on this trip. I thought you might want to spend some time with me, but it's all about Tommy." I rolled my eyes.

She put a hand on a hip, her face hard. "You know Tommy and I are working hard to make this trip a success, right? That comment about the film was so ... unhelpful."

I didn't answer. Inside, I was starting to curl up.

"I thought you were into Buddhism. I thought you understood about helping others, thinking positive."

I used my "I'm-so-weary" voice. "Buddhism isn't about positive thinking, Cass. Buddhism is ... life is suffering."

"No, that's *you*, Ellie. *You're* into life is suffering."

"Life is suffering—First Noble Truth, Cass," I raised my voice. "That's what it says in the scriptures, I'm not making it up. Have you looked around? Have you seen the *dogs*? They're starving. You just don't like it. You want everything to be all positive and fake."

"Being positive isn't fake, Ellie. It's *helpful*."

"Not if it's forced."

"I thought it would wake you up—getting fired and everything. You're acting *exactly* the same. You're passive. You don't help yourself."

"I'm going to sleep," I said. I turned my back on her. She rustled around with the light on for a while, then finally turned it off.

Now I'm in the bathroom, writing. One lightbulb and it smells like a sewer. This notebook isn't any different from the other notebooks, is it? Cass is right: I am not a new person. I am a fucking mess.

Friday, August 15, 1 a.m.
Kathmandu

For two nights, I slept.

I'm not going to sleep tonight. Jesus, what am I doing here. I should never have come.

She isn't my friend.

I couldn't get along with Celeste. I can't get along with Cass.

It's me.

I think I should go to Tibet. I have no desire to climb stupid fucking Everest with all these wholesome jocks.

Or just die.

1:30 a.m.

I am a loser.

2 a.m.

I might as well climb the fucking mountain. If my oxygen runs out, that will be it.

2:20 a.m.

Positive thinking. Christ. She's not even understanding what the movie is trying to *say*.

2:45 a.m.

The truth is, she's choosing Tommy over me. I thought she wanted *me* to come.

9 a.m.

When I woke up, Cass wasn't in the room, so I went down to the Bakery Café for breakfast. Fairly empty so I guess it was late. Same wood tables, screen door that slapped shut, smiley Nepali girl who serves the food.

That woman Kelly was there. I was still angry, and I thought I'd make friends with Kelly and show Cass it isn't just about her. I sat down at the table next to her.

"So I heard most of the group went on some practice climb yesterday?"

Kelly raised her eyebrows. She was wearing sensible shorts, a cotton top, and had a cotton band in her hair to soak up sweat. There were still dark circles under her eyes but she looked tanned; a little more relaxed. "They did?"

"That's what Cass told me."

Kelly shook her head. "Not me."

"Oh. Cass told me it was everyone." Kelly picked at a piece of buttered toast.

"I liked what you said about the movie last night," I said. "I liked it—the film."

She grimaced. "I think Tommy wanted to show that film because some people are getting antsy."

"Oh yeah?"

"James and Courtney. They were complaining last night. About the delay. I guess they took vacation from work and they don't have that much time."

"Oh. Why *are* we delayed?"

"Tommy can't find enough oxygen or everyone. Without that ..."

"Oh."

Kelly isn't very talkative. After breakfast, she said she was going to Svyambunath. She didn't invite me.

Now I'm sitting here looking through the guidebook, deciding what to do.

I know Cass wasn't really telling the truth about the expedition, now. Not everyone is as gung-ho as she says, and not everything is going so well. It makes me even madder that she would put it all on me. In my head I tell her she isn't my friend. Then I take it back. If she isn't, who is?

The rest of last night was bad. I didn't go back into the bathroom again to write in my journal, but I couldn't sleep either. First, I got madder and madder at Cass in my head until I was screaming at her. I screamed at her that Tommy was shallow; I didn't know why she was following him.

Then I remembered something Calvin said when I first started going to his lectures, that it wasn't just ourselves that aren't inherently real—it was everything else also. Hadn't we noticed how someone could be our best friend one moment and our worst enemy the next?

It's true, isn't it? One moment Cass was my best friend, then I hated her guts. So much for equanimity.

I am so far away from that.

I've decided: I'm going to Zhiba today. They have meditation classes in the afternoon. If anyone has helped me, it's Pema. I need to go to the place she comes from. It's an hour walk. I need to tire myself out. I need to stop my fucking mind.

11 a.m.

Dear Calvin,

I am on the ghats: huge stone steps with all the colors from mud to the brilliant yellow and red of saris. Heat unbearable; water bright in the sun. About six feet away from me is a water buffalo. He is tied by a rope to a metal pole buried in the cement. It's a short rope—maybe three feet. Just beyond his reach is a puddle of water. He keeps trying to reach it with his tongue. The rope won't allow him. He stretches his neck, angles his chin to reach the water. His tongue almost reaches it, but the rope has no more slack. He gives up, tries again, gives up, tries again. He is so thirsty. Foam has formed at the corners of his mouth.

Samsara.

Out of the country, you said. The best thing for you, you said. Now *I* am out of the country; I still can't stop talking to you in my head.

But you did give me things—that time you talked about time stopping. Yesterday, I passed a young woman selling fruit at the market, staring off into nothing. At the center of every mandala, a vanishing point, you said.

I promised myself I would stop writing to you.

The words keep coming.

When I write to you, I think it is a form of prayer.

5 p.m.

My legs are killing me now. It took me two-and-a-half hours of walking to get to Zhiba—so humid my fingers swelled like sausages. Quite a walk: streets full of chickens, dogs, people hanging laundry from rooftops.

I was so happy to get there, just to sit down. The meditation room was huge: blond-wood floor; picture window as big as one wall with a view of the rest of the compound; no furniture except the shrine at the front. Nice and cool out of the sun, with overhead fans spinning. We sat there on purple buckwheat cushions, about eleven of us Westerners. Silence—just a few clearings of throats. The teacher was a French guy named Rene who has ordained there. I liked him: Keds under his monk's robe; convex body; thick French accent; Adam's apple that slid up and down the front of his throat like the slide on a trombone. He gave us a meditation method: pretending our bodies had exploded and we were just consciousness in outer space.

It helped. I feel calmer now. I stopped screaming at Cass in my head.

The best part was the dharma talk. He told the story of the Buddha again for the newcomers. He said that when we Westerners travel, we are like Siddhartha. We've been living in complete luxury—cars and houses and appliances—and then we come here to a place like Nepal, with all its poverty, and we see how the world really is.

"For me a wakeup call," he said. "I am Swiss, so if you don't know Swiss people, we are like … no possession is too much? My fadder … he is big for gadgets. Every month, he is coming with a new one. First there is coffee maker, then television that is maybe … one-and-one-half meter? Just before I leave, he brings home a machine to make popcorn for when we watch the large TV."

Lots of titters by then. Recognition.

"So when I come here I think my God, where have I been—this is how most people live—there isn't enough to eat; people suffering … I have been sleeping, you know? This is what life is for—just to be comfortable? To have a machine to make popcorn?" He looked around, nodding. A few people laughed, embarrassed.

A woman raised her hand and said, "I listen to you and I'm thinking how you were a traveler and then you decided to ordain as a monk, and I'm wondering if you think traveling is spiritual. Sometimes I think I am doing something spiritual, and sometimes I think it's just indulgence, you know?"

Rene laughed. "One day I ask this question to Rinpoche. This is before I ordain. Rinpoche says everything we do is spiritual if we are learning. He says this is the spiritual life—knowing yourself. Really knowing yourself." Then he made a joke. "This why meditation, but once you start meditating, you don't want to know yourself anymore, because you start to discover who you really are—so boring." He laughed. His whole body shook.

I liked him.

Now I'm sitting here in the Bakery Café nursing my hot lemon and listening to the conversations around me. Everyone has stories—day-long train rides; treks full of leeches; bad toilets.

The truth is, even being mad at Cass, I'm kind of happy. The poverty is bad—really bad—but it's different from New York. I haven't seen anyone step over a person lying on the sidewalk.

I'm remembering the couple from yesterday, Giselle and Conrad. The way she was laughing was the same way Rene was laughing—as if they'd both seen themselves dead, and now they were free.

I think I should go to Tibet. *You're too passive, Ellie.* I've been depending on Cass. I need to stop.

And then I will come back and I will hand Calvin the phurbu.

He will open it and he will know who I am.

241

6 p.m.

When I got back to the hotel, Cass was there. For a few minutes neither of us spoke. She asked me how I was, and I said tired. Finally, she sat on the edge of the bed and asked, "Can I talk to you?" and I said, "talk away."

Big sigh. Her hair was up in a ponytail because of the heat. "I shouldn't have attacked you like that," she said.

"Why did you?"

"I don't know." She colored. "I guess I wanted you to make me look good. With Tommy."

I kept my face neutral. "How could you not look good with Tommy? You're completely devoted to him. You met him at the airport for God's sake."

Her eyes traveled the wall, miserable. "I don't know if he really wants my help or if he's just being kind to me."

"*Kind* to you? *You're* being kind to *him*. I don't see anyone else going with him all day to look for climbing equipment."

"I'm not even sure he wants me to come with him." She looked at me, red-faced. "I offered and he said 'Awesome,' but does that mean he really wants me there?"

"I don't know, Cass. Sometimes it seems like it's more about Tommy than the mountain."

"I just like what he stands for."

"What's that?"

"Action. I like action."

"Just acting without thinking isn't ... I'm not sure I admire that." She didn't answer.

"Anyway, I'm sorry." Her eyes flickered around me helplessly. "You're my friend and I should have treated you better."

"Thank you for saying it." I looked right at her. "You made me feel like shit."

She learned forward earnestly. "Ellie, you matter. I don't want to make you feel bad. I don't want to do that."

I turned my face away.

"Forgive?" she asked. I wouldn't look at her, but she moved so she was right in front of me. "Forgive?" she asked again. So I gave in. I nodded. She hugged me, standing, and I put my face in her shoulder and I almost cried.

After that, I told her about Zhiba and Giselle and Conrad, who'd been to Tibet.

"Wow you've had some ... adventures," she said.

I showed her the map they gave me. "I know you don't want to think about Tibet yet, but it sounds pretty cool," I said. "It *just* opened. It's ... pristine." I kept talking: "mountain lakes, monasteries, nomads ..."

"You're making me want to go," she said.

"Good."

I sat back and looked at her. "So how have *your* two days been?"

"Not so great, actually ... there's just no oxygen, and we really need it. Frustrating. *We* want it for a good cause, but the Nepalis just sell to whoever can pay the most. Today Tommy yelled at some people—some Nepalis who said they were selling to another company who could pay more. Then when we were outside he got mad at himself that he lost his cool." She glanced at me nervously. "I like that, y'know? That he's real. That he makes mistakes."

I raised my eyebrows. All the times I went along with Calvin. I was in his cloud.

9 p.m.

A weird dinner with the group. Tommy said he knew "some of us" were frustrated with the delay, but he wasn't the kind of climber who took stupid risks, and he wasn't going up the mountain without the right equipment. "That would endanger *everybody*," he said, looking around.

Then out of nowhere he started talking about sacrifice, and how just being here we were already accomplishing our mission, and how not all of us might summit, but that didn't matter; just participating in this project *was* summiting. People were eyeing each other during the talk. I kept looking at James and Courtney; both of them had their eyes wide open like they were hearing something alarming and asked to speak with Tommy "after dinner." Kelly just looked sadder than usual and Dilly nodded her head up and down, looking very serious but also crestfallen. Finn looked annoyed. Ray tried to look supportive.

There were questions. How long did he think the delay would be? What about our visas ... couldn't they run out? What were the criteria for deciding who would summit and who wouldn't? It was obvious what James and Courtney thought: they took turns talking about preparation and how it seemed like the most prepared ones were the most logical ones to summit. Tommy nodded, looking apologetic.

"So what was *that* about?" I asked Cass when we got back to our room. She looked embarrassed.

"If we can't find the oxygen, one or two people maybe have to stay at base camp and not attempt the summit."

"Oh."

She sighed. I looked over: her face was all red. "I think Tommy wants *me* to do that."

"But you're so into it," I said.

She shrugged. Her face—pinched. "You heard what he said. Sacrifice."

"I would be happy to stay at base camp," I said. "We both know I'm not much of a rock climber."

Cass gave me a perceptive look. "Yeah?" she asked.

"Definitely," I said.

"That would be great," she said. "If you really don't mind." "I'd *rather*," I said.

After that, she suddenly wanted to talk about Tibet. She said I was right, the border is open. She said she thinks she wants to go with me.

"Really?" I asked.

"Absolutely."

Yay.

Saturday, August 16, 1 a.m.
Kathmandu

I'm in the bathroom again—that sewer smell. Sound of Cass breathing. I can't believe I can't sleep because I'm *happy*. Or relieved at least. I hated being mad at Cass. And now she's saying she wants to come to Tibet!

But it whipped my mind up. I kept going around and around that conversation Cass and I had when I came back to the room. She was happy when I said I was willing to just go to base camp. Now I'm thinking that I don't even want to go to base camp. It's ten days walking. I'm thinking about Calvin's postcard: *Vite, Vite* ...

I shouldn't care, but if I'm going to Tibet anyway ...

I think I'll get my Chinese visa tomorrow.

Going to Tibet will be like walking into one of Calvin's slides. It will be like entering a legend.

I wonder if the phurbu is really there. I wonder if I will get it.

Sunday, August 17, 12 p.m.
Kathmandu

I am sitting looking at a small open-fronted store across the street. There is a cabinet with a clear plastic front, the words *Photo Copy* painted on it in red, and a man standing next to a tiny copier. Two Bollywood Movie posters on top of the roof. A man on a bicycle with a big metal box on front: Ganesha Bread.

Just now, I was at the Pilgrim's Bookstore, looking for a *Lonely Planet* guidebook for Tibet. I couldn't find anything so I went to the front to ask. The guy I met was named Leo. He must have been forty or so: white yoga pants; balding on top with a little corkscrew ponytail. There weren't any. "Border opened a few weeks ago," he said.

I was feeling brave, so I asked a question: On the wall there was a framed quote: *Every journey is in some sense a pilgrimage— Lama Govinda.*

I pointed to it. "So do you think traveling is a spiritual experience?" I asked.

He widened his eyes. "Absolutely. If you have the right intentions? If you stay open?"

I looked at him: a long hook nose; narrow brown eyes. "Have you traveled a lot?"

"Six years." He shook his head. "Nothing like it. Traveling forces you to live in the moment." He opened his jaw, snapped it shut again.

"Going to Tibet, huh?" he said when I asked for the guide. "The Hermit Kingdom," he nodded. "I know what *you* need." He gave me a photocopied guide. "It's so hot off the press it hasn't even been printed yet. But I think you might need it." When I told him I was going alone, he sold me another book, too: a book about

246

mountaineering. "Lots of practical advice for high places," he said. He told me I need to take Diamox, a blood-thinner, to avoid altitude sickness.

I felt guilty about all the time he gave me. I felt like I should buy another book so I asked him what books he would recommend about Buddhism.

What the Buddha Said. Funny—it's one of the ones Pema recommended.

Here is what I am thinking: there are other people who know things besides Calvin. And they are better people, too. That guy Leo just wanted to help me, and he didn't try to get into my pants.

3 p.m.

I started reading that photocopied guide to Tibet—so much magic! There is a building that is a three-dimensional mandala; a place in the side of a mountain that you can touch, and you are getting a blessing from the goddess who lives inside.

I want to go.

Monday, August 18, 9 p.m.
Kathmandu

Things keep happening.

We all gathered in The Bakery Café tonight. Tommy looked grave. He said that there were "issues."

"Some of the vital equipment just isn't available," he said. "I'm just going to say it. Someone has to volunteer not to go."

I said it right away. "I will."

Tommy's face deflated with relief. I saw the way the others were looking at me too: James and Courtney with their faces set—good, because *they* weren't going to be the ones to give up the chance. Finn obviously thought I was an idiot. Cass's face stricken with admiration.

I didn't feel anything. What difference does it make?

Then Tommy talked about that's what this was all about—the cause, not the climb. Making sacrifices was what it was all about.

So it turns out I'm going to take a bus to Pokhara tomorrow with everyone's extra stuff. Tommy feels there's too much weight; he knows someone in Pokhara who he can trust to keep it for them until they get back.

I said yes. It didn't matter to me.

Then I thought about Calvin's postcard: *Vite, Vite ... you have a month*.

Now that it's decided, all I want is to go to Tibet.

Tuesday, August 19, 12 a.m.
Kathmandu

In the bathroom again. So happy I can't sleep: Cass said she is definitely meeting me in Tibet!

About an hour after I left the restaurant, she came back to the room and stood in the doorway looking at me. Her red hair was damp in the heat.

"Thank you," she said meaningfully.

I smiled faintly.

"No big deal," I said.

"It *is* a big deal. It was a *great sacrifice.*"

"Everyone else wants to go a lot more than me, and they're in better shape. You've put so much into it. You really want to go."

She cocked one eye shut, looked at the ceiling then back at me. "Well guess what—I'm only going to base camp."

"Seriously?"

"There isn't enough oxygen. Tommy said he didn't know what he was going to do. He was kind of freaking out, so I said I would give up my oxygen." She gave me a defeated look. "That means I can't go up."

Several flies buzzed at the window.

"Are you upset?"

She shrugged. "I'm still part of the mission, right? That's what matters, right?"

"You could still be upset."

She smiled. "I could be, but I'm not going to let myself. What's the point of making the sacrifice if I'm just going to be all morose about it?"

"I wish I could control my feelings like that."

Bleak smile.

249

Then I blurted it out. "So I have something to tell you," I said.

She waited. I drew a breath. "I'm not completely done with Calvin."

Cass sunk down on the bed. "Oh?"

"The reason I'm going to Tibet is to get something for him. That's why he gave the pledge money for me." I watched her face. "Are you mad?"

"Mad? I'm going with you. I'm not missing Tibet!"

"Really?"

"Hell yeah. If I'm not going to get up the highest mountain in the world, I need to do second best."

"I already figured out where we can meet. Tingri—it's on the Tibet side of Everest. I'll show you on the map."

I scootched over to her bed, sat next to her, spread out the map the Australian couple gave me. Of course, Cass had no trouble reading it. She put her finger on Everest, then traced a line across.

"Okay so this is Tingri. I'm going to have a Tibet visa so I can go there. You said the closest town is Lhotse?" She moved her finger slightly. "Look how close it is!" She looked at me significantly. I half-smiled.

She moved her finger down to the border of Nepal and China. "If you came in from Kodari to Zhangmu, you'd be maybe a day away. You'd get a bus up here to Lhotse ... you'd have to get a truck or a bus to take you."

"Do they *have* bus routes do you think?"

She looked at me with eyebrows raised. "I don't know," she said. Suddenly a sly look. "Maybe you'll have to rent a yak."

The pleasure rose in my face. "That'll be easy. I'll use my fluent Tibetan to negotiate the price."

Cass narrowed her eyes, amused. "So why are we going there again?"

I sighed. "There's this thing called a phurbu. It's like ... a ceremonial knife. Magic. It belonged to Calvin's teacher and he left it in Tibet when the Chinese invaded and he fled to India. Calvin wants it because whoever has the phurbu is his teacher's dharma heir. He gets to run the Buddhist Center and everything."

"Dharma heir. How can you inherit something like that?"

250

I shrugged. "I don't know. It's a Tibetan thing."

"Damn. You Buddhists with your secret handshakes and magic knives. I thought it was about compassion. I thought it was ... *holy*."

"It *is* about compassion, but ... there's other stuff too."

"A magic knife, huh? What can you do with it?"

We were punchy. She started singing it: *what can you do with a magic knife*. It *did* sound pretty funny.

"This is like *Indiana Jones* or something," she said. When I told her about Eckerman's people also trying to find the phurbu, she got even funnier.

"Oh my God," she said. "We're going to have to get lassos. Now we're going to need *fast* yaks so we can ride across the Tibetan tundra with them in hot pursuit."

The rest of the night was jokes.

We might have to hole up in the mountains for a while to elude our rivals.

Who was going to play us when we got back and wrote the movie script.

I am in the bathroom of a hotel in Kathmandu at 2 a.m. and I am having a party with myself.

Wednesday, August 20, 11 a.m.
En Route to Pokhara

The ceiling of the bus to Pokhara is lined with filthy plaid uphol-
stery. That is what I'm staring at. I follow the yellow vertical line
with my eye, from one side of the ceiling to the other, taking in the
blue lines that cross it, trying not to get sick.

Concentrate.

Tommy said that it's a three-hour trip.

I just have to hold on.

I probably shouldn't be writing. Just a few lines.

The day started early. Tommy outside our hotel in a taxi with
bags of stuff that other people didn't want to take to Everest.
Kathmandu at that time of morning was gray; roosters crowing
behind every other house. We drove to the bus station, one huge
circle of dusty ground crossed with tire tracks, a corrugated tin
roof on one side over booths selling chapatis or rice and dal, bottles
of some kind of drink: orange, black. Already baking outside.

The *Lonely Planet* guidebook talks about "bus touts." I guess
that's their name for the teenage Nepali boys who run the buses
like conductors. Ours has a goatee and a mop of black hair with
a baseball cap perched on top. He has one extremely long pinky
fingernail and keeps the rupee bills we use to pay our fares woven
between his fingers. It's clear he loves his job, bossing everyone
around; throwing the luggage up top with quick movements;
flicking through the thick wads of rupee bills woven around his
fingers to make change. Tommy bought me two seats, although he
said I shouldn't expect to keep them once the bus got going. Two
teenage Nepali boys in jeans and ragged tee shirts tied the bags on
top of the bus where there was already a bleating goat and a giant
basket of very quiet chickens.

The way it works here, you sit in the bus and wait for it to fill up, then you go. It took a while: mostly it was families with large baskets of food.

Cass came to see me off. At one point, Tommy leaned over me, fixed me with that earnest stare of his, and said that he had never gotten to know me as well as the others, but now he wished he had. He could see I really had "character." Then he told me my "mission": drop off the bags at the hotel he'd given me the name of, stay with the stuff.

"How long do I need to stay?" I asked. "Aren't you guys going to be gone like a month?" A flicker of annoyance—maybe that I had other plans.

"The owner is named Nina. You could leave it if she's there. I'll send someone to pick it up in about ten days."

After that, Cass came on the bus and sat next to me. I could see they were about to leave, and I didn't want her to be gone. "Next stop Lhotse," she said. "Eight days and I'll be there." She was in a good mood. Outside the bus station had started to wake up: people walked back and forth across the dirt parking lot, hung out at the dark wood booths that sold chai in little clay cups and fruit in plastic bags.

"I'll see you soon, Indiana," she said when she left.

4 p.m.
Pokhara

According to the LP Guidebook, people come to Pokhara for the views. I can see why. The lake is glass and goes on forever; light blue mountains in the distance; a shimmer of heat.

When the bus stopped, everything happened at once: the bus touts unloaded all the bags that Tommy had sent me with, throwing them on the ground. Then it was gone.

I wasn't prepared for Nina, the owner of the Peace Eye Guesthouse. I had pictured some middle-aged hippy in bell bottoms and embroidered Indian shirts, like the ex-pat who ran the café where I ate when I walked to Zhiba. But Nina looked she should be running a gallery in the East Village.

Slim, elegant black pants, a tee shirt that says *The Clash*, and Keds; large eyes and the long face of a Byzantine Madonna. One long, blonde braid that hangs down her back; narrow hips that swivel as she walks.

When I gave her the note from Tommy she made a funny face. "So you're another victim of Mr. Positivity," she said.

I laughed out loud. "I didn't make the cut," I said.

"Better off." Nina nodded. She wrinkled her nose. "Man with a mission." She shook her head. "The worst kind." When I laughed, she gave me an ironic look.

"He said you were trustworthy," I said. "He said you'd be willing to store all this stuff."

She narrowed her eyes. "How much money did he send you with?"

I held out a wad of rupees.

She eyed it, then nodded. "Looks about right."

"Pandenla will help you," she said. She called inside in her husky voice and a sleepy-faced Nepali teenager in black pants and worn green tee shirt came out. "Pandenla, this is ..."

"Ellie," I said.

The bags from the expedition were laid out in a semi-circle on the ground behind me. Nina waved her hand over it. "This all goes in storage," she said.

He moved unhurriedly, in a way I've seen Nepalis move over and over again. No one is ever in a rush.

The guesthouse has a little rickety deck with railings and picnic tables with umbrellas so you can eat outside; there's also an inner dining room, dark with bare windows. Those in the front have a view of the dirt road and the lake. To decorate, there are faded color photographs of mountain ranges and scenes from treks.

I like my room. I'm in the back; Nina said it would be quieter. "A bunch of Aussies here now," she said. "They can get rowdy." She winked at me. I have my own bathroom too: the toilet is on a cement slab raised from the ground, and it smells ... but this means I can be by myself.

I'm sitting here now on my sagging bed. So quiet compared to Kathmandu ... there are kitchen sounds coming from below and some voices outside, but otherwise nothing.

I should try to enjoy myself. The lake is beautiful.

I am going to Tibet.

Soon.

8 p.m.

At dinner, Nina introduced me to the group of Aussies that is staying here. They were just the way she described them: rambunctious. There was a brunette in a halter top, always laughing; another girl with shaggy hair who seemed to be the one to make the jokes; two guys in shorts and Hawaiian shirts, legs covered with curlicues of black hair. When I met them, all the usual questions: where was I going? where was I coming from? New York City got a big rise— there were jokes about how there aren't enough restaurants. Tibet got a rise, too. How did I find out the border was open? Did I have a visa? They were back from the Annapurna trek. Lots of funny stories about dysentery.

It didn't feel good to be with them—they're too jolly. After dinner, they invited me to go for a Fosters with them—evidently there is a bar here that imports it just for the Aussies—but I said I was too tired.

When they left, Nina came in to clean up the tables.

"A pretty jolly group, eh?" I asked.

"Aussies are always the party animals. National personality." She eyed me from the other side of the room while she bent over a table, wiping it down.

"How long have you been here?"

She cocked her head. "Give or take six years."

"So you must see all the nationalities. Do you have a favorite?"

"I think my favorite nationality is Nepali." She turned her back to me, bending over a chair, then stood up.

"The French are difficult and persnickety; the Germans are loud; the Dutch are cool; the Scandinavians underdress ... for Asia; the Israelis are annoyingly aggressive." She gave me a lopsided grin, closed one eye. "I usually say we don't have rooms left."

Done wiping, she sat across from me. She's so obviously a New Yorker. I wonder what she's doing here.

"Do you like running a guesthouse?" I asked.

She sighed. Her eyes traveled the ceiling. "Well, it allows me to stay here."

"And you want to stay?" She didn't answer. "What do you like about it so much?"

She sat down. "It took me leaving the States to see how the real world lives." She shrugged. "When you have less, you live more in the moment. Pandenla ... he's been with me four years. He doesn't worry about 'making it,'" she widened her eyes. "He just lives."

"You're from New York, right?"

She gave me a side smile. "How could you possibly tell?"

We both laughed.

"You don't miss it?"

"Do I miss squatting in a studio on Avenue B with no hot water and junkies climbing up the fire escape to rob me?" She shook her head. "Just so I could live The Life." Gazing at that black tee shirt and the braid, I thought how, in The Village, she would have been one of the cool ones, like the people I gazed at when I was in that Italian bakery with Cass writing dream statements. The kind of person I never was.

She got up again to wipe another table.

"I don't have to live The Life here. I can just make art."

Now I'm upstairs in my room.

I wonder what it's like to be her.

Brave.

9 p.m.

So here I am, another room. Eight days till Cass gets to Lhotse. I guess I'll leave here soon, too.

I kind of wish I didn't say yes to Pokhara now. I did not want to be with those other tourists, but without Cass, I'm scared.

I like Nina. She's obviously a lot stronger than me.

Like that's so hard.

Thursday, August 21, 4 p.m.
Pokhara

I took a walk around the lake today, mostly wondering how I got myself into this; why I said yes when I really wanted to start for Tibet. Completely different from Kathmandu: green fields, dirt roads, brown, leaning shacks; the wall of blue, white-capped mountains in the distance. Relaxed.

At some point the path around the lake veered off and I followed it. I climbed a hill and then I was looking down on a green, marshy expanse of fields, the fields separated from each other by shallow grass borders. There was a procession of black umbrellas coming, tromping along in a snaky line; a wedding procession I had met up with earlier, much closer to the guesthouse. I guess the umbrellas were for the sun, or maybe they were expecting rain later. They looked ridiculously out of place. In a few moments they all took different paths and then the effect was even more comical. From far off, with their umbrellas, they looked like they were in an impressionist painting, trying frantically to scatter off a background where they did not belong.

So that made me happy.

5 p.m.

There's going to be a lot of notebook-writing here.

I tried to meditate. I followed the steps that Rene taught us: imagine your body has exploded into space and you are just consciousness. Of course it fell apart. I thought of Calvin, imagined myself handing him the phurbu.

I spent an hour looking at the mountaineering book that Leo recommended to me. So many warnings—the altitude, rock slides, mudslides, avalanches. I suppose I should prepare more seriously. There's probably equipment I could buy here. Trekkers must come through here all the time and sell the stuff they're done with.

Friday, August 22, 12 p.m.
Pokhara

There are basically two choices, both for breakfast and lunch: rice and dal or an omelet and toast. For some reason Pandenla makes it with the crusts cut off. He seems to do everything, but always calmly. His face is always composed and quiet, his hair uncombed, his hands slow. I wonder if he lives here. Probably.

I think the Aussies have decided I am anti-social because I didn't go with them for the Fosters; they didn't try to talk to me today at breakfast. What did I expect? But it still made me lonely.

Nina passed through while I was waiting for my food. I had two of the books Pema gave me out on the table and she came over to look. She sat down and started to thumb through *Buddhism in Action* while we talked.

"Where did the Aussies go?" I asked.

"The Tibetan temple," she said. She shrugged and gave me a bored look. "They all go there."

"Oh," I said. "Maybe I should go. I'm going to Tibet soon."

She looked up. "I *heard* the border was open. I was thinking of going myself, but ..." She turned and gestured at the room. "There's this."

"Are they nice—the Tibetan temples? Have you been?"

Raised eyebrows. "They're fine. I'm a little jaded because all the Westerners go there. They read a few paragraphs in the *Lonely Planet* guidebook and then they go to the Tibetan temple and they think they know everything about Buddhism." She raised her eyebrows and peered at me over her glasses. "Instant conversion." She held up the book. "Where did you get this?"

"It's from the East West Bookstore," I said. "A Buddhist nun recommended it."

Nina's looked at me open-mouthed. "Oh my God!" For a moment, I thought she was sick, she gasped so loud. "The East West Bookstore!" she said. "Jesus what a blast from the old days. I used to spend whole days in there."

I laughed. "Yeah?"

She shook her head from side to side. "I was all into Hinduism, then I was all into Taoism, then I became obsessed with Zen." She opened her eyes wide. "I guess there's a theme there, huh? Salvation." She leaned back and laughed, her voice silvery. When she sat up again, I looked at her face, her eyes folded downward into half-crescents. She wasn't beautiful, but I liked looking at her.

"And now?"

"Now I'm a feminist. Now I read Angela Carter."

"Who's that?"

She gestured toward the bookshelf, read some titles: *The Bloody Chamber, Nights at the Circus.* She looked at me. "Fractured fairytales."

"Magic."

Nina gave a half-smile. "The reason I like Angela Carter isn't because of magic. The reason I like her is that the women always save themselves."

"Oh." I laughed. "I guess that *is* better."

She shook her head, holding my eyes. "You don't like the story— change the story." Her fingers tapped the tabletop. I noticed the fingernails were chewed down to the white.

Restless.

I can't believe she knows the East West Bookstore.

She stood up. "Well I'm going to paint," she said. She picked up a canvas that had been leaning against the wall and stuck it under her arm, then left.

3 p.m.

Another walk around the lake: that is basically all there is to do here. After that, I cracked the mountaineering book, read about altitude sickness.

I have to decide whether to get a tent or not. I've been looking at Calvin's map, realizing how vague it is. The map from Conrad and Giselle has distances, at least. It looks like the distance from Lhotse to the monastery is about 20 kilometers. Ten miles. I suppose if I started early I could walk it in a day.

Survival.

I am turning into Cass, now.

5 p.m.

I should not have come to a place where I would be alone. There has been enough of that.

This afternoon, I read more from *Buddhism in Action*, the chapter on negative emotions.

If you are sad, just say to yourself, I am sad, it says. There doesn't have to be any drama. It will pass.

Of course it doesn't work.

I thought about Nina holding up that Angela Carter book: the women save themselves.

That is what I should do, isn't it?

Cass is probably very happy right now. She'll be in her element, conquering the obstacles she encounters, talking with Tommy about crimps and oxygen levels and Diamox.

Saturday, August 23, 3 p.m.
Pokhara

Today I hung around the guesthouse, hoping I would see Nina, but she didn't show up, so I ended up taking a walk around the lake again. Red ground and stone buildings with thatched roofs, green everywhere, especially the long-tailed banana trees. The poverty is serious, even more than Kathmandu.

Coming back, I passed the hippies who were swimming nude, eyes slit with the enjoyment of their own audacity, and in the shallow water, the buffaloes, wallowing up to their necks. Their horns curve out from their heads like solidified streams.

If I want the phurbu, I should go. "A month until Eckerman's people get there," said Calvin. What am I waiting for?

4 p.m.

Yet another walk around the lake today.

I think my whole life has been this. I don't know what I want, so I follow other people's suggestions. Here I am in Pokhara because I followed Cass, then Tommy. And I'm following Calvin's slides to Tibet.

When I got to my favorite outlook, the hill that overlooks rice fields, I remembered Celeste talking to me about the prostitutes. She said they had trauma. She said sometimes you don't even realize when you've been traumatized—you don't even feel it; that's your protection.

I think surprise is traumatic.

When you see something coming, you can brace for it. When it sweeps the ground from under your feet, it's hard to trust your own footsteps anymore.

The surprise was after Max left.

My mother's nervous breakdown began the day after: a Saturday. She came down for breakfast. She made herself some toast and when the toaster binged, she put the toast in her mouth without buttering it and began to chew, mechanically, staring straight ahead.

Saturdays were my mother's days to get the house in order. Generally, after breakfast, she swung into action. But that day, she did not move. At noon I asked her if she wanted lunch and when she said she didn't, I made her a grilled cheese anyway. My mother took the fork and pushed the bread down; yellow liquid cheese squeezed out the sides. She pushed her fork into the melted part then lifted it to her mouth, then put it back down without tasting.

The crying started after that.

It sounded, at first, like a shrill, prolonged hiccup. For a minute, I thought she was choking. Her ribcage rose, froze, and over it I saw her red, startled face.

Then it slammed down again, and the first sob escaped. The words shuddered out: "I thought he loved me. He said he luh-uhved me."

"It's okay, Mommy."

"He. Said he. Luh-uhved me."

"It's okay, Mommy."

My mother, the person who had come down in the mornings and talked on the phone while sinking her hands into a bowl of raw chopped hamburger for meatloaf later that night; who would shout with laughter in the supermarket.

I put my arms around her. "It's okay, it's going to be okay," I soothed.

"Stop saying that," she sobbed. "It's not okay. It's not going to be okay."

I think knowledge comes in layers. On the top layer was anger, but under that, there was trust. He was my father. We had spent all those hours together. He had talked to me about the astral plane and all religions ending up in the same place. After three weeks, I decided to go to him.

I had seen a slip of paper on my mother's bureau with his address on it. I got the local roadmap out. If I took Route 12 to 456, I could get there in about two hours.

Walking along Main Street, I was picked up in about fifteen minutes by a middle-aged lady with a pantsuit on. I could tell what she was thinking: what was I doing out here, a nice young girl like me? The rest of the trip went pretty smoothly: a golf club salesman; a young guy in a pickup truck who let me off at the end of my father's road.

The movie in my head went like this: I came to the door and he started to cry, he was so relieved to see me. He knew he was wrong. He hugged me to him hard; my face smashed against his chest. I could smell him; his familiar Dad-sweat.

His house was at the end of a long road. I had to walk a couple of miles and my thighs were throbbing when I got there. I hadn't eaten anything, and I was shaky; at the same time, I had that energy you get when you're running on empty: get there get there get there.

The house looked like a barn: unpainted wood, with big square windows and a front porch with a railing. My stomach was churning when I knocked on the door.

He came after the third knock. He just looked at me. He looked the same: blond hair, gaunt face, worn jeans. My father.

He didn't back out of the doorway.

"What do you want?" he asked.

I had thought of so many things to say on the way there. Now I just stood there.

"Mom is having a nervous breakdown," I finally said.

Behind him on the wall, I could see one of his paintings: *Delicious Abstract*, all red and what looked like a pair of blue sunglasses in the middle of it all.

"That's not my responsibility anymore," he said.

I didn't speak. I looked at my shoes. My legs ached from all the walking.

"Dad," I said. "I'm sorry I wrote you that letter. I don't know what to do."

"Figure it out, Ellie," he said in a loud voice, as if he were talking to a room of people. "You're on your own now. Didn't you say that you didn't want me in your life anymore?"

"I didn't mean that."

"I come home and find a letter from you like that."

"I'm sorry!"

"Sometimes we have to take responsibility for the things we say, Ellie."

"You did bad things!" I said. "You had affairs. You left Mom."

"That's none of your business, Ellie."

"I'm in this family too." I could hear my own voice—high, defensive. "It's part of my business."

He shook his head from side to side. "I really had high hopes for you," he said.

"I'm still me," I said. I could feel my throat closing.

He shook his head. "It's never going to be the same, is it?" For a moment, he looked sad too, but then I realized what it was: pity.

"Dad!" I went back in the dark. He said he couldn't drive me—his car was gone. "Can you give me something to eat at least?" I asked him. He went into the kitchen and came back with a couple of pieces of bread.

When I got home, my mother was standing on the front porch, arms folded, face wrinkled from crying. "I was about to call the police," she said. "Where were you?"

I went upstairs to my bed and curled into a ball.

The disciple of the Noble One beholds not feeling, perception, the impulses. "This is not mine, this am I not, this is not my self."

Sunday, August 24, 7 p.m.
Pokhara

I have been thinking about what Pema said to me that last time I saw her: the dark things are as important as the light things.

Is it true?

Pema became a Buddhist nun because her friend killed herself. My father left, and I went looking for wisdom.

And then Calvin.

A blow comes, and then you try to heal.

Monday, August 25, 3 p.m.
Pokhara

Well, I finally had a chance to talk with Nina. I was sitting on the deck of the Peace Eye Guesthouse, reading one of the books on her shelf: *The Great Way is not Difficult*. The first line: *Life is a catastrophe.*

I heard footsteps scuffing the pebbles on the path and looked up. There she was: black pants in spite of the heat; a cut-off shirt with *The Specials* blazoned across it. It was hot; there was a mist of sweat on her upper forehead and her tendrils of dirty blond hair were sticking to it. She was carrying a big cardboard box but when I said her name, she put it on the floor and sat down in the rocking chair next to me.

"Whatcha reading?" she asked. I held the book up. "Oh that's a good one." She sat back in her chair and rocked, looking out at towards the lake. "Hot."

"You must be boiling in those pants."

She looked down at her thighs and laughed. "Yeah I guess I could come up with something more comfortable. It's kind of my identity … what I have left from my New York self. Also the Nepalis don't really wear shorts if you've noticed."

"Yeah why is that?"

She shrugged. "It's a more conservative culture."

She looked over at me. "So what do you like about the book?"

"I like 'life is a catastrophe.'" She crinkled one eye, nodded.

"Yes that about says it, doesn't it? I liked that too. I was having a rough time when I read that book. That line stuck with me." We both gazed out toward the lake. At the horizon jagged white peaks pushed into the sky. Through the trees it was possible to see some buildings on the other side of the lake.

"Was that when you first got here?"

She glanced over at me, then back. "It was, as a matter of fact."

"Why was it rough? Just ... adjusting to a new place?"

She sighed, surveyed me briefly. The look was not exactly friendly.

Then she said, resolutely: "I was jilted."

"Oh." We both stared at our feet and the wood floorboards of the porch.

"Worst pain in the world," I said. "So ridiculous. It's just one person. But ..." I shook my head. A fly buzzing off to the side. "Was it ... at the altar?"

She laughed. "No. I followed him here. Like a little ... teeny-bopper." she wrinkled her nose in distaste at herself.

"I'm sorry," I said. "That sucks."

Pause.

"And then you decided not to go back to New York?"

She sighed. "I was in shock," she said. "I didn't know what I was going to do. I came here just to rest. I had that book with me. One day I was taking a walk and I found myself looking at this man from the village. He was wearing shoes, but one of them was missing half of the upper sole. I just had this thought: *he's wearing half a shoe.* And then I realized that I would never see that back in New York, and I just ... was humbled. I mean ... life is a catastrophe for practically everyone. I decided I wanted to have that in front of my face. So I stayed."

"Humility, the queen of virtues."

A man on a bike slowly passed on the road in front of us. Nina smiled at the air. "I like that. Where did you hear that?"

"The East West Bookstore!" I said. I raised one eyebrow. "Source of all wisdom."

Nina laughed too. She has a funny laugh: surprised.

"Remember I told you about meeting a Buddhist nun there?"

"Yes. I remember now."

"She was the one who said it to me. But I think it's from some ancient Christian saint or something."

I could hear Pandenla inside, stacking dishes.

"So are you glad now? That you stayed?"

She nodded. "I am glad. It was really tough at first, but now ..."

She looked over at me. "Mostly in New York, I was broke. And miserable."

"Why was that?"

Self-deprecating smile. "Trying to find myself."

"Hmm. I guess I'm doing that."

"You're more likely to find some answers here than over there, I can tell you."

It was hot enough to want to go in by then. I wanted to stay out on the porch, but Nina's leg was jiggling, ready to move.

"Did you find yourself?"

She laughed. "I stopped looking." She stood up. "Gotta go."

7 p.m.

That was quite a talk with Nina.

I'm lucky I met her.

I'm *really* lucky.

Now I'm talking to two people in my head: Calvin and her.

Tuesday, August 26, 1 p.m.
Pokhara

It rained today. Everything was silver. From where I sat, on the porch of my hotel: droplets bounced up from the dark brown road; a long, slick, green banana leaf nodded in the breeze; a man on a bicycle whizzed by, shirt and pants soaked, plastered to his body; a mother in sari hopped over puddles, holding her daughter by the hand. They were both laughing.

Watching it, I thought about Leo, the guy at the Pilgrim's Bookstore: *Every journey is in some sense a pilgrimage.*

Time stopped. Happiness.

Wednesday, August 27, 3 p.m.
Pokhara

I have no words for this so I will just start.

Nina invited me to talk with her while she painted. We went to the lake; it was a ten-minute walk from the guesthouse; she had an easel and I carried her paints.

Humid. I was huffing while we walked. The green around us vivid; the dirt on the path red.

"I'm so amazed that I met someone I can talk to about these things."

"I am too, actually. There are plenty of Westerners who *think* they understand Buddhism." We passed a small store, doorless, with shelves of household goods in bright plastic containers, large sacks of rice with *USA* stenciled across them.

"You think I understand it? It's so ... contradictory."

"Well let's put it this way; you don't misunderstand it." She cocked her head to the side.

We passed a young boy, dark-skinned, with stitched-together pants.

"Have you met many Nepali Buddhists?"

"Some."

"How different is it?"

"Much more devotional. There's a lot of Rinpoche worship. Guru! You hear that word all the time around here."

I echoed her, laughing. "Guru!"

"Have you ... did you ever have a guru?"

"I did actually."

"Here?"

"Back in New York."

I laughed—I could hear the nervousness of it. "I did too."

A feeling in my stomach. I pushed it down.

Nina surveyed me, amused. "We're turning into the Coincidence Twins."

I could see the lake through the trees; glass. Long, multi-colored boats that tourists could rent were gathered around a dock.

"Are you glad ... I mean, was it helpful?"

She raised her eyebrows. "Not sure that would be the word for it. It was ..." she looked at me. "An experience." She stopped, so I did too. She held my eyes.

"I was in love with mine, actually. I hate admitting that. Such a fucking cliché."

My stomach froze.

"Are you still in touch with him?"

Pause. "That was the person I was telling you about the other day. When I said I was jilted. The one I followed here."

"Oh yeah?"

"We were supposed to go trekking, and then ... he wouldn't take me. "

My stomach flipped. I think I was starting to know.

"... From one day to the next, he said I couldn't come with him."

"What reason did he give?"

"We were supposed to go trekking. I stayed out one day and got sunburned. It wasn't that big a deal; it would have faded in a day or two. But he said I couldn't start out on a trek in that condition; that there would be too much sun exposure on the trek."

I was looking at the lake, but I wasn't seeing it. My stomach had collapsed.

Calvin in the loft on 14th Street: *Two days before we start, she falls asleep in the sun ...*

"I'm just wondering. The person you feel in love with ... it wasn't Calvin Ross, was it?"

Her hand flew to her chest.

"Oh my God. My entire body chemistry just changed. You know Calvin?"

Finally I eked it out. "I was in love with him too. I am, still." My face burned. We had arrived. Nina set down her easel. I looked over the lake without seeing it. "I think he talked about you. He said there was a girl he took to Nepal to go trekking. He said you got a bad sunburn so he couldn't take you." I looked over at her: a crooked smile.

Nina put a hand to her heart. "Jesus I can't believe it! My *blood* is jumping."

We were quiet for a moment.

"I got the sunburn, but that wasn't why he wouldn't take me."

"Oh?"

"Calvin wanted to fuck someone else." Her own queasy smile.

I stopped inhabiting my own body. "He said you got sun poisoning, and you couldn't go. He said pain was an opportunity."

She laughed angrily. "Easy to say when the pain is someone else's."

From far away, I heard my voice, reedy. "I thought it was just me."

She gazed at the lake. "I did too, but later someone in the group told me—it was an assembly line. A new girl every month. I'm sure there was a lot of overlap ..."

Nonononononono.

I did what I always do; I ran.

"Ellie, stop," Nina called after me. But I had to go.

One thing at a time:

A girl in a pink blouse and navy-blue skirt.

A man in a striped Nehru hat.

Through the old village, out into the countryside. Old wooden houses; colorful laundry hanging from lines; Nepali families looking at me suspiciously. Walk until the body rebels. Name things: woman in sari, boy on bicycle, road, fence, field.

Now I am in my room again. I hope Nina does not come. I can't talk to her now. Maybe I'll never leave.

7 p.m.

Dear Pema,

I am in my hotel room in Pokhara. I wonder if you were ever here.

I need to write to someone.

273

I need it to be you.
Everyone is your teacher, you said.
Right now, you are my teacher.
You are not here, but you are teaching me.
And I need to know you are there, a direction to turn to.
Everyone has to make their own path, you said.
But there has to be a light.
I am still in Pokhara, waiting to leave and meet my friend Cass in Tibet, but something has happened.

I suppose you guessed that I slept with my teacher, Calvin. I have discovered that I was not his only lover. I was one in a line of many.
A surprise.
It shouldn't have been, but it was.
Thank you for being you and being there. Right now I need that.

8 p.m.

I am not leaving this room.
I am not going to eat.

9 p.m.

I sit here and talk to myself: *You were nobody to him.*
I draw the blade across my heart.
I need to keep doing it. I need to learn.

10 p.m.

How stupid I was. Everything was pointing at it.
It was obvious and everyone saw it except me.

10:30 p.m.

Nina came and knocked on my door.

"Ellie?"

"I can't talk now. Thank you, Nina," I called. I could hear my voice in the air.

I don't get to leave.

I don't get to eat.

I should not live.

11 p.m.

I disgust myself.

Truly.

Thursday, August 28, 2 a.m.
Pokhara

Dear Calvin,

You are not a person to be trusted.

I met Sunburn Girl. She has a name: Nina.

I remember what you said about her when she got the sunburn and you wouldn't let her trek with you. *An opportunity*, you said.

It's so easy for you, isn't it.

When you told the story, it was all about your wisdom, letting her deal with hard times, become stronger.

But you didn't wait to see what actually happened to her, did you?

You just left her here, in Nepal.

An assembly line, said Nina. I remember now.

Jane with the tragic face and long hair down to her waist. Monica from Brazil who cut herself. I remember watching Jane in a lecture, sitting on a chair with a hand on each knee.

People don't matter to you, do they?

Well, women don't.

Here is the worst thing: I still don't hate you.

1 p.m.

I went down to breakfast today. I had to eat.

Nina was waiting. When she saw me, she enfolded me in her arms.

Then she let go and looked at me.

"I spent most of the night thinking about this," she said.

I smiled, bleakly. "I didn't sleep either.

"C'mon, eat."

Breakfast was toast. Nina watched me.

"It doesn't feel real," I said.

"It does happen," she said. "People go on the road and then there are incredible coincidences. When I first got here? I went on the Jomosom trek. I'm navigating this very tricky place where the path has washed away, hauling myself by pulling at grass ... I look up and there's my friend Teresa from art school."

I looked at the toast Pandenla had made me.

"But of course we're special," she giggled. "Two concubines of the Guru of 14th Street."

I smiled. "The dakini-ettes."

"The devoted disciples of the Master of the Great Wand." I did laugh. It felt good.

Then I remembered: *assembly line*. The pain was physical.

It should be funny, right?

When I was done eating, she took my arm.

"Ellie," she said. "C'mon. Let's take a walk."

We walked into town to buy me supplies for Tibet. For the first time, Nina looked like an ex-pat: Nepali patchwork pants with the ubiquitous black tee shirt. The blonde braid swayed behind her back when she walked. There was about half a mile of muddy road before we got there. When people passed, they nodded; most people know her around here.

"For at least two years, I thought he would send someone after me," she said, smiling at the sky. "*Now* you come. When I'm not waiting anymore."

Vivid green grass, low trees; an occasional cement block house.

"The thing I hate is thinking about him all the time," I said.

She nodded, her arms crossed in front of her. "I'm very familiar with that syndrome. Sickeningly familiar." Glimpses of the lake as the road curved back toward it.

"So who's still in the cult?" she said. "Judith? Edwin?"

"They're still there."

She laughed, shaking her head. "Judith is never going to give up on Calvin. No matter how badly he treats her."

"You think it's a cult?"

She shrugged. "I don't know if it matters what you call it. It is what it is."

"I thought he said so many true things," I said.

"Yeah that's the weird thing, isn't it?" she looked up and I followed her: a crow.

"*One* of the weird things."

"Did he say that thing about everything being on fire?"

"Yes."

"You know that's not original, don't you?"

"It isn't?"

"It's the Buddha's Fire Sermon. It's famous. When he left me, I started reading a lot. It helped me realize that he didn't come up with all those profound truths. He stole them. "

"Oh?"

"How did you meet him, anyway?"

"Art school. Calvin was teaching there."

"Oh yeah. I forgot he used to do that."

"Did he ... seduce you?"

"Yeah."

"Did you go to that apartment on Spring Street?"

"Sometimes. Sometimes we went to the loft."

The first signs of town appeared; an open-fronted store in a wood shack with a corrugated metal roof. Two men in black pants and white button-down shirts worked on a porch, handing off cement blocks. A young woman in a sari passed, holding a black umbrella against the sun.

"Why does he do it?" I asked. I could hear my voice, vulnerable.

She put her arm around me. "That's a question I asked myself a lot. Then I decided it wasn't the right question to ask. I'm never going to figure it out. What mattered wasn't why. What mattered was that I needed to stop defining myself in relation to him."

2 p.m.

Nina said I would need a wool hat in Tibet. "It's freezing in the mountains," she said. We went to a shop with old down coats hanging from the overhang; one sorry-looking sleeping bag slung over the back of a chair. Startling to be in town, with all the signs and activity. There was a woman in a paisley sari with a banana cart on wheels; a tiny shop said *Legal Consultant Service*. There was a wood child's desk with a small pile of dusty books.

We ate lunch at a place called the Butterfly Restaurant. Rickety wood tables on a sloping wood porch, where the owners were happy to see her, and we were served by a young girl in a shalwar kameez who was all smiles. "Pandenla's sister," Nina said. "She used to come by all the time." We had momos—delicious. I asked her a few things: where did she get the start-up money for her hotel? (her mother); was there a lot of corruption? (yes). But I couldn't focus.

When the plates were cleared, it was just us again. "How did you stop?" I asked. "Thinking about him?"

She looked across the road. "Time. You just have to wait."

"How long?"

Nina looked at me, tapped a palm against the surface of the table. "Long," she said.

"But it does end?"

"It does end," she said.

"Do you think love is an addiction? When I told Calvin I loved him, he said 'love is an addiction.'"

She looked at me thoughtfully. "I think we ask a lot of love. Especially women. But I also think Calvin is a fool to throw away real love."

I guess my face was starting to crumble, because she put her hand out and pushed a piece of hair out of my face.

"It's not you, Ellie," she said. "It has nothing to do with you."

I waited to talk.

"I don't understand no-self," I said. "I mean if you are aspiring to not have a self, shouldn't you just ... let people hurt you? That is what I thought. Calvin would hurt me and I would think, *well, if I really want to be egoless ...*

"I don't think no-self and egolessness are the same thing. She looked at me, blinking. "I don't think it's really about not having an ego. I think it's about— being bigger." She held my eyes. "Trying to be nobody is very unhealthy."

4 p.m.

Nina has gone to do an errand. I am in the shade, looking out at the lake. It stretches on forever, glazed with light. The blue mountains are a wall that look at themselves in the water. Nepalis stand in groups and stare down at the water.

I meant to walk, but it's just too hot. The sun is unreal.

We must have sat in that restaurant for another hour, talking.

Nina is different from me. She fought more.

When he told her he couldn't see her as often, she wrote him a letter in blood.

"In blood?"

"Yeah. I cut my finger open and wrote."

"What did he do?"

Her mouth clenched. "He paid attention."

"Are you glad you met him?

She nodded. "I am. If Calvin hadn't given me that experience, if he hadn't made me fall in love, then left me on my own, I would never have grown like this."

"Did he talk about tantra? Use all the negative emotions in the service of enlightenment?"

"He did."

"I think it's true. The bad things ... push you. So hope for the worst, huh?"

She laughed, surprised. "Yeah that's one way of putting it. Hope for the worst."

"I wish I could be like you. Strong."

"No you don't. You're you."

"I wanted to be lovable," I said. "I really wanted that."

I must have sounded bad. Nina pulled her chair over next to mine.

"*I* like you," she said. "And I can see why Calvin liked you."

"Why?"

"You're a searcher, Ellie."

6 p.m.

I'm the only guest at the Peace Eye Guesthouse now. Nina thinks a new group will show up tomorrow. She's in the kitchen now, with Pandenla. I'm on the porch, writing.

After her errand, Nina came to get me at the lake and we walked back. It took an hour in the heat; we spent it making fun of Calvin.

Nina noticed things I never did:

"Did he talk about Eckerman all the time?" She smiled conspiratorially.

"Yes."

"Did he talk about all his lectures from the past and how great they were?"

"He did actually." I laughed.

It feels good—we are beyond him. But it isn't true, is it? At least not for me.

Everything's changed now. Now I want to learn how to be like Nina.

One more day here. I wish I could stay.

9 p.m.

The mosquitos are driving me crazy. It's impossible to sleep with the window closed. Nina gave me a mosquito coil to burn. It burns my nostrils.

More talk after dinner.

I told Nina about my "mission."

"Did he ever talk about the Ralung phurbu when you were with him?"

"Jesus! That fucking phurbu! He kept waiting for China to allow tours of Tibet so he could go look for it."

Her eyebrows furrowed.

"That's why you're going to Tibet?"

"He paid for me to go on the Everest expedition so I'd go to Tibet and get it for him."

She thought, looking off in the distance. "You don't have to go, you know. He doesn't deserve that from you."

"Well I have to now. I'm meeting my friend there."

"Seems a little dangerous for you on your own. What if your friend doesn't come?"

"Cass will come."

She turned her head to me, frowning.

"You're doing all this for Calvin. I'm not sure that's wise."

"I guess I convinced myself I was doing it for me."

"And now?"

"And now I have to meet my friend." Nina got up to open the window some more, then sat down. "And I guess I still want to get it," I said. "I want to hand it to him. I want to put it in his face and let him know I'm more than he thought I was."

Nina closed one eye, shook her head. "He will never do that Ellie. He will never be impressed. He's only impressed by himself."

We could hear Pandenla in the kitchen, pushing plates.

"When it first happened, when he first left me, I honestly thought I was going to die. I wanted to."

"You ...?"

"Yeah." She looked at me, her face scrunched up small. "But you know what I decided?"

"What?"

She nodded her head. "I wasn't going to let him do that to me."

I didn't say anything.

"Be careful in Tibet, Ellie. You haven't trekked before. It's harder than you think."

Friday, August 29, 1 a.m.
Pokhara

I slept for a while, but the mosquito coil burned down and the bugs came in. I might as well write.

I wish I wasn't leaving. Almost every minute, I think of another question I want to ask Nina. We are the only two people I know who have been in Calvin's bloody chamber.

But Nina thinks I should leave soon if I'm going. She looked at the maps Calvin and the Australian couple gave me. "I think you should leave four days to get to Lhotse," she said. "You don't know what kind of transport they've got over there."

A day and a half now of unwrapping our experiences. It reminds me of how it was when my father left; my mother and I sitting at the kitchen table while she wept, both of us in disbelief.

I am remembering something she said, just before I went upstairs. "Why did he tell those stories about teacher and student?" I asked. "The Milarepa story? I thought he was telling us something. I thought that meant I was supposed to stay with it; I was going to learn."

Nina looked at me solemnly. "You have learned," she said.

"What? Not to trust?" My voice cracked then. "I don't understand why he couldn't love me."

She raised her head. "Love yourself, Ellie," she said.

11 a.m.

I can't believe I just made a friend I will have to leave.

But I can't leave Cass stranded in Lhotse.

Today, Nina came up to my room and we spread everything out on the bed while Nina stood with a checklist in her hand and I held things up as she called them out: Tent, sleeping bag, canned food, vitamins.

She put her hand on my sleeping bag. "I'm not crazy about *this*," she said. "It feels pretty thin."

"How much am I going to be using it? One night?"

"It gets pretty cold in the mountains at night," she said. "Sweat all day and freeze all night." She shook her head. "Well I guess it's too late now. Do you have wool? You need wool. You know about altitude sickness, right? Do you have Diamox?" I showed it to her, but she gave me more. "And water," she said. "You need a LOT of water. You've got iodine to purify it, right?" I showed her and she nodded. "It would be good if you had something antibiotic."

"Oh. Tommy never mentioned that."

"I've got some."

She looked at my stuff, thinking.

"Food," she said decisively.

"I can't bring *food*."

She looked at me. "You get into the mountains and you don't know what you're going to find ... or not find. You need to bring stuff you can just eat ... or cook easily: ramen noodles, bread ... and you need more canned stuff. I've got stuff in the kitchen."

She came back with it and dumped it on the bed. My pack weighs a ton now.

She put her arm on my shoulder. "Well I guess you'll be okay." She tightened it. "If something happens to you, I will have to go kill Calvin myself."

I think we both didn't want to admit we were separating.

"My friend Cass told me that every mountain in the Himalayas has its own god or goddess," I said. "Is that what the Nepalis believe?"

"That's what they say," said Nina.

"So you have to make sure you don't offend them?"

"You don't offend people, Ellie," she said.

Monday, September 1, 2 p.m.
Lhotse, Tibet

Tibet!

I did it.

By myself.

The town of Lhotse has one dirt road down the middle of it. Shacks line one side of it. Everything is dust. There is a kind of general store here where you can buy batteries that leak and Chinese candy. I have been buying the ones called White Rabbits—they taste like vanilla tootsie rolls, but chalkier—a cross between candy and Kaopectate.

The town is sunk in a kind of bowl with low, dust-colored mountains all around us. Farther out, higher, white-topped mountains dip and rise—ocean waves stopped mid-motion. On the way here, pyramids of sandy soil and land in all directions with nothing growing on it. I have never been in a place that looked so much like the moon.

The Tibetans wear faded Mao jackets or traditional chubas and are very happy to see Westerners. The Chinese in this town are all soldiers in khaki uniforms with curiously delicate white shoes, and they despise us. Yesterday a khampa passed me on the road. Khampas are the wild men of Tibet: long hair, lots of oversized coral jewelry. He was carrying a giant dried sheep leg and held it out to me as if to shake hands with it. We both laughed.

At dawn, loudspeakers on the road blare martial music. The work starts: Tibetans on flatbed trucks are driven out of town somewhere. Some are in actual rags; they still seem genuinely happy. I saw one using a cement block as a pillow and grinning. I think they do road work. The trucks come back to town in the late afternoon, and they are covered with yellow dust.

There is one hotel made of concrete: cement block bathrooms, hard beds, a giant concrete fountain shaped like a daisy in the courtyard that does not work. No other guests.

Nina was right about food: there are no restaurants, even at the so-called hotel. It was good she sent that bread and the tuna with me. I'm eating it. But that means I'm eating up my trekking food.

Wednesday, September 3, 9 a.m.
Lhotse

I can't believe how different it is here from Pokhara. Pokhara was lush; here it is like the surface of the moon.

A town like the Old West; dirt roads, wood shacks.

And I'm freaking out.

Cass isn't here.

It's been two days.

I was so happy. I got here by myself. We were going to be together. Fuck. Where is she?

2 p.m.

I am upset because Cass isn't here, but I need to remember something: coming here, I was happy.

A fairly epic journey. The town just across the Nepali-Tibetan border, Zhangmu, is basically a truck stop. All mud, that place: it's laid out on the side of a slope that goes straight up. Crawling with Chinese soldiers in their khaki uniforms and white cloth shoes. I showed my visa, one Chinese soldier took a half-hearted look through my backpack, and that was it ... so I guess I won't have to worry about carrying the phurbu back out.

Twenty or so Westerners sleeping in a Tibetan "hotel," which was basically a room full of camp beds with an outhouse outside, and a very friendly Tibetan couple running the place. Not like Nepal, where people travel in groups that keep to themselves. All the Westerners were together in one big room. It was actually fun.

Everyone wanted to go to Lhasa, but there were no rides. People were talking about getting a ride on the back of a pickup truck, but most of the Tibetan drivers didn't want to take anyone. Finally, a Hino bus showed up. That's when the fun started.

We all banded together to convince the driver, a laughing, skinny Tibetan guy in a beret, that he should take us to Lhasa. A circus, I kept thinking: a whining Swedish woman, an Australian hippie mom with a very unhappy four-year-old, a guy named Oud, a drop out from the 1960s, dressed in paisley elephant pants and an embroidered cotton Indian shirt who kept saying "Oh, MAN."

We finally struck a bargain with the bus driver and chugged up the road—straight up. Jungle-y forest all around us and then all of a sudden we were on the moon. Oud convinced me to give the Tibetan driver a Talking Heads tape for the tape deck. We sailed up the road to David Byrne singing "Road to Nowhere."

I felt like I was in a movie.

Now it's just me. Kind of a let-down; everyone else went on to Lhasa. If I wasn't going on this mission for Calvin, I could have gone with them.

Where is Cass? I can't believe I'm the only Westerner here.

Today I walked for three hours.

I'm trying not to eat too much of the food I brought. Why isn't there a place to fucking eat?

Ridiculous to worry that Eckerman's students would have gotten here before me. I'm the only Westerner here.

4 p.m.

There is a dzong about six kilometers out of town. That is where I am now.

It's a deserted fortress. You can see it from town: a rectangular tower of brick and high walls, on top of a sand hill.

An hour or more of walking to get here. In my head, I talked to everyone I know.

When I first arrived here in Lhotse, I was triumphant. I made it! Now I am wondering what the fuck I am doing here. What an idiot I was, coming here on a crazy mission to get some lost artifact for Calvin.

I think of what I must look like to people from the outside: utterly deluded forlorn girl who treks off to Tibet to please a man who will never love her.

Last night something came to me: hungry ghosts. They appear on the Buddhist wheel of life, which is painted next to the front door of every temple. There is the Buddha realm, the god realm, the human realm, the animal realm. And then there are the hungry ghosts, with narrow throats, large bellies bloated from malnutrition. They are perpetually hungry, but cannot get food down their constricted throats, cannot nourish themselves.

That is what I have made myself into.

Everyone has needs, Ellie. That's what Celeste said to me at one of our sessions. *It's like you're trying not to have them.*

I suppose I have been trying not to have them.

Trying to be nobody is very unhealthy.

10 p.m.

So it turns out I am not the only Westerner staying at the Chinese hotel after all. This afternoon I saw two young men sitting in the courtyard on the edge of that giant daisy-shaped fountain that never spurts any water. One of them had a short beard and was in overalls; the other in jeans. At first, I worried they were Americans—students sent by Eckerman maybe. But then I talked with them.

They are Dutch. Luuk is very handsome with a cleft chin like Sean Connery. Jeroen is the one in overalls; plain, but much kinder.

Lucky I ran into them—they have found a "restaurant"—a Tibetan couple that has set up an eating shack on a side street. We went into the kitchen and pointed at the things we wanted in our stir-fry, then sat outside at a rickety table set up in the dust to wait for the food. Yay. Hot food.

Luuk and Jeroen have traveled from China. The Chinese in Tibet are horrible, they said; soldiers everywhere. They saw Chinese soldiers making a joke out of driving a hairs breadth away from a Tibetan doing full length prostrations on the road. They themselves had to duck when Chinese soldiers started throwing empty beer bottles at them. For fun.

"They are the cats; the Tibetans are the mice," said Luuk.

"What is the word?" said Jeroen.

"Bullies?" I offered.

"Yes, bullies."

We talked about what we were doing here; the Dutch were thinking of approaching Everest from this side, but they aren't going to go, now.

When they asked me why I was here, I told them. I think they were startled. We spread my map over our rickety table and looked at it.

"This map isn't so detailed," said Jeroen.

"It's old," I said.

"Perhaps it is dangerous, this idea? To use an old map? You don't prefer to hike to a lake?"

He's probably right, but I'm here now. I have to go. Tomorrow I will go looking for the trail again.

I asked to see the guestbook in the hotel. I wanted to see if Cass's name was there by chance, or one of Eckerman's people. But the front desk person wouldn't show me. Maybe Eckerman's students have already arrived? Maybe they have the phurbu?

11 p.m.

I am trying not to think about the strangeness. This cement-block room. This cot. The lights won't stay on past seven at night in this "hotel," so I am writing by flashlight. I don't want to be here alone.

Cass.

Please.

Show up.

Thursday, September 4, 4 p.m.
Lhotse

Today when I woke up, I went looking for Luuk and Jeroen, but I couldn't find them anywhere.

Another day alone.

What is there to do but walk? It is beautiful in a way: the mountains rear up like giant walls all around.

About two kilometers down the road, I saw a Tibetan woman doing full-length prostrations along the main road. She wore leather knee pads and a brown apron over her chuba for the dust. Her black hair was in a braid down her back. So hot—how can she stand it? She looked like she was swimming on land. Stand, look straight ahead, crumble to her knees, dive toward the ground, place forehead against the dirt, repeat.

Humility, the queen of virtues.

It made me remember the Dogtooth Buddha. Calvin told us that story when I had already been seeing him several months. A son goes away and asks his mother what she wants him to bring back to her. She says she wants a tooth from the Buddha. He promises to bring it, but then forgets. On his way home, he remembers his promise. He sees a decaying dog, brings her the dog's tooth, tells her that it is the tooth of the Buddha.

She worships it for months and months. When he comes to see her, it's glowing.

I thought I knew what it meant: *just believe.*

I remember what Pema's teacher said: Westerners always want to get there through knowledge. They forget about devotion.

Full length prostrations: that's devotion.

I have been devoted, just to the wrong person.

But maybe it's just a matter of being devoted.

6 p.m.

I have to remember—even if it was kind of stupid to come here, *I'm still here.*

I was reading the Xeroxed Tibet guide Leo gave me—it says that if I trek, I am likely to run into nomads.

Nomads!

They live in large yurts, travel to find forage for their yaks.

Exotic.

9 p.m.

I can't fucking believe this.

Calvin was right about the Chinese. I fucking hate them. Today the man at the front desk told me I am not allowed to stay more than four days. How can that fucking be?

"Why?" I asked.

"Regulation," he said.

I met Luuk and Jeroen coming up the road from the general store. They got the same message. "Well we leave anyway." Luuk shrugged.

I don't know what I'm going to do. I've been waiting three days. Where the fuck is Cass?

10 p.m.

This is a crisis.

I guess I could go to another town and come back, but I don't know if there will be food there. I've already eaten almost half of the trekking food Nina gave me.

Fuck.

I shouldn't have come here.

All I do is make mistakes.

Friday, September 5, 10 a.m.
Lhotse

I'm doing it.

I left a note for Cass at the front desk. I hope they give it to her.

It's been three days.

I told them I needed to stay. I told them I was meeting a friend. They brought a soldier to talk to me.

"Miss!" he kept saying.

I don't want her to come here and look for me, but I don't know what else to do.

I have copied my letter into my notebook in case she does not believe me:

September 6, 1986

Dear Cass,

I have copied this letter to you into my notebook in case they don't give it to you at the front desk.

The Chinese made me leave. They said I could not stay at this hotel anymore, and there is nowhere else to stay.

What happened to you? I waited three days.

I hope you are okay. Everest is a dangerous mountain.

I'll be back in two days.

Wait for me.

Love, Ellie

Friday, 11 a.m.
On The Trail to Ralung

I should not be taking long breaks. But I have to write, or I'll lose it.

Three hours of walking, constantly up.

I am in a desert. A salt landscape: cone-shaped salt hills; salt plains to the horizon. For an hour the path led through the irrigated fields outside of town. How beautiful the trickling sound of the water was.

My heart is pumping—exertion, but also fear. I'm really doing this, alone. With my map drawn on a piece of loose-leaf paper and my complete lack of trekking experience. Three weeks ago, I was typing labels in an office in New York City. My shoulders ache, although I have tightened the belt around my hips as tight as it goes. Away from the irrigation ditches, the only sound is my dry footsteps. The air is cool, but the sun beats down relentlessly with no trees to block it.

My chest hurts. I never did get in shape like Cass told me to.

So far, the path matches the map Calvin gave me. Nine kilometers to the top of the pass, then six down. Calvin drew prayer flags at the top so I would know when I reached the pass; I guess it will be hard to miss. And there's only one trail, so I must be on it. From the pass, I should be able to see Ralung.

What if it's not there?

When I walk, it's hard not to think about what's in my pack and how heavy it is. Maybe Nina was right about the tent, but it weighs a ton. Ten boiled eggs—I got the Tibetan couple at the "restaurant" to boil them for me last night—so there's that on top of the food Nina gave me. A half-gallon of water—Nina said water is important. *Very important*, is what she actually said. I want to just get there, get the phurbu, and come back. Maybe Cass will be there when I get back to Lhotse. We can go to Lhasa, then back to Nepal.

Ellie, stop writing and *walk*.

12 p.m.

The intrepid explorer treks through the Tibetan hinterland ...

The mousy secretary treks through the Tibetan hinterland ...

The idiotic American tourist treks through the Tibetan hinterland ...

It's been two hours. I need to stop.

It is still straight up. My chest hurts. I have to not think about my shoulders.

The scrub on the side of the mountain is something like sagebrush—the kind out in Arizona where my mother lives. Only a few thin trees, but they do cast a whispery shade. When the pack comes off, my whole body loosens. But I will have to put it back on again. It's like carrying a tower on my back; if I bend over, I feel like it will pull me headfirst into the ground.

I don't know how far I've walked. According to the book, the average walking pace is six kilometers per hour, but this is sixty degrees up ... so maybe two miles? On the map, the pass is labeled 10,000 feet. I'm thinking of what the mountaineering book says: if you start getting altitude sickness, you need to descend. Best would be to force myself to get to the pass, then just go down the other side and get to Ralung in one day. If I can make it the eight kilometers, my feet will hurt going down, but I'll get there.

I can't wait to stop walking.

Even the exertion hasn't stopped me thinking. For the past God-knows-how-long, talking to Calvin in my head. Handing him the phurbu and seeing the look on his face. And then going over those conversations with Nina. *I did learn*, she said. Then to Calvin again: *did you ever have good intentions toward me.*

What kind of person are you ...

You won't get away with it.

But he will. He has.

Transcendence. That's what I was going for, right? *Consciousness that can survive even in a slaughterhouse.*

Jesus. Look at me.

2 p.m.

Two more hours of walking. It's been rough: at least a 60-degree angle up.

At least there are switchbacks, but of course that makes it longer. My shoulders are killing me.

The mountains rise all around. Everywhere I look, an ocean of land-waves.

Not one person since I started.

I think I might actually make it to Ralung today. I keep picturing myself handing Calvin the phurbu. He will do what he always does. Open his eyes wide. "Ho-*ho*!"

Something like that.

3 p.m.

Nina told me it wasn't a good idea to go alone. So did that guy Conrad. I had the picture of myself handing the phurbu to Calvin in front of his entourage, and I just walked toward it.

I'm thinking of my talk with Nina. I told her I that I didn't understand all those stories about sacrifice, believing in the teacher, if you weren't supposed to do that. "Like Milarepa," I said. "His teacher tortured him, and then at the end, it was all praises."

"I think those stories are aspirational," she said.

She was a lot smarter than me.

If it is just something to aspire to, why even tell the stories?

"Oh, so you wrote him 'you' letters, too," she said later.

You-letters. My head is a you-letter.

4 p.m.

I made it to the pass. Freezing but I made it. The landscape unfurls all around, a carpet of earth. The air is blue. The land rising all around, dull colors: brown, green, brown. The prayer flags flap in the wind—blue, green, yellow, red squares of cloth—from a crazy network of ropes—telephone lines gone wild. They are the sign that people have been here; you need that in a place like this. I took a picture of myself in that ugly green down coat; propped the camera up on a few rocks. It took a while and now my hands are freezing.

I don't see Ralung. That kind of freaks me out. I see the track at least. It goes down straight, dark brown, into the valley, then gets lighter and turns a corner between two peaks.

I hope it goes there. I hope I see someone. Anyone ... except maybe a Chinese soldier ...

7 p.m.

Jesus fucking God I made it. My legs are wood. My shoulders want to come *off*.

The town of Ralung is abandoned; grassy and silent. There is part of a road, and three or four abandoned buildings of white stone. The side of a mountain stretches up behind the town, dark brown. I think I can see a pile of rubble up there. According to Calvin's map, it's where the monastery is supposed to be.

Not good.

When I got here, I walked along the road and shouted. A lot.

Nobody.

I still had some light to pitch my tent.

I'm pretty sure this is right: there is the flat rock right in the middle of town; the stream right next to it.

I don't like this.

The phurbu is probably not here, which really sucks.

I hope I can walk tomorrow. I want to go right back.

8 p.m.

If Cass were here, it would be completely different. It would be an adventure.

Whatever. I'll leave tomorrow.

9 p.m.

Once the sun went down it was FUCKING FREEZING. I'm wearing practically every item of clothing I brought.

10 p.m.

Here is something I should know about myself: I am the kind of person who will do a thing like this.

I will go to the 42nd Street Library to read about sorcerers, and then I will come to a place near the end of the earth to look for something that I do not even want for myself.

10:30 p.m.

Nina was right about the tent; it's a good thing I have it.

11 p.m.

All these empty houses. I wonder what happened here. If there was a massacre, would I see bodies?

11:40 p.m.

It just occurred to me that this might be a place I am not supposed to be. What if it is being patrolled by Chinese soldiers?

They shoot Tibetans who try to cross the border.

11:45 p.m.

I've noticed something: I'm living in the moment.

Saturday, September 6, 9 a.m.
On The Trail to Ralung

My legs hurt seriously. Breakfast was a 151 Chinese army biscuit and water. They aren't so bad—basically shortbread.

Better in the morning. Beautiful here: the ground is level and grassy—there must be water somewhere—aching blue sky, and the mountains rise on all sides, an ocean frozen in time and solidified.

I walked around. Things are actually in quite a state of ruin: grass poking through cement block foundations; dark wood sagging houses.

It's still weird.

I wonder when it happened; how long after Calvin's teacher left. Quiet.

But I don't want to stay here. I need to look for the phurbu, then go.

11 a.m.

Un-fucking-believable: I have it. It was exactly where Calvin's map said it would be—so easy it was funny. I was right that the rubble on the mountainside was the monastery—pretty clear after I got there and saw part of a wall painted with a giant fresco of a goddess.

I got there around ten and started looking around. I followed the map—the phurbu was supposed to be in a metal box buried under the altar. It took me awhile to figure out where the altar might be. There was a long piece of metal and I used that to dig. At first, I was worried I didn't have the right place, but the map said it was three feet down, in a metal box. I kept sticking the piece of metal into the ground there and I finally hit something metallic.

299

I felt bad digging around in a holy place. More and more I'm thinking the monastery must have been destroyed by Red Guards during the Cultural Revolution. Terrible.

It only took about an hour. I don't know why the ground was so soft, but it was. I didn't realize it would be that big; the tin box was about three feet long, and when I opened it, there it was—the phurbu Calvin has been talking about for all these years.

It's black, about sixteen inches long. I thought it would be smaller—it's going to be hard to fit it in my pack. I have been looking at it off and on—there are four small faces on top facing in all the directions, all crowned. Then it slopes down to what looks like a long dart. Definitely scary looking—the faces all have fangs.

According to him, it's magic.

According to him, everything's magic.

So it's done.

I want to go back.

I want to get out of here.

I told Cass overnight. I'm going back—today.

1 p.m.

Walking for two hours. I can't wait to get back: the Chinese hotel I complained about seems luxurious now. A real bed! And they've got to let me stay there the extra night ... please.

It's weird when it's just you, your body and your breath. My thoughts still go while I walk, but it's less.

Ten hours of walking between me and that bed.

C'mon Ellie.

1:30 p.m.

Nomads! Just like that guide said! The road turned a corner and there they were. They have round tents of white canvas, the circumference of the roof decorated with blue interlocking diamond shapes. There were a few yaks—they put embroidered red harnesses on them and bells. I didn't see them yesterday—I guess they moved in overnight?

It made me so happy.

2 p.m.

Jesus fuck I FUCKING HATE dogs, but I FUCKING HATE TIBETAN MASTIFF DOGS the most. First of all, they are HUGE. Second of all, they come after you even if you are just walking along the path. Why do they have those dogs? I remember Conrad and Giselle laughing about them.

Fuck.

The nomad camp was far away, but the dog followed me anyway. I yelled at it, but it wouldn't go away. I threw a stone at it—not smart.

It lunged at me and then I felt the pain. I don't know which was worse: the fear or the pain.

I think I was screaming. I ran. I can't believe I ran *uphill* with my pack on. You would think one of the nomads would have heard me and stopped their dog.

Fucking dogs.

I've been here for a while now. The adrenalin just grips you. I really had to force myself to breathe more slowly.

Now I feel the bite. Fuck.

I ran far, even with the pack on. Now I'm halfway up the mountain, toward the pass. It stopped chasing me.

The bite is deep. And it hurts like hell.

2:30 p.m.

I looked at my foot. It's throbbing but it will stop.

My ankle is maybe a worse problem. Running uphill with the pack wasn't the greatest idea. I can't put weight on it.

There is not going to be any more walking today.

This is fucked.

Stupid to come here alone.

The ankle is swelling. I looked all through the pack for the antibiotic Nina gave me to put it on the bite. It's not fucking here.

3 p.m.

Headache, now. I remember how they described it in that movie about climbing Everest: like a nail being hammered into your head. The sharp pointed tip is drilling into the side of my skull.

This is so ridiculous.

The bite is really hurting. I washed it, but it's pulsing. AND I CAN'T FUCKING FIND THE IODINE EITHER so I have nothing to disinfect it. I packed it. I know I did.

Fuck.

I tried to stand. Dizzy, and I can't put weight on the leg. I guess I am not going to get to Lhotse today. Thank you Nina for the tent.

There is no way to reach anybody. There is no way to get help.

I was thinking maybe I could signal the nomads, but they're a long way away.

At least I stayed on the path.

Ha ha. Now I'm *wishing* Eckerman's people would come. Who else is going to come here?

A long shot.

You are fucking ridiculous Ellie.

An assembly line. What an idiot I am.

3:30 p.m.

"That's how it's going to be, folks," said Tommy, after we watched that first movie about Everest. "At this altitude, you will have the brain of a reptile."

4 p.m.

I am halfway to the pass. A green fuzz of grass at some points in the slope downwards, but mostly brown, then a ring of white-capped mountains circling the horizon. Down below, I can see the nomad tents, white with blue interlocking diamond patterns. The sky is ridiculously blue.

I am in a place. I am breathing. I am alive.

Calm down, Ellie. You can survive this.

4:05 p.m.

Funny that Cass is not here. She would love this; the challenge.
  I hope she is okay.
  I hope *I* am okay.

4:20 p.m.

Still here. I didn't want to keep living, but I don't want to die.
  It's so anonymous.

4:25 p.m.

Breathe.

4:50 p.m.

I keep talking to people in my head. Celeste, my mother, Cass,
Pema:
  I was prepared. It only takes one little thing to go wrong.

5 p.m.

Breathe, Ellie.
  Lie down, and just be.
  I'm trying to calm myself.

5:30 p.m.

I keep thinking of that sign at the Pilgrim's Bookstore in
Kathmandu:
  Every journey is in some sense a pilgrimage.
  I think it's true.
  I think I have been on a pilgrimage.
  Even from the beginning, when I started going to the 42nd Street
Library.

Looking for something.

I am looking at the mountains and I think I know what it was:
I was looking for my father.

It was Cass who told me about the opening. We were still at school, then.

"Is your father named Max Adkins?" she asked. Then she showed me the flyer:

Max Adkins: Where the Meanings Are.

My first thought: So he made it. My second thought: how pleased with himself he must be. My third thought: he doesn't deserve it.

After that, I knew I would go. I would figure out a time when the gallery would most likely be deserted. A weekday, just after it opened.

A Thursday. Trying to pay attention to outside things as I went down there: a woman wearing purple cloth shoes. A sign that simply said *Courage*. A manhole cover with plastic orange netting around it.

Breath getting short as I got closer. But for nothing: when I arrived, it was only a young woman sitting at a white counter, reading. Galleries are always as clean as hotel bathrooms. Everything white; blond wood floors, silence, awe.

The first surprise was the paintings. They were figurative.

That hit me right away when I stepped into the room. Away from me, Max had made a 180-degree turn.

And I didn't know why.

He only had one room in the gallery. On one wall there was a canvas with a woman seated on a couch staring at the painter; I guessed that was his new girlfriend. But it was impossible not to go first to the centerpiece: a huge canvas on the back wall with nothing else around it.

The house in Laurel. I walked right up to it, owning it: *mine.*
Every detail: The conical turret on the right side; the blue wood shingles; the white picket fence around the front; the rhododendrons that had never done well on the side.

Everything: my father's studio with its tiny window in the door; the playground in the back with the lilac bushes, the crooked merry-go-round.

In the painting, my parents stood off to the side, a kind of American Gothic.

And then there was me. I was all over the painting. At the side of the house; a face in a window; a figure at the back. In all of them, I was doing the same thing: destroying. In one corner, with an axe, chopping at a window sill; at another pouring gasoline onto a wall.

Broken Home—the name of the painting. And then one of those paragraphs that you always find in galleries. Art-talk, my father called it.

Max Adkins, formerly an abstract artist, has turned to figurative painting to illuminate the ambiguities that exist within our personal histories.

Max was making it all my fault.

Not possible. Not allowed.

Twisting it.

We tell each other stories in order to live.

It wasn't long after that I went to the East West Bookstore and saw Calvin's sign.

Maybe it was an accident. Maybe I was looking for Max and ran into Calvin.

Maybe that is how I've ended up on this mountain.

The trickster is going to show you who you really are.

6 p.m.

There is food, but I'm not hungry. I looked at how much water I have. I brought enough for a day. That was how long I thought it was going to be. *Keep hydrated,* said Nina.

7 p.m.

I put up the tent. It took forever—tents are designed to be put up by two people and I couldn't stand for very long, but I was determined. It wasn't easy crawling around but it's a good tent and I was able to string the poles together sitting down, so I only had to stand on one leg to stretch the ropes.

The headache is worse, but I took aspirin. At least I remembered that.

I'm nauseous, but I'm going to try eating one of the hard-boiled eggs for the water in it. I don't think not eating is the best idea.

I've risked my life for an asshole.

8 p.m.

How funny; now there is nothing to do because I can't walk.

I decided to take out the phurbu and look at it.

Frightening. Black and dull. The main face is baring its fangs. It is wearing a crown made of skulls. Not a normal blade: more like three blades that intersect in the middle and come to a point.

It's big: almost as big as a shoebox.

I have risked my life for this.

You have to rescue yourself, said Nina. I have not done that, have I?

9 p.m.

So here I am in the tent, writing by flashlight. I just looked at the mountaineering guide again.

I guess I probably have altitude sickness on top of the bite.

It says that if the symptoms get worse, you have to go down. I don't see how I can do that unless I crawl.

And that means leaving everything behind: my pack, the phurbu. After all this.

10 p.m.

This is bad.

I looked at my leg again. There are blisters around the bite.

I looked at the "First Aid" section of the mountaineering book.

Under "dog bites" it listed symptoms: blisters, the first sign of gangrene.

10:30 p.m.

I need to go down. Tomorrow. Even if I can't walk, I have to go down.
  I need water.
  If it is altitude sickness I need to go down.
  If it is gangrene I need a doctor.
  I could go toward the nomads but the dog might kill me.
  Fuck.

11 p.m.

Those Victoria Holt books I read when I was twelve or thirteen. At the last minute, the woman is always rescued by the man who really loves her.
  If it's love, in the end, you will know.
  If he saw me suffer enough, he would come for me.
  No one is coming.

12 a.m.

Rest. Why did Nina say I needed food?
  I don't need that.
  So tired.

3 a.m.

It's 3 a.m. There's light outside, but the cold is unreal. It's only fucking September! I looked at my leg.
  Worse.

3:30 a.m.

Gangrene. That means losing the leg.
  Even if I get to Lhotse, is there a doctor there?
  Don't panic Ellie. I shouldn't panic. That doesn't help.

Sunday, September 7, 10 a.m.
On The Trail to Ralung

Well, I slept a little. I feel a bit better now.

I can't eat, but I drank some water. According to the mountaineering guide, that's the most important thing.

Maybe I'll heal. I don't see how crawling is going to help anyway.

And what about the phurbu? Am I just going to leave it after all this?

12 p.m.

I think I am in bad shape. I feel asleep for a while.

Terrible dreams. The goddess of this mountain came down to me. She rode across the sky, white-faced, her robe ending in elegant curlicues. She said her name: Tsering Ma. Of the Five Sisters.

"We have been here since before the Earth knew its name," she said.

White swirls came out of her mouth.

2 p.m.

At least I slept. Maybe I'm getting better? But there is another blister around the dog bite.

I looked at the symptoms again

Blistering around the wound

Redness, swelling and pain around the wound

Oozing from the wound.

I have all of them. And the headache too.

2:30 p.m.

I guess I have a fever. I have that feeling and I can't stop shivering.
My head feels like it's made of iron.

In one of the survival stories Cass talked about, a man actually crawled down Everest.

3 p.m.

The mountain goddess came again—Tsering Ma. Naked, with skin the color of dried blood. She was walking along the top of the mountain as high as a New York skyscraper.

Then she flew down to talk to me. She was naked so I tried to be polite and just look at her face.

"I shouldn't have done this," I said. "Shouldn't have come here."

She didn't answer. She gazed at the sky. "What did you think tantra was, anyway?" she asked.

She was so real. That's what scares me.

I told her I didn't want to die. I asked her to save me.

"A little late," she said. I cried a little. "You think this is hard? When I was in the charnel grounds, bones were everywhere. Flesh fluttered in the breeze like flags."

She stood up, took a step backward. She started to dance. Her knees bent and her calves shot up behind her thighs, faster and faster. It looked like Irish step dancing, but mechanical, batteries that couldn't be stopped.

You think this is bad? She kept repeating it. *You think this is bad? You think this is bad?*

Maybe I'm just dreaming really vividly because of the fever?

I should try to get to Lhotse. If I can't walk, I should crawl.
Seriously.

8 p.m.

Another dream or hallucination; I don't know which.

Cass came, but she did not look like Cass: green body, skirt of tiny silver skull heads, wild, blue snaky hair, but I knew it was her. She told me I was going to be alright. I said I was sorry I had left without her, and I hoped she was alright too.

But then she turned into the goddess. A naked body nine feet tall, shiny black skin. Around the head, where the face would be, a cloud of flies.

The worst, though was her face: flayed. I wanted to throw up.

She sniffed. "I smell your fear," she laughed. "Stinky. Look at me," she said. I did. "I know what you want," she said. "You want magic. You want something better than reality."

I was weeping.

"Why should you have something better than reality?" she screamed. "Why do you deserve that?"

Monday, September 8, 11 a.m.
On The Trail to Ralung

Dear Notebook, you may be the last person I talk to.

I am crawling to Lhotse.

It came to me: just like the man Cass told me about who crawled down Everest.

Save yourself.

I did it. I set my eyes on one rock. I pulled myself, stopped, kept going.

You see everything this way. The ground is a mountain range.

The leg throbs but I don't care. I'm going.

When I got here, I took a break.

Looked at my watch: one hour.

Dying is being wiped away.

12 p.m.

A ladybug. They have them here. It makes its way along the ground. Waddles.

I rolled over on my back to look at the sky.

Everything so beautiful.

Never get rid of the ego.

...

I

...

Please.

September 16, 1986

Dear Cass ... Thank you for not dying. I couldn't survive that.

I wrote you so many letters in my head when I was on the mountain. I couldn't believe you didn't show up to Lhotse. I waited, then they told me at the Chinese hotel that I had to leave the hotel, so I left. I made the trek. I hate myself for that.

I guess now you know all about Nina and her connection to me.

Nina saved my life. When the guy from Tommy's team came for all the stuff and Nina heard what happened to you on Everest, she knew you weren't coming to meet me. She hired a car to take her to the border, then got a truck driver to take her to Lhotse.

I was hallucinating. I thought I saw the mountain goddess.

I'm ashamed to tell you the next part. When Nina found me, I wanted to go back for Calvin's phurbu.

"It's your leg or that stupid phurbu, Ellie," she said. So much was a daze, but I do remember that.

I had the most horrible dreams when I was on that mountain.

At least I chose my leg.

I'm lucky. Nina knows the mountains. In Lhotse, she hired some Tibetans to carry me back in case I couldn't walk when she found me. Otherwise, I wouldn't have made it.

Here's the funny part: Remember I told you about that rival group that might also be looking for the phurbu? They came. They were the ones who hired the car that was waiting at Lhotse, and that was the car that took me to Kathmandu and saved my life. Nina traded with them: she told the group who had hired the car where my tent was, so they could go get the phurbu.

The doctors told me it was a matter of hours when it came to my leg.

So you almost died too—edema of the lungs. I can just imagine Tommy's panic when you started wheezing. I guess he really does know what he's doing, though. He got you the helicopter right away.

My Cass. I'm so glad you're okay.

I'm sorry you're back in New York. This trip has been a big disappointment for you. I know how much you wanted to be part of what Tommy was doing. And I know you wanted to come to Tibet.

I'm in Pokhara now, with Nina. After three days in the hospital, the doctors said I was going to make it, and she took me. She said the only thing more dangerous than being up on the mountain was being in that hospital. It *was* primitive compared to hospitals in the States, but they saved the leg. Today I walked ten steps.

You asked what I'm going to do. I don't know.

I might travel—Nina is thinking of taking some time off and going with me. I might sign up for a retreat at Zhiba. I might just stay in Kathmandu for a while and see what comes up. Whatever I do, it won't be coming right back to my life in New York. I'm away, now. Away is good. You were right. I was stuck in my life. I needed to do things.

December 12, 1986

Mom,

I know you are expecting a call from me soon. "Every two weeks," you admonished me in Pokhara, and I've always kept my promise, wherever I am. This time, I decided to write, though. There are things I need to say from a distance.

Growing up, I was always so different from you. You were the one who everyone knew—laughing in the supermarket, exclaiming at funny coincidences. And me—what was it you used to say about me? *Mooning.*

I've had a lot of time to think. In the end, we aren't so different, are we? We both loved someone who didn't love us back.

Maybe you don't remember: it was a month or so after Dad left. Your friend Myra came over. She had just gotten a divorce, too. I was relieved when she came: an adult to take over from me. The two of you must have spent a week sitting at the kitchen table all day, drinking Gallo wine out of juice glasses and talking.

You went over the mistakes you'd made in your marriages: thinking someone would change just because they said they would; believing in the person time and time again, even after they betrayed you. After a while you had slogans: *It's what you do, not what you say. Three strikes you're out.* You and Myra let me sit with you sometimes, and I remember what I thought: that these were things to remember. I was going to be grounded, realistic. I wasn't going to let anyone treat me the way Dad treated you.

But it turns out that, more than I wanted to be strong and take care of myself, I wanted the fairytale. I met Calvin and I thought he could turn me into more than I was, and I wanted that badly. I wanted it more than anything else.

The worst thing was seeing you shatter. When Dad left, you sobbed so hard I thought you were going to stop breathing. Your face would get red and crumple and then it would start—a storm I couldn't stop. Maybe I shouldn't have written that letter to Dad. It made me mad, the things he did to you. But maybe I should have stayed out of it—I don't know.

One of the principles of Buddhism is nonattachment. You're not supposed to cling to things—possessions, people, even ideas. But when I was on that mountain, I talked to you. I asked you to come for me, which was ridiculous. You didn't even know where I was.

And then, those weeks when I was healing at Nina's place in Pokhara, you came. Cass had called you. I didn't even know you were coming, and then there you were, my mother.

You were yourself again: busy, laughing. Once I got better, you wanted to do things. Once you saw the poverty, you wanted to do something about it. And you were so proud of yourself because when Seth called wanting to get in touch with me, you told him he wasn't good enough for me.

You were the mother I remembered.

It's been three months: India, then Thailand, and I've had a lot of time to think. I'm starting to realize: you've moved on from those first days when Dad left us, but I'm still there. Still there, seeing you fall apart in front of me. Still trying to hold the pieces of you together with my hands. Maybe that's what love really is—what happens to the other person also happens to you.

I was mad at you when you moved away with Travis—I was *really* mad. I didn't know why you left me. I didn't think it was fair. I guess I understand now, though, how a person might want to get away from herself, because that is what I'm doing now.

A week ago, I was on a train from Varanasi to Delhi. I was in a berth with an Indian family. The father spoke English and we compared the price of eggs in every single place either of us had been. When we stopped at a station, hundreds of arms reached out of the train windows to buy little clay cups of milk tea sold by the chai-wallahs. When people were finished drinking, they threw their tiny cups against the tracks and they broke with a very pleasant sound.

I was happy.

Well, I'll call you from Bangkok.

Love, Ellie

March 8, 1987

Dear Calvin,

In the third world, it is the donkeys who suffer the most.

In Jaipur, in India, they load up the donkeys: burlap sacks over their backs, a pocket on either side, and each pocket is loaded with piles of bricks. The donkeys stagger down the street. Terrible to see.

And here in Lombok, the donkeys pull small carriages, animal-powered tuk-tuks, loaded with far too many people. Yesterday, I saw a donkey sliding on its hooves downhill on a paved road, the carriage twisting around it and pulling it down behind it.

Now I am in a beach hut in Lombok with dozens of other Western backpackers. We sit with our feet on the railing of the cabin looking out on a blue-perfect sea, drawl out the names of the places we've been.

It has been almost one year since I got your letter with the prepaid COD envelope. I have carried that envelope with me to so many places: to Jaipur and Udaipur and Srinigar and Dharamsala in India; to Bangkok and Koh Phan Gan; to Bali and now Lombok. I have tried many times to write back to you, but then I have had to stop. Now maybe I am ready.

By now you know: Eckerman has the phurbu.

That is probably all you care about, but I want to tell you.

I want to tell you that Nina saved me. Coming back from Ralung, I was bitten by a nomad's dog. I was on the way to gangrene. I would have died on that mountain, trying to get you the thing you wanted.

But then Nina came. I still wanted to go back to get it for you. I remember being on the ground and looking up at her. "It's that phurbu or your leg, Ellie," she said. What did you tell us? *The Buddha is awake.* Pain wakes you up. I think that dog bite was a gift.

Here is what Nina said to me about Eckerman getting the phurbu instead of you: *He can think of it as an opportunity.*

So many letters I never sent to you. When I was in Kathmandu, I sat on the ghats, watching the agony of a water buffalo that just wanted a drink in the hot sun. And here is what I wrote: that when I address myself to you, it is a form of prayer.

Almost a year, and I still write to you in my head. I make beauty out of what I see because you have always made me want to give the best of myself to you. It has occurred to me lately: maybe that was really what I fell in love with—what you brought out in me.

Every morning when I wake up now, I time how long it takes before I start thinking of you. In the beginning, a nanosecond. Now it is up to five minutes, and the other day I realized I hadn't thought of you until I was eating breakfast.

I keep thinking about what you said: *The trickster is going to show you who you really are.*

It did work that way. I saw what I am: seething. A fire that won't go out.

Before I came here, I went to Borobodur. I looked at the statue of a bodhisattva with a tiny Buddha on its forehead and remembered. You showed us a slide of the tiny buddha at the top of the bodhisattva's head. You said the Buddha is what the bodhisattva is thinking about.

All this time I have been doing the same, meditating on my teacher.

Just yesterday, I understood what that meant:

Really I have been teaching myself all along.

May 14, 1987

Dear Max,

Sometimes we need to go far away to see things clearly. I am now about 15,000 kilometers away from home: the island of Lombok. A sandy paradise with a coral reef and a beach where European backpacker women go topless; we sleep in wood-platformed tents on cots, get up in the morning and saunter over to the outdoor pavilion to drink coconut juice and eat fresh papaya for breakfast, all for pennies a night.

I have met a lot of people in my travels. Some are on summer vacations, some have taken a year off. A few of them are never going home again. One I met calls himself Newfy, a thin, leathery-skinned guy with a ponytail whose pack was smaller than anyone else's. I did not like him, but I found him fascinating. He has been traveling for eight years. He is never going home, probably. It's as if he's found himself in lostness.

From this far away, perhaps it is possible to see home clearly. What it is supposed to be, anyway. The place that will always be yours. Here is what Mom said about home: it's the place where people love you. I know what you would say about that: sentimental.

Three years have gone by since we last spoke to each other. I have been so angry at you. So angry I couldn't find any words.

Here is what I want to say to you, Max: when you don't know who you are, it is difficult to be.

I have been thinking of the painting you made; the one of our house in Laurel. The house and the way you painted it, faithfully, with the white picket fence, the blue wood shingles, the rhododendrons, the conical turret on the right side. The real Laurel; the Laurel that will always be mine.

318

You did not invite me to the gallery, but I went anyway. Then I saw the painting.

Here is what I want to say.

You leaving was impossible.

It was impossible, but somehow I endured it. I went into your studio, fingered things, remembered.

But there was something more impossible than your leaving. That was when I went to your opening, the opening I was not invited to, and I saw you had made a painting in which I was the one who destroyed everything, burnt everything down. *Me*, killing everything.

It was like the moment when Sleeping Beauty pricks her finger. Everything fell asleep. I couldn't feel myself anymore.

When you went to California, when I heard from Mom about the things you did, I told myself that you were wrong and I would not let you get away with it. I hated you. Hating you was the way to hold on to you. I was so sure that when I confronted you, it would all be untrue.

Here is something I want you to know: Ever since you cut me off, I have had the same dream, every few months or so. In this dream, I am in your studio with you. You are painting and telling me a story and I am lying on the floor listening as I used to do. And then we begin to rise. You are still talking to me although I no longer understand what you are saying. And we are both floating in golden light.

I have thought about that. I kept asking myself what the light meant. One day I was looking through a book of Renaissance paintings and I looked at the light coming out of the halos and I realized. There is golden light in that dream because you are holy to me. I was a little girl and I was not happy but I had you.

But maybe that is just what I thought, and not what was.

Now I have traveled and traveled and traveled and I am here on the other side of the world and I write because I have something to tell you, and here is what it is:

The only reason I ever hated you was because I loved you so much, Max.

Do you remember the day when I was eight? I had gotten in trouble for something at school, unfairly. I had been crying, and you just looked at me. "Ellie is soulful," you said. I remember how I felt: I was carrying something very precious inside of me. I did not know how it got there, but it must be there.

Mom never described me as soulful. She said I was "sensitive," and it was never a good thing. She hissed it at me: *so sensitive.*

But you left. And you didn't just leave: you tore up the path I might have walked on to get back to where we were.

Here is what I think: What we can't have, we worship. That is a way to have it, even if we can't really have it. We look at it, hold it in our gaze, and then it is as if we have it, because we think about it all the time.

Maybe what's sacred to us is our wish.

But you can mistake what you want for what is. Ever since you left, I've wanted it to be the way it was when it was you and I in your studio together. I wanted to lie there and listen to the sound of your brushstrokes and wonder over the things you said to me. A happiness I can't describe. Golden air.

When I lost you, I found myself with nothing. Then I met my teacher, Calvin. One day in class someone asked him what religion was for, and he said, "Religion is for when you have nothing else." Then he told us the story of the Buddha's son.

The Buddha's son, Rahula, was born right before his father, Siddhartha, left the family home forever. Maybe you know the story—Prince Siddhartha had a perfect life—a palace, a wife, a son—but then he discovered that he wasn't living in the real world. The real world was suffering. The real world was death. He couldn't accept it and he left. He went on a quest and finally he discovered the secret of rising above this fact. He became enlightened. He became the Buddha. He had disciples and taught vast multitudes of people. He wandered and begged for his food and taught. And one day, late in his life, he returned to his own palace with his begging bowl. His son, Rahula, met him at the door and asked him for his inheritance.

And what did the Buddha do? He held out his begging bowl. That is what you gave me, Max. The begging bowl.

Thank you. Thank you for the opportunity.

June 29, 1987

Dear Pema,

Sometimes I think the luckiest day of my life was when I met you. It's a funny thing how traveling is the best thing I have ever done, but there is also so much tedium. When I come to a new city, I am always full of the expectations I have gotten from the guide-book, but I also think about what is waiting for me at the American Express office. I know that there will always be a letter from you.

The last one was so very helpful.

I think about you so often. It has come to me, this year, what it was the Buddha offered.

Freedom.

In my travels, I have met so many Westerners. Some are away for a short vacation; others, like me, have been going for a year or so. Then there are the diehards, the one or two who never stop.

What you do is ridiculous, Pema. 10,000 full length prostrations. Sitting in meditation for hours. Isolation. All that to save yourself so you can save the world.

But of all the people I've met this year—those who have climbed Kilimanjaro, gone diving with the Bahau people in the Philippines, taken steamers to islands where they are the only Westerners— you are the one who is the bravest. You have made an offering of your life.

I have been gone one year in Asia. On the island of Sumba, it is the monsoons again. Where I stand, a wood farmhouse, surrounded by fields that glisten in the wet. Off to the right, a boy runs beside a hoop, guiding it with his stick along a shallow wall. Three women trudge by, covered by blue plastic. At the food stall, a radio wails.

The profiles of two men, talking, off to the side. At a short distance, two little girls sit motionless at the corner of a rice terrace.

The world is created anew every minute.

Acknowledgements

This book would not have been accomplished without my writers' group: Marcia Bradley, Patricia Dunn, Jimin Han, Gloria Hatrick, Deborah Zoe Laufer, Maria Maldonado, and Alexandra Soiseth, talented writers and true friends all.

Special thanks are due to Deborah Zoe Laufer, my champion throughout, who asked the right questions and offered her unerring sense of story; and to Jimin Han, whose encouragement helped me keep going, and whose careful reading improved the book in its final iterations. Patricia Dunn helped me navigate the world of publishing.

At the Sarah Lawrence MFA program, I am grateful to Kathleen Hill, Joan Silber and Myra Goldberg for wise teaching and the generosity to read my work almost twenty years after I graduated the program.

In my research for the novel, I relied on several important works. Donald S. Lopez Jr.'s *Prisoners of Paradise* helped me understand the ways in which Western agendas have often distorted the understanding of Tibetan religious texts and practices in the West. Richard Avedon's *In Exile from the Land of Snows* chronicles the genocide of Tibetans by the Chinese government, and Tsering Woeser's *Tibet on Fire* lays out the many ways in which Tibetans are still systematically oppressed by the Chinese government today.

Many thanks to Jessica Bell at Vine Leaves Press for the kind care she extends to all her authors, and to Amie McCracken and the rest of the team at Vine Leaves Press for the work they do to support writers. Special thanks to Melanie Faith, for understanding my intentions with this story and working with me to make sure they were manifested.

For much-needed ongoing technical assistance, gratitude to my friend Debrah Malater.

To my dear friend Vera Krivoshein, who rescued me in the first place—thank you.

And finally, to my mother: your open heart has taught me so much about love.

Vine Leaves Press

Enjoyed this book?
Go to *vineleavespress.com* to find more.
Subscribe to our newsletter: